Advance Praise f

"Real-life murder and hysterical Satanic Panic played out to a [illegible]y metal soundtrack—a must-read for anyone who wants to understand teenage alienation and violence in suburbia. This is the darkest and truest Long Island story."

—Nick Mamatas, author of *The People's Republic of Everything* and *I Am Providence*

"Extremely well-written and artfully laid out. Through his research, Pollack takes us inside Ricky Kasso's and Gary Lauwers's world like never imagined. *The Acid King* stands in the same league as Dave Cullen's *Columbine*."

—Peter Filardi, screenwriter of *Flatliners, The Craft, and Ricky 6*

"If you're looking for a compelling read that you won't be able to put down, *The Acid King* fits the bill. Pollack deftly weaves the tangled narrative that the media created about the crime into a finely crafted tapestry that is incredibly entertaining and informative. The tragic stories of Ricky Kasso and Gary Lauwers kick off the so-called Satanic Panic, but Pollack manages to show the human (and inhuman) parts of the story without the sensationalism. A definite must-read for true crime aficionados."

—Jeff Heimbuch, horrorbuzz.com

"The story of this very specific sort of suburban anomie almost only could have taken place in New York, and specifically Long Island—the other underside of Gatsby's Long Island where drugs, drink, failure, and anger ultimately throbbed through Satan and murder. This is what happens when the *Me* Generation takes its sobriquet a little too seriously. *The Acid King*—Jesse P. Pollack's magnum opus to the horror of it all—is a recommended read."

—Eugene S. Robinson, editor-at-large for ozy.com and author of *The Inimitable Sounds of Love: A Threesome in Four Acts*

"*The Acid King* paints a chilling picture, one filled with twists and turns as dark as any found in the Aztakea Woods. Pollack has delved deep into the past and carefully revealed the many layers building up to this shocking murder, while also giving us a glimpse at the human side of those involved. For as sensationalistic as his crime was, many of us have known a kid like Ricky Kasso. And following his journey—from childhood into darkness—is at once frightening, saddening, and thought-provoking. Pollack meticulously balances the legendary aspects of the story with the bare truths behind it. He spins a tale that builds a dreadful suspense as it travels to its terrible conclusion. But it also remains relatable, rooted in our memories of teenage feelings of awkwardness and rebellion, as it tells the foreboding tale of what happens when the rebellion goes totally sideways. *The Acid King* is a gripping and engrossing look into an infamous American legend. It is a must-read for anyone looking to explore the deeper truths behind this notorious crime."

—Heather Shade, author of *Weird Texas: Your Travel Guide to Texas's Local Legends and Best-Kept Secrets*

"I was a teenager in the mid-1980s and was aware of the events surrounding the murder of Gary Lauwers by Ricky Kasso. I remember the resulting 'Satanic Panic' and the sudden scrutiny of my generation's music, fashion, and recreational choices. The legend stuck in my mind over the years, but in reading *The Acid King*, I realized there was a lot the legend left out. Pollack carefully outlines not only what happened that fateful night, but also the lives of the participants leading up to it—and of the survivors after the fact. I came away from reading it still horrified by the murder, but seeing it from a wider perspective. This is a story of kids neglected by parents who also screwed things up on their own with drugs, petty crimes, and apathy. Maybe the scariest thing Pollack points out are the people latching onto a 'Satanic' influence, based on kids toying around with words and images, but not necessarily doing the unthinkable as a result. This is a fascinating and authentic look at a slice in time, and Pollack makes the facts as interesting as the legend—if not more so."

—J. M. Austin, senior editor, *Weird NJ* magazine and author of *Weird Hauntings, Weird Encounters, and Weird Ghosts*

"Pollack did an incredible amount of research for *The Acid King*, and it shows in the finished product. Finally, someone has filled in the gaps that were left by all the previous attempts to talk about what happened in Northport, Long Island, in 1984. There is no speculation about the power of Satan, no accusations about the evils of heavy metal music. Instead the book presents a sobering look at the reasons behind this tragedy and how it has impacted the lives of those left behind. Wisely, Pollack doesn't overshadow the story with his own personal spin, but steps aside to let those who lived through the events tell their own stories. There are no clear-cut villains or heroes in *The Acid King*. Pollack manages to show the humanity of everyone involved, including the 'Acid King' himself, Ricky Kasso. This approach is refreshing, especially in a world where opinions have become increasingly polarized. *The Acid King* is absolutely riveting reading. Anyone who is interested in the legacy of Satanic Panic, true crime stories, or the ongoing problems of troubled teenagers needs to get this book."

—Leslie Hatton, author of "All Hail the Acid King: The Ricky Kasso Case in Popular Culture" as featured in *Satanic Panic: Pop-Cultural Paranoia in the 1980s*

Simon True: Real Stories. Real Teens. Real Consequences.

Deep Water by Katherine Nichols

One Cut by Eve Porinchak

59 Hours by Johnny Kovack

Simon True

THE ACID KING

JESSE P. POLLACK

SIMON PULSE
NEW YORK LONDON TORONTO SYDNEY NEW DELHI

SIMON PULSE
An imprint of Simon & Schuster Children's Publishing Division
1230 Avenue of the Americas, New York, New York 10020
First Simon Pulse edition October 2018
Text by Jesse P. Pollack
Cover image of warped spiral by mastaka/Thinkstock
Images of spray paint by johnjohnson13/Thinkstock

For information about special discounts for bulk purchases, please contact
Simon & Schuster Special Sales at 1-866-506-1949 or business@simonandschuster.com.
The Simon & Schuster Speakers Bureau can bring authors to your live event.
For more information or to book an event contact the Simon & Schuster Speakers Bureau
at 1-866-248-3049 or visit our website at www.simonspeakers.com.
Cover designed by Sarah Creech
Interior designed by Greg Stadnyk
The text of this book was set in Chaparral Pro.
Manufactured in the United States of America
2 4 6 8 10 9 7 5 3
Library of Congress Control Number 2018939389
ISBN-13: 978-1-4814-8229-5 (hc)
ISBN-13: 978-1-4814-8228-8 (pbk)
ISBN-13: 978-1-4814-8230-1 (eBook)

For Ann—the star I sail by

CONTENTS

WHO'S WHO

Ricky Kasso: a frustrated and bitter teenager; a seeker attracted to darkness

Gary Lauwers: a lost soul doomed by the desire to fit in

Jimmy Troiano: Ricky's closest friend; impulsive and intimidating

Albert Quinones: a brawler caught up in a perfect storm

Johnny Hayward: Gary's best friend and protector; tough, but a dreamer

Matthew Carpenter: a force of kindness in Ricky's life; a symbol of his past

Rich Barton: a loyal kid; the keeper of Ricky's secrets

Jean Wells: a troubled but brave girl

Paul McBride: the young leader of a strange and controversial brotherhood

Tony Ruggi: a social worker desperate to make a difference where others failed

Pat Toussaint: an aging alcoholic obsessed with the occult

Dick Kasso: a man fueled by ambition for his children

Lynn Kasso: a wife and mother caught between two worlds

Officer Gene Roemer: a small-town, no-nonsense cop

Chief Robert Howard: head of the village police department; a hopeful realist

Detective Jim McCready: a gumshoe bent on solving every case that came his way

Detective Louis Rodriguez: an investigator with a reputation for securing confessions

Detective Lieutenant Robert Dunn: an overdramatic county homicide squad chief

Eric Naiburg: a lawyer with an eye for a good case

William Keahon: chief of the Suffolk County District Attorney's Office's Major Offense Bureau

David Breskin: a young writer searching for meaning

These are the town's secrets, and some will later be
known and some will never be known. The town
keeps them all with the ultimate poker face.
The town cares for devil's work no more than
it cares for God's or man's. It knew darkness.
And darkness was enough.

—Stephen King,
'Salem's Lot

AUTHOR'S NOTE

The story you are about to read is true. While some names have been changed, no scenes were invented. All dialogue has been re-created from nearly one hundred hours of recorded interviews, in addition to police reports, print media, television broadcasts, and notes provided by the journalists who originally covered this case. Extensive efforts were made to track down the origins of the innumerable myths, legends, and tall tales surrounding the events that took place in Northport, New York, during the 1980s. It is the author's hope that this book will help destroy the half-truths, misinformation, and lies that have plagued this story, while providing some form of closure for those who were affected by the tragedies of the summer of 1984.

THE ACID KING

Prologue

I grew up in a seaside town where the devil lives.
Bonfire lights in the woods at night said to "be afraid. . . ."
—Wheatus,
"From Listening to Lightning"

FORTY MILES EAST OF MANHATTAN, THERE LIES A small picturesque village on the north shore of Long Island. The locals are kind—quick to tell you who cooks the best breakfast at one of the many restaurants on Main Street, or whose kid is the star athlete on the school sports team. They work hard, running the mom-and-pop shops downtown, fishing for lobster in the marina, or operating one of the many bars and restaurants on Main Street. Some residents jokingly call the village a "quiet little drinking town with a fishing problem." Most of them go home to average houses, some of which are old Victorians that have stood on the Island for over a century, while others are of the newer and grander variety.

Surrounding these otherwise unremarkable homes are a few small, scattered patches of woods, making up the tiny bit of wilderness left in suburban Northport, New York.

Not too long ago, the newer neighborhoods made up of upscale houses and condominiums were yet to be built, and as such, the woods sat undisturbed by time. As they so often tend to, local teenagers quickly discovered the advantages of hanging out inside a vast sea of trees, far out of view from their parents and the authorities. The woods became a popular lovers' lane, along with the perfect place for clandestine drinking and pot smoking.

Soon after, rumors of much more sinister activities began to take flight in Northport. In the early 1970s the villagers began to whisper about a coven of witches meeting inside the forest near Franklin Street, holding midnight ceremonies after an evening of robbing graves. For the citizens of Suffolk County, this gossip was nothing new. The Island has long possessed a storied history of accusing residents of occult activity, going all the way back to 1658 when Goody Garlick of East Hampton was charged with the crime of witchcraft—a full thirty-four years before Salem, Massachusetts, became infamous for its own witch trials.

The location of Northport's rumored rituals didn't help to quash these rumblings, either. The woods filling the southwest corner of the village seemed to be surrounded by an almost supernatural aura in recent years, all thanks to a set of strange ruins deep inside the wilderness. These eerie abandoned structures reminded passing teenagers of the ancient Aztec temples they read about in their high school history books. Soon they began referring to the area as "Azteca Woods." As word was passed back and forth from kid to kid, the name eventually evolved into "Aztakea."

While the ruins had given birth to a name, they certainly failed to reveal any answers regarding their origin. Even today, the citizens of Northport continue to disagree on what the crumbling structures were or where they came from. Some will tell you about a religious fanatic who set up shop in the village sometime during the late 1970s and had a stone chapel built in the woods. The preacher—referred to as "Reverend Shitbird" by his detractors—made a habit of driving around and blasting his sermons through a large speaker jury-rigged to the top of his car, hoping to recruit young followers. Residents soon became uneasy about the man's behavior and had the village police department chase Reverend Shitbird out of town.

Some who grew up in Northport maintain that the dilapidated building was erected decades earlier by an Italian religious order. The project was intended to be a home for local orphans of World War II, but was supposedly abandoned halfway into construction when the order's funding was pulled.

Others insist the church was merely a ruse during Prohibition, with the chapel being used to smuggle alcohol into the village.

Perhaps the most unsettling version of how the strange stone structures came to appear inside Aztakea Woods is a tale told by some residents about a Universalist Christian minister who arrived in Northport in the 1920s, asking for money to build a temple in the woods. The village agreed, and construction soon began. A roadway was carved out and a marble floor was laid. A barrel-shaped chapel with a Gothic archway was crafted from stone and brick, complete with windows in the shape of a cross.

Then, one day, the project suddenly stopped, and the minister vanished—along with the remainder of the money he had been lent.

Sometime later the minister returned to Northport completely penniless. He tearfully apologized to the townsfolk for spending all their money, but swore to complete the church if he was again loaned the remaining funds required. Wisely, the village refused to put up another dime, despite the half-finished temple still sitting in their woods. The minister walked away from the meeting completely dejected and ventured back into Aztakea Woods to visit his church one last time. He was found hanging from a tree a few days later.

With each resident presenting their respective story as the "true" version of the facts, it is hard to say what truly occurred in Aztakea Woods during the first half of the twentieth century. The abandoned church was eventually razed to make room for houses as more and more people moved to the small maritime village, and the definitive story, it seems, has been lost to time. With the construction of North Road, Northport may have been done with the planned church—but Aztakea Woods was far from done with Northport.

During the summer of 1984, these woods became the guardian of a terrible secret that would horrify this tiny bedroom suburb of New York City and help ignite a worldwide panic—the echoes of which are still being felt today.

Part One

JULY 1984

Our youth has gone to the ends of the earth
to die in the silence of the truth.
—Louis-Ferdinand Céline,
Journey to the End of the Night

Chapter 1

SUNDAY, JULY 1, 1984
4:45 P.M.

"THERE'S A BODY IN THE WOODS BEHIND GUNTHER'S TAP Room."

The line went dead.

Larry Springsteen stared at the telephone receiver cradled in his hand. The fifty-four-year-old lieutenant for the Northport Village Police Department had to think quick. Everyone in town knew Gunther's. As Northport's favorite watering hole, the bar had made a name for itself as one of writer Jack Kerouac's favorite drinking spots. But a body? In *Northport*? Nothing ever happened here. Hell, that was the reason most people moved here in the first place. As far as Springsteen knew, no one in Northport was even *missing*.

The woman on the other end of the line had sounded young. Maybe it was a prank?

Either way, Springsteen had to follow up. If there really was a body in the local woods and the police brushed a tip off as a crank call, there would be hell to pay. Springsteen dialed the home of Officer Gene Roemer, who was off-duty that day. He told Roemer about the strange phone call and asked him to come into work to help trace it. Roemer obliged and soon the two were working on a trace at the small village hall that housed police headquarters on Main Street.

Unfortunately, their efforts were unsuccessful. Too much time had passed since the anonymous caller hung up. Springsteen and Roemer organized a brief search of the area behind Gunther's, but no remains were found. Maybe the call really was a prank? Roemer and Springsteen decided to continue their investigation the following morning, and both headed home.

Any optimism the two policemen shared was shattered the next day when another call came in—this time from Sister Mary James, the head nun at the Madonna Heights School for Girls in Dix Hills. James told the police that one of their students, Jean Wells, had returned to the school after a weekend in Northport and told a counselor that her friend, a teenager named Gary Lauwers, had been murdered and buried in a place called "Aztakea Woods." Once the call ended, Springsteen telephoned his boss, Northport Village Police Chief Robert Howard, and alerted him to the situation. Howard had just begun a monthlong vacation, leaving Springsteen in command. Springsteen, however, thought his chief needed to be directly involved.

When Chief Howard arrived at the station, he placed Officer Roemer in charge of the investigation. At forty-two years old, Roemer had been with the department for nearly twenty years and had proven himself to be an outstanding officer. His first move was to drive over to the Lauwers residence on West Scudder Place to see if Gary was even missing. Chief Howard joined him.

Once Roemer and Howard arrived, Gary's mother, Yvonne Lauwers, insisted that she speak with the two on her front lawn. Over the past year, Gary had gotten himself into some serious legal trouble—mostly robbery and assault—and his father, Herbert Lauwers, forbade his wife from even mentioning their son's name in the house. Standing outside, Yvonne told Roemer and Howard that she had not seen Gary for some time.

"Well, you know," she said. "This is not unusual. Sometimes I don't see him for two or three weeks."

"That may be," Roemer replied, running his hand through his thick graying hair, "but how about doing me a favor? I can't really do this kind of investigation without a missing person's report. As soon as he's located, the law says we gotta tear this up and it never happened. We can't release it to anybody because he's a minor."

The fifty-six-year-old mother of three relented, and filled out the required paperwork for Roemer. Now armed with the documentation he needed, Roemer could continue his investigation. He wanted to question Jean Wells immediately, so he headed south to Madonna Heights School for Girls, only ten miles outside of Northport.

When Roemer pulled up to the large white mansion at the

end of the long, paved driveway, he found Jean's parents waiting for their fifteen-year-old daughter. When Jean emerged from her classroom, they began to chastise her.

"What did you do wrong *now*?!" her mother and father demanded.

Officer Roemer stepped in.

"Your daughter did something very courageous," he told the distraught couple.

Sitting down with Jean, Roemer asked how she found out about Gary's murder. She replied that she had gone to the Northport movie theater around noon the previous day to hang out with her friend Karen. The two had made plans to meet at the Midway, Northport's local head shop, and then walk downtown to see a movie. Afterward, they planned to grab lunch at Phase II Heros on Main Street.

Also joining them on that fateful day was Karen's boyfriend, Jimmy Troiano. Jean was slightly intimidated by Jimmy. An eighteen-year-old high school dropout, Jimmy had a reputation for being a tough guy who dabbled in drug dealing and the occasional burglary. His physical appearance was also unsettling to some. Since he was a young boy, Jimmy Troiano's face had been adorned with a large scar, along with a grin marked by a mouthful of unnaturally sharp teeth. The canines were the result of genetics, but the scar came from a childhood injury on a local playground. Some say a seven-year-old Jimmy took the chained hook from a swing set and jumped off the top, tearing his cheek open in the process. Others maintain he merely fell. Either way, Troiano's face had earned him the unflattering nickname "Drac"—short for Dracula. Before he dropped out of Northport High School in the middle of his sophomore year, Jimmy's classmates made sure "Monster Mash" was played in his honor at their ninth-grade dance.

Once Jean arrived at the Midway, she exchanged small talk with Karen and Jimmy before asking the question that would change their lives forever.

"Hey, I haven't seen Ricky since I left for boarding school," Jean said. "How's he doing?"

"Ricky" was Ricky Kasso, Jimmy Troiano's best friend. Ricky's taste for ingesting and selling LSD had earned him the tongue-in-cheek nickname "the Acid King." In reality, Ricky's kingdom was sparse. For the last three years, he had been bouncing back and forth between his parents' home and living on the streets. His father, a strict disciplinarian, had no tolerance for his son's drug-fueled rebellion. By spring 1984, Ricky was seventeen and homeless, with no job or education. He survived by sleeping on friends' couches, inside public restrooms, and even in a sewer trench at the Port Jefferson railroad station. What little money he had from selling drugs usually went to buying more.

"Oh, Ricky? He just killed some guy," Jimmy replied. "What's his name? Um . . . um . . . *Gary*."

"Gary *Lauwers*?" she asked. Jean knew Gary well. The two had been friends since they were in elementary school.

"Yeah," Jimmy replied nonchalantly.

"*What?!*" Jean exclaimed. "That's not *funny*, Jimmy!"

"Nah, I'm serious!" Jimmy insisted. "Do you wanna go up and see it?"

"'No!" Jean replied. "What are you talking about?!"

The three stood in the rain as Jimmy told them how there had supposedly been a "bad drug deal" between Ricky and Gary, so he and Ricky decided to ambush him. Jimmy and Ricky, along with their friend Albert Quinones, then lured Gary into Aztakea Woods and stabbed him to death. Karen laughed, thinking Jimmy was pulling a prank on Jean. She had no reason to believe the things her boyfriend was saying. The laughter caused Jean to temporarily relax and they all headed downtown to catch their movie. However, sitting in the darkness of Northport's small theater, Jean couldn't stop thinking about what Jimmy had said to her.

What if Gary really *was* lying dead up in Aztakea?

After the movie, Jean skipped lunch with Karen and Jimmy and called her mom from a pay phone, asking to be picked up right away. Once she got home, Jean quietly snuck over to a neighbor's house and asked to use their phone. She called the Lauwers residence and Gary's mother, Yvonne, picked up.

"Hi, Mrs. Lauwers, this is Jean," she said. "Is Gary home?"

"No, Jean, he's not," Yvonne replied. "I haven't seen him in two weeks."

Jean felt a chill dancing up her spine. She hung up and immediately called the Northport Village Police Department.

While Jean's story seemed believable to Roemer, he still wondered if the girl was simply the butt of a cruel joke. After all, he knew about Kasso, Troiano, and the trouble they liked to cause.

"Jean, is it possible Jimmy may have been lying to you?" he asked. "We checked the woods yesterday and we didn't find anything."

"Oh, of course!" the pretty young blonde said, desperate to believe Roemer's suggestion. "Jimmy *definitely* could have been telling me a story. . . ."

Roemer left Madonna Heights wondering if this investigation had become a fool's errand. He now had the names of the victim and the alleged killers, but no hard evidence. When he returned to headquarters, Roemer called the Suffolk County Police Department, asking for help locating Gary Lauwers's remains. However, Suffolk County turned down this request, telling him that teenage gossip wasn't enough to warrant their intervention. Undeterred, Roemer scheduled another search of Aztakea Woods for the following afternoon.

When he returned to Madonna Heights the next morning, Roemer asked Jean Wells if she would be willing to take a polygraph test. She agreed without hesitation. When Jean arrived at the Suffolk County Police Department in Yaphank for the test, Roemer first had her meet with detectives from the homicide bureau. Upon hearing her story, the detectives decided Jean was credible, canceled the test, and agreed to help the Northport police search Aztakea that afternoon.

Unfortunately, this search also came up empty. Due to severe thunderstorms, the police dogs could not key in on any kind of scent that might have led to a body. Tired and frustrated, the investigators decided to go home and try again the next day.

Chapter 2

THE UNMARKED POLICE CRUISER CRAWLED UP Church Street and made a right onto Franklin. This afternoon would mark the third day spent roaming Aztakea Woods in search of Gary Lauwers's body. The rain had finally let up overnight, leading to more manageable conditions, but some of the investigators had become frustrated. Most of them wished they were home. It was Independence Day, after all, and some had begun to suspect they were on a wild-goose chase.

As more unmarked vehicles from the Suffolk County Police Department arrived, Officer Roemer grabbed his walkie-talkie. Suffolk County Homicide Detective Kevin James McCready, known to fellow officers as "Jim," sat next to him, clutching his radio. Normally, the walkie-talkies would have been tuned to the Northport Village Police Department's frequency, but special care was being taken to ensure the search was kept secret, to not tip off the suspects or the press, so a separate frequency was used.

Soon after, a wave of car doors opened, releasing a small group of Suffolk County Police cadaver dogs, each partnered with an investigator. The dog teams were assigned specific areas, and after some brief discussion between the detectives, they entered Aztakea.

It didn't take them long to find what they were looking for.

"Hey, guys, come on over here," a voice called out through the static of Roemer's walkie-talkie.

Roemer and McCready exited their car and ran into the woods. About a hundred yards away from the opening path, they found a cadaver dog named Reb pulling on something embedded in the dirt. Roemer bent down for a closer look and realized Reb was chewing on a blood-soaked scalp. He pulled the dog away and radioed for the Suffolk County Crime Lab in Hauppauge to get to Aztakea right away.

As Roemer lowered the walkie-talkie, he came upon another gut-wrenching realization—he had walked on top of this spot the day before, but the bad weather had prevented him from realizing it.

Forensic scientists from the Suffolk County Crime Lab, along with police photographers and videographers, quickly descended on the scene. As tripods were set up, the forensic scientists started digging into the soggy ground. They soon realized how little work they'd have to do. Only an inch of soil and leaves covered the decaying corpse lying underneath.

As more and more dirt was removed from the grave, the situation became increasingly grim. Chief Howard peered into the opening in the ground and was horrified to discover that Gary Lauwers's head had all but rotted away, leaving little more than a skull lying next to the festering body's feet. His first suspicion was that Lauwers had been killed by decapitation. The idea made the forty-three-year-old police chief sick to his stomach. In the two decades since he had joined the Northport Village Police Department, Howard had never gotten used to the sight of a dead body—and the maggot-infested remains lying before him didn't change this.

Unlike Howard, Roemer and McCready didn't have time to ponder the cause of death. Exiting Aztakea, they walked back to their car and began their search for Ricky Kasso, Jimmy Troiano, and Albert Quinones. While Ricky and Jimmy were nowhere to be found after hours of searching, Northport Police Officer Tommy Schramm received a tip that Albert Quinones was at his home on Maple Avenue. While Roemer and McCready were more interested in locating Ricky and Jimmy, they definitely didn't want Albert fleeing once word got out about Gary's body being found. The two picked up Schramm, who was in plainclothes, and devised a plan wherein he would peek into a window at the Quinones residence, confirm Albert was present, and then meet the investigators at the Lewis Oliver Dairy Farm, two blocks over on Burt Avenue. There, the three would discuss their next move.

Around one a.m., the unmarked police car gently braked in front of a two-story house on the corner of Maple Avenue and

Oxford Street, about three doors down from the Quinones home. Schramm got out, and the car drove off. He then casually walked down the quiet, tree-lined block until he came to the small brown house marked "85." Turning left onto the concrete walkway on the side of the house, Schramm approached a side window next to a wooden gate leading to the backyard. Peering inside, he saw Albert's sister Wendy and a friend, sixteen-year-old Mark Florimonte, sitting in the living room. Albert was absent. Almost immediately, Wendy and Mark locked eyes with Schramm, and the two dashed toward the front door. Schramm backed away from the window as the teenagers came barreling out onto the porch, running after him.

Sitting in their car two blocks away, Roemer and McCready heard their portable radios come alive. Someone inside the Quinones residence had called the police to report a "prowler." Meanwhile, Wendy and Mark were chasing Schramm farther away from his rendezvous point. Roemer and McCready quickly realized Schramm wasn't headed their way and began searching for him.

The two eventually found Schramm, who jumped into the back seat as the cruiser sped off. While the twenty-seven-year-old officer sat catching his breath, Roemer and McCready began to wonder how they could bring Albert in for questioning without alerting his sister and friend. If one of them tipped off Ricky or Jimmy, finding the accused killers would become much more difficult.

Roemer chuckled.

He turned to Schramm and said, "Hey, Tommy, I got a good idea. . . ."

The three then drove back to the police station, where Roemer told Schramm to get downstairs and put his uniform on.

A short while later a marked Northport police cruiser pulled up in front of 85 Maple Avenue. The vehicle began shining its spotlight around the area, pretending to look for a burglar. Albert and Wendy Quinones, along with Mark Florimonte, saw the searchlight and approached the vehicle as a newly uniformed Tommy Schramm stepped out of the driver's seat.

"You guys see a prowler around?" Schramm asked.

"Yeah!" Wendy and Mark replied in unison.

Schramm asked the two to describe the man they had seen earlier, all while nodding along and trying not to laugh. When Wendy and Mark finished their descriptions, the officer offered a suggestion.

"Why don't you get in the back of the car?" Schramm said. "That way, if you see him, we can get him."

The three agreed and hopped into the police cruiser. Albert and Wendy sat behind Schramm, while Florimonte buckled himself into the passenger seat.

Schramm began to drive, pretending to search for the mysterious "prowler" on the darkened streets of Northport. Looking out the rear passenger-side window, Wendy Quinones noticed a parked car with two men—Roemer and McCready—hiding behind it, and alerted Schramm, who then decided it was time to bring Albert in.

First, however, he had to get rid of Wendy and Mark.

Turning to Wendy, Schramm said, "You and Mark get out of the car, and Albert will stay with me. We're about to do some police business, and I might need some help."

Wendy Quinones, tired of riding in the back seat of a police car, replied, "Oh, that's good! Thank you very much!"

The two exited the car, and Schramm drove back to the corner of Laurel and Main, making small talk with Albert. Once they arrived, Schramm parked the vehicle, picked up his radio, and called out to Roemer and McCready.

"I got him," Schramm said calmly.

Albert looked around, noticeably confused.

Suddenly the cruiser's door flew open as Roemer and McCready pulled Albert from his seat. The two put him into their unmarked car and headed straight for the Suffolk County Police headquarters in Yaphank, about forty minutes away.

Once there, Albert was brought into a private room by Suffolk County investigators and extensively questioned regarding Gary's murder. Terrified that the police were trying to frame him, he refused to talk. After two frustrating hours, the detectives ended the interview and released Albert. Despite the lack of cooperation from the teenager, the investigators went to work obtaining an arrest warrant for Ricky and Jimmy.

Meanwhile, back in Northport, the police were staked out on Main Street, silently observing a Fourth of July gathering of teenagers inside Cow Harbor Park. Mingling with the crowd were Ricky and Jimmy. The officers were tasking with keeping an eye on the two while Suffolk County worked on getting arrest warrants for them.

Later, around four thirty a.m. on Thursday, July 5, the moment of truth finally came. Suffolk County detectives were given the go-ahead to apprehend Ricky Kasso and Jimmy Troiano. At some point during the night, however, the two had vanished.

An hour later, Northport Police Sergeant Ed McMullen drove up Bluff Point Road, passing the Northport Yacht Club on his left. He observed nothing out of the ordinary on this dead-end street, so he turned around and continued his patrol elsewhere. A few minutes later, a battered old Pontiac driven by two stoned teens pulled up in front of a house across from the yacht club and parked. They rolled their windows down to bring relief from the muggy weather, and hung their legs outside the car.

Around seven a.m., the Northport Village Police Department received a call from a homeowner on Bluff Point Road. She told the officer that a strange vehicle was parked in front of her house, and that two young men were sleeping inside it. Sgt. McMullen returned to the area and parked behind the maroon sedan. Thanks to a tip from one of Ricky's acquaintances, McMullen, along with the rest of the investigators, was on the lookout for an "old purple car." Standing before the Pontiac, he was confident that these were the guys he was looking for, but he had to be positive before calling for backup.

McMullen approached the vehicle and found Ricky Kasso sleeping in the back seat and Jimmy Troiano asleep in the front. McMullen instantly recognized the two from their prior run-ins with law enforcement for burglary, vandalism, and drug use, and rushed back to his cruiser to alert dispatch. Officer Roemer was then contacted via the secret police frequency.

"They got your guys down on Bluff Point Road," dispatch radioed.

Acting quickly, Roemer, along with Chief Howard and more than a dozen other officers, arrived on Bluff Point Road and charged toward the Pontiac. Despite the flurry of action, Kasso and Troiano remained asleep in the car until the investigators opened the dented doors, guns drawn. Ricky and Jimmy were quickly cuffed, tossed into the backs of separate cars, and driven away. The detectives looked forward to interviewing the accused killers and finally getting some answers about what had happened to Gary Lauwers.

Nothing could have prepared them for what they were about to hear.

Chapter 3

THE CARAVAN OF SQUAD CARS AND UNMARKED vehicles sped away from Bluff Point Road and toward Suffolk County Police headquarters in Yaphank. When they arrived, Ricky was placed in a cell while Jimmy was questioned by McCready and Detective Lieutenant Robert Dunn, commanding officer of the Suffolk County Homicide Squad. Seated across from each other in the small interrogation room, Troiano and McCready were total opposites. Jimmy had long, unkempt hair and homemade tattoos, and he wore a smelly bootleg tie-dye Grateful Dead shirt and ratty blue jeans. McCready, on the other hand, wore a freshly dry-cleaned suit, an ironed dress shirt sporting an impeccably knotted tie, and well-combed hair that was neatly trimmed around his chiseled face.

Visibly upset, Jimmy started talking. He told them the basics: his full name, date of birth, and former address. "Former" because he, like Ricky, had been recently thrown out by his parents, and the two were now living in the rusted-out Pontiac. After some pressing, Jimmy began to discuss the incident in question.

"I'm not sure when, but Gary took ten bags of angel dust out of Ricky's pocket," he told the detectives. "I heard that Ricky was passed out at the time."

McCready and Dunn now had Kasso's motive.

"About the second or third day I got out of jail," Jimmy said, "I was with Ricky in the New Park in downtown Northport."

Troiano had just been released from the Suffolk County Correctional Facility after burglarizing a home.

"Ricky beat Gary up because Gary had taken the dust," Jimmy continued. "Ricky wanted Gary to pay him for the dust, and Gary kept putting him off. I think that was the third time Ricky beat up Gary."

Finally, the moment the investigators had been waiting for arrived—Jimmy's account of how Gary Lauwers was killed.

"On Saturday, June 16, about seven o'clock," he said, "I met up with Gary, Ricky, and Albert Quinones."

Still high on PCP from the night before, Troiano incorrectly recalled the date of the murder as being June 16. Unbeknownst to the police, it had actually occurred three nights later, on June 19. Completely unaware of this error, McCready and Dunn didn't think to correct Jimmy as he went on.

"We hung out for a while and decided to go to Dunkin' Donuts," he said. "We got donuts and cigarettes and then walked up to Aztakea Woods. On the way, Albert said that Ricky was going to beat up Gary. After we got up there, Albert told me Ricky was going to kill Gary."

This revelation surprised the interrogators. Based on the limited information they had gathered, McCready, Dunn, and the rest of the investigators had assumed the murder was a spontaneous rage killing. Now Jimmy was saying it had been planned all along.

"As we sat there watching a small fire," he continued, "Ricky kept telling Gary to donate some of his clothes to the fire. At first, he told Gary to donate his socks. Then, he wanted Gary to donate his undershorts. Ricky kept telling him to donate things. Gary finally donated his jacket sleeves. Gary then told Ricky that he thought Ricky was trying to start a fight with him. Gary then told Ricky that he would fight only if it was one-on-one and no weapons. Ricky and Gary started to fight as Albert and I watched. Suddenly me and Albert heard Gary say, 'I love you, Mom.' I turned and saw Ricky stabbing Gary in the back. Gary tried to get away from Ricky and ran. Ricky ran after Gary and dragged him back by the legs. Ricky had dropped the knife after stabbing Gary. After he dragged Gary back, he found the knife and stabbed Gary in the back many times. Just before I heard Gary say, 'I love you, Mom,' I heard Ricky tell Gary to say, 'I love you, Satan.' I heard Gary say this once after Ricky had stabbed Gary in the back."

Ricky Kasso had long been obsessed with the devil—and the police were well aware. Only three months before, Ricky had been arrested for trying to steal a skull from a nineteenth-century grave. When he was arrested, his pockets were searched, and a list of the dignitaries in Hell was found in his wallet, along with steps on how to conduct a ritual.

"He told me to help him drag Gary's body away from the clearing and into the woods," Jimmy continued. "I did this with Ricky and then I saw Ricky bending over Gary, saying something about Satan. As he was saying this, Gary's head moved, and Ricky bugged out and started stabbing him in the face. He stabbed him plenty of times in the face. We all then covered Gary with leaves and branches. As we walked away, Ricky realized he lost his Satanic star necklace. We looked around for it and couldn't find it. We then kicked dirt on the bloody spots on the ground to cover it up. As we walked away, Ricky was laughing about what happened. It was about three o'clock in the morning when we left. We went over to Albert's house on Maple Avenue. Ricky took a bath and cleaned up. He put on the same pants, but I think he put on a different shirt. We went back downtown, and then during the day, I went to Kings Park."

When asked about the murder weapon, Troiano told the three that when he returned to downtown Northport later the next night, Ricky told him he had thrown the knife into the harbor earlier that day. Troiano was, however, able to describe it.

"The knife has about a four-inch blade. It locks open and says 'Flasher' on it in gold letters," he said. "The handle is black hard plastic."

McCready and Dunn ended the interview by asking how Gary's remains went from being hidden under a pile of leaves and sticks to its eventual burial in the shallow grave.

"Last Saturday, around eleven o'clock in the morning," he replied, "Ricky and I went back up to Aztakea and buried the body. We took turns digging, and Ricky then pushed the body in the hole."

Jimmy then described how Gary Lauwers's skull ended up down by his feet.

"When Kasso and Troiano pushed him into the grave, he was so badly decomposed that the head just fell off—and they *kicked* it into the grave," Robert Howard later told a television interviewer. "The head was not cut from the body. . . ."

Later that morning Albert Quinones, who had just been rearrested downtown, encountered Jimmy in the hallway of Suffolk County Police headquarters.

"Tell them everything, Albert!" he yelled to the muscular boy with the mop of black hair.

Assuming Jimmy had been cleared of the crime, Albert decided to talk. He was brought into another room and told the police about Gary's murder. Albert's statement mostly mirrored Jimmy's. He described how Ricky had lured Gary to Aztakea and how the drug debt was paid off and seemingly forgotten. He talked about the donuts and how the four tried to get a fire started in the damp woods. He told the detectives how Ricky gave Gary a knife and told him to cut the sleeves from his denim jacket to use as kindling. Albert then surprised the interrogators by saying Ricky had killed Gary at the behest of *Jimmy*, insisting he saw Jimmy tell Ricky to slice the boy's throat. Despite the unexpected revelation, no one was shocked that Jimmy had failed to mention this important detail—thereby incriminating himself—but the detectives weren't about to interrupt Albert over this matter. They sat quietly, jotting down notes in their legal pads as Albert described how Ricky had forced Gary to get down on his hands and knees and say he loved Satan as he repeatedly plunged the knife into his friend's body.

The lurid story concluded with Albert telling the investigators how he had helped Ricky and Jimmy cover Gary's body with leaves, and how he'd even let Ricky come back to his house—where his mother and two sisters were sleeping—so he could wash Gary's blood from his body and borrow a shirt. Despite what Jimmy had told investigators earlier, Albert made no mention of advance knowledge of Ricky's intentions to kill Gary. At the same time, the detectives weren't naive enough to believe Albert would deliberately incriminate himself during questioning. However, since they still had nothing solid to charge him with, they decided to let Albert go.

Shortly afterward, Detective Louis Rodriguez of the Suffolk County Police Department was asked to take Jimmy back to Northport so more crime scene photos could be taken. Rodriguez, along with a few other investigators, then headed toward the village. Once there, they briefly stopped at the police station and then drove to Skipper's Pub, one of Northport's Main Street restaurants, for lunch before the trip to Aztakea. The investigators hoped the friendlier environment would help Jimmy loosen up and divulge more information. He was shocked when the detectives ordered him a hamburger and a Coke.

"People think we use these horrible tactics to get people to make statements," Chief Howard later told an interviewer. "We bought James Troiano a hamburger. A big hamburger and a Coke. He couldn't believe we were being so nice to him."

As Jimmy chowed down on the first decent meal he'd had in weeks, Ricky was brought to see Detective McCready back in Yaphank.

There, Ricky gave a statement that was nearly identical to Albert's and Jimmy's, save for one important detail—Ricky claimed that all three knew in advance that Gary was going to be killed, and that Jimmy actually *helped* him do it. Ricky told the detectives that Jimmy held Gary down while he was punching and biting him. Echoing Albert's statement, Ricky confirmed that Jimmy had told him to slice the boy's throat and had later handed the murder weapon back to him after he dropped it.

This changed everything. With these new details in mind, McCready now wanted a second statement from Jimmy.

After lunch, the detectives drove Jimmy to Franklin Street to take photos of the Aztakea crime scene. Here, events took a controversial turn. Around this time, Detective Rodriguez had been made aware of Kasso's confession and how Troiano seemed to be much more involved in Gary's murder than initially assumed. Sitting in the car, Rodriguez questioned Troiano further and eventually got a second and more damning statement out of him. Not only did Jimmy supposedly admit to handing the knife back to Ricky after he dropped it, but he also claimed to have broken Gary's ribs during the attack, and even helped Kasso drag Gary back to the campfire after he had briefly run away.

With this new confession added to the record, Jimmy was arrested shortly after taking the requested photos in the woods. He was then driven back to Suffolk County Police headquarters, booked, and placed in a cell.

The group of investigators were proud of the work they had done. In less than a week, they had successfully followed up on Jean Wells's tip, identified the location of Gary Lauwers's remains, secured a witness statement from Albert Quinones, and safely apprehended the two suspects. Adding Ricky's and Jimmy's confessions to the ever-growing pile of evidence against the two gave the detectives an overwhelming sense of confidence. All in all, this seemed to be an open-and-shut case for the courts.

Ricky Kasso, however, had other plans.

Part Two

A BRIEF INNOCENCE

Childhood is the kingdom where nobody dies.
Nobody that matters, that is.
—Edna St. Vincent Millay,
Wine from These Grapes

Chapter 4

THE BOY WHO WOULD BECOME THE ACID KING WAS born Richard Allan Kasso Jr. on March 29, 1967, in Long Island's Huntington Hospital. The child, affectionately called "Ricky," was the firstborn son of Richard Sr. and his wife, the former Lynn Pechman.

On the surface, the young husband and wife seemed to be a natural couple. Both taught at Northport High School and ostensibly complemented each other well. What Lynn lacked through her more reserved nature, Dick made up for through his aggressive passion for sports. Initially Dick indulged in this love through coaching, but his athletic obsessions eventually spilled over into the Huntington home he shared with Lynn. On the night her water broke, Dick forced his twenty-five-year-old wife to wait until he was done watching a sports game on television.

Only *then* would he drive her to Huntington Hospital so Ricky could be born.

As the years went by, the Kasso family grew larger. In 1969 Lynn gave birth to a daughter, Kelly Lynn, and within the next four years, two more sisters were born; Jody Lee in 1970, and finally Wendy Lauren in 1973. The family eventually moved from Huntington into a quaint, four-bedroom home on Seaview Avenue in Northport. To some, life might have appeared cramped inside the small Dutch Colonial house the Kassos called home, but matters were alleviated by Kelly and Jody sharing a bedroom. The two always seemed to come as a pair from then on, which created a vacuum between Ricky and Wendy. This, however, allowed for a strong bond to form between them.

In family photos, Ricky is almost always seen standing with Wendy, happily engaged in the sacred role of his sister's protector. The two even began to resemble each other more than they did their other siblings. Kelly and Jody stood out from the pack with their golden blond hair and cherubic faces, while Ricky and Wendy shared identical shades of earthy brown hair, piercing blue eyes, and even the same thin, straight nose. Ricky doted on Wendy, playfully nicknaming her "Windy." If Kelly and Jody were bothering his youngest sister, Ricky would let Wendy stand in the doorway of his second-floor bedroom so she could call them names. If they tried to come after her, Ricky would yell at his sisters, chasing them away.

When Wendy was a student at Northport's Ocean Avenue Elementary School, she was given a chicken egg to carry across the school gymnasium on a small plastic spoon during an afternoon of activities and games. She soon began to stress over the responsibility of the task, but Ricky, who was watching nearby, saw the fear on Wendy's face and quickly ran to her aid. Placing his hand on his little sister's back, Ricky kept his sister steady as she made her way from one end of the gymnasium to the other, never once dropping her egg.

"Ricky loved Wendy," recalls Sue Sterling, a family friend. "He would say, 'My Wendy! My little Wendy-Lou!' If she was upset, he would take his hand and rub her hair, saying, 'It'll be okay, Wendy-Lou! It's all right! Don't cry!' He idolized her."

Sue first met the Kassos in the early 1970s in her hometown of Argyle in upstate New York. A few years earlier, Dick's parents had given him and Lynn a small red cabin on Argyle's Hemlocks Lane, and the family began spending their summers there. The cabin itself was far from extravagant, containing only a couple of rooms barely larger than an average closet, plus a living room that doubled as a kitchen. However, the unobstructed view of the wilderness surrounding the midnight-blue waters of Cossayuna Lake was the best vacation this nuclear family from Long Island could hope for. Every June, on the last day of school, the Kassos would pack up their Dodge station wagon and make the four-hour drive upstate.

Good-natured and always smiling, Ricky had no difficulty making friends in Argyle. Once the family settled in, Ricky, Kelly, and Jody would join Sue and her brother Bruce for a multitude of summer activities. There were games of tag, speedboat rides, and swimming races held to see which kid could make it to the lake's floating barrel dock the quickest.

Unfortunately, as the youngest sibling, Wendy rarely got to join in on the fun. Most of her time was spent with her mother, but occasionally, Ricky would bring Wendy out to the barrel dock with him. Placing his hands underneath her armpits, he would then let her jump in and out of the water a few times before bringing her back inside.

Once the sun set on a typical day in Argyle, the Kasso children, along with most of their friends, would dry off and gather around a large campfire Dick built near the edge of the water. There, everyone toasted marshmallows as Dick told ghost stories. Afterward, he would take his small motorboat out onto the lake for a round of night fishing. Hearing him approach, all of Dick's children, along with Sue, Bruce, and others, would race down to the dock to see what he had caught—usually northern pike or largemouth bass.

Ricky often passed the time in Argyle by working at the Mallory family's dairy farm. Ricky was friends with the Mallorys' sons, Tony and Danny, and was more than happy to lend a hand. One of Ricky's favorite duties on the farm was "Woodchuck Watch." Several troublesome woodchucks had been laying waste to the farm's corn crops, so the Mallorys allowed Dick to load up his station wagon with all the kids and shoot the rodents with his shotgun. When one of the children spotted a woodchuck, Dick would fire. Some were launched into the air and others would land sideways, leaving Ricky and the others rolling in fits of laughter.

After summer ended and the Kassos returned to Northport, the halcyon image of a Norman Rockwell existence continued. Ricky often rose at six in the morning so he could join the other boys on Seaview Avenue for a quick game of football before school. Nothing could have made Dick happier. His own father, Alfred Kasso, had once played as an outfielder for a minor-league baseball team and Dick, wanting to keep the family tradition alive, held high athletic aspirations for Ricky. Seeing his child grow into a young man who loved competitive sports was nothing short of a dream come true for Dick Kasso.

Ricky often enjoyed playing with his neighbor from two doors down, Grant Koerner. Grant was three years younger than Ricky—a gargantuan age difference for children under ten—but the two never seemed to mind. Their days were often spent playing with green plastic army figurines in Grant's backyard sandbox or launching model rockets in the Ocean Avenue Elementary School parking lot with their friend Dave Johnson.

When Ricky wasn't sending cardboard rockets on imaginary trips to the moon, he spent his days inside Ocean Avenue as a less-than-average but likeable student. Dick Kasso didn't mind Ricky's C-average grades as long as his son maintained an active interest in sports.

"Nothing else could compete with my father's love of sports," Wendy says. "Not even his kids. Sports were his entire *life*. He was highly competitive and winning mattered to him. He wanted all his kids to be the same way. He had four kids who each had a natural ability to play sports well, but not all of them necessarily *wanted* to. Everyone *had* to be on a team. If what you were doing wasn't related to sports, it wasn't important."

Wendy eventually realized this the hard way. When she was a young girl, she joined her school's choral group. After spending weeks practicing, she raced home to tell her parents about her upcoming concert. Lynn was excited for her youngest child, but when she told Dick to save the date, her husband replied coldly, "It's not a sport. It doesn't matter. I'm not going."

Unbeknownst to Dick, Wendy was in the next room and heard everything. She was heartbroken. From that day on, Wendy Kasso knew if she ever wanted to gain her father's affection and approval, she would have to focus on sports like Jody, Kelly, and Ricky did.

For Ricky, at least, this was initially manageable. There were plenty of opportunities to play sports in the village. He tried his hand at basketball for the Northport Nets and Little League baseball with the Northport Mets. For the most part, Ricky was an average baseball player. Unfortunately, as he grew older, *average* became less acceptable in his father's eyes. If Ricky's playing wasn't up to par, Dick had no problem calling his son out for it. On several occasions, Ricky found himself publicly humiliated by his own dad, who would leave the bleachers and loudly chastise him on the field while the game was still being played.

Ricky's coach, Harry Schock, always stepped in when this occurred.

"My dad tried intervening between Ricky and his father during our Little League games," says Harry's son, Richard Schock, who also played for the Northport Mets with Ricky. "This guy used to scream and degrade his kid. My dad would have to say to Dick, 'Hey, calm down! It's just a game! The kids are here to have fun!' Dick wanted Ricky to be the next Willie Mays or Johnny Unitas. The man had a screw loose."

Watching these conflicts left a lasting impression on the other boys on the team. One such boy was a short, fair-haired classmate of Ricky's whose life—and death—would become forever linked to his own.

His name was Gary Lauwers.

Chapter 5

"WHERE'S GARY?"

Nicole Lauwers was used to this question.

On April 30, 1967, her mother Yvonne had given birth to her third and final child, a little boy, in Huntington Hospital. Nicole badly wanted her youngest brother to be named Christopher, but Yvonne decided to call him Gary instead. As a consolation prize, they used Nicole's suggestion for his middle name.

Nicole adored her baby brother, Gary, despite their fourteen-year age difference. If she had a movie date downtown, she would bring him along. One might expect teenage boys to resent this kind of "third wheel" situation, but Nicole's dates never objected, always asking where the little blond toddler was if he didn't show up with his sister. When the weather was nice, and Nicole didn't have any plans, she would take Gary downtown to play in the park or buy handfuls of candy at the local sweet shop.

For Gary, having Nicole around was almost like having a second mother, and he loved every minute of it.

He came to rely on his sister as a source of positivity in his life as he grew older. His parents were Belgian immigrants and he sometimes failed to connect with them or his older brother, Michael. When Gary started attending school, he quickly discovered that his classmates weren't going to fawn over him the way his sister and her friends did. His father worked hard at a Manhattan bank to provide his children with nice clothes to wear, and thus, Gary often arrived at school wearing classy turtleneck sweaters and a blazer. The boys clad in sports tees and flannel shirts were not impressed. They soon targeted Gary, shouting "Faggot!" as he walked down the halls of Ocean Avenue Elementary. Nicole recalls Ricky Kasso, whom Gary had met during his second year at Ocean Avenue, being one of these boys. However, others who knew them maintain the two were friendly during these years.

Gary's father did his best to alleviate matters by letting his son join the Cub Scouts, accompanying him when his pack traveled upstate. Herbert Lauwers hoped that getting away from the village for some time spent camping and fishing would help Gary forget about the boys terrorizing him at school. This seemed to help for a while, but as soon as Gary entered puberty, his problems worsened. While he never grew to be particularly tall or athletic, Gary possessed other traits that several of his female classmates found attractive. His mop of golden blond hair set him apart from the other boys, while the charming smile highlighting his freckled face made him easily approachable. Once Gary's tormentors noticed the girls flocking his way, they doubled down on their bullying, often punching and shoving him in the hallway.

"This was a much more brutal time to go to school," says Richard Schock. "Teachers used to actually *encourage* fistfights. If you had a problem with a classmate, your teachers—not just the coaches—would say, 'Well, go out on the field and fuckin' duke it out!' I remember one time I got into a fight in front of Northport Junior High School with a kid and we were knockin' the shit out of each other. It was *brutal*. The teachers were all rooting and betting on who would win."

One such teacher was a mathematics instructor named Arthur Worm, whom students like Ricky Kasso particularly despised. A World War II veteran with a buzz cut and gruff voice to match, Worm took a literal hands-on approach to teaching. If he caught one of his students sleeping in class, he would grab their head and bang it on the desk. This, he told his class, was *discipline*.

Gary's older brother, Michael, had experienced similar problems at Northport Junior High School nearly a decade before. Michael's problems eventually faded away, but Gary's troubles seemed to be a permanent curse. His friends recall him constantly trying to fit in, but never quite achieving this. Many felt he was trying too hard, and, as a result, was picked on even harder. Gary tried to compensate through his ever-present sense of humor. He would crack jokes, make up silly songs, or do funny voices.

Unfortunately, the bullies weren't laughing.

"He was like one of those yappy little dogs," Beth Brewer, a former classmate of Gary's, says. "You'd want to tell him, 'Oh, just stop talking, and everyone will stop being mean to you!'"

Frustrated and helpless, Gary sought an alternate way of coping. One day he noticed some of the other middle school outcasts passing a joint back and forth at the loading docks behind the nearby Ground Round restaurant. With nothing to lose—as far as he was concerned—Gary joined them, and asked for a drag.

Matthew Carpenter, a friend of Gary's and Ricky's, understands why Gary turned to drugs.

"Being an outcast in Northport wasn't very cool," he says, "so I turned to drugs and alcohol. Suddenly I had instant friends."

It was not long before Gary Lauwers began joining his own instant friends at the loading docks every morning before school, numbing himself to the looming misery in a cloud of marijuana smoke.

Chapter 6

IF DRUGS WERE TO BLAME FOR THE HORROR THAT eventually befell Northport, the turning point in Ricky Kasso's life came one day in the fall of 1977. Ricky, then a ten-year-old fifth grader, was offered a joint by a friend's older brother. Ricky's first encounter with drugs had a profound effect on him. With just a few quick puffs, his world changed. The jokes his friends told were funnier, the music he played sounded cooler—his food even seemed to *taste* better.

For a while, Ricky's pot smoking remained an occasional indulgence. After all, how much privacy to smoke could a ten-year-old have? This all changed, however, when Ricky turned twelve. By then, he had found classmates who were also smoking marijuana. As always, Ricky would leave early for school, but no longer for the early morning football games he used to love. Instead he was meeting his friends at the loading docks so they could get high before class.

Smoking pot was now an everyday routine.

Ricky soon became curious about trying other substances. Most of his friends were more than happy smoking marijuana, but Ricky was craving something different—something *stronger*. By seventh grade, he was ready to take his drug use to the next level. For him, this meant LSD and the small purple tablets street kids called "microdots." Ricky and his friends mistakenly thought the tablets were mescaline, a natural hallucinogenic chemical found in the peyote cactus, but the microdots were actually low-grade LSD mixed with PCP and sometimes strychnine, a very toxic alkaloid. No one recalls when or where Ricky Kasso tripped on these for the first time, but by 1979, he was swallowing hits of acid and handfuls of purple microdots like candy.

One day Ricky walked into his junior high school art class high on purple microdots. Taking his usual seat next to Matthew Carpenter, he grabbed a sheet of paper and began quietly sketching a dragon. Matthew looked over at Ricky's creation and broke the ice.

"Whatcha drawing?" he asked.

"A dragon," Ricky replied.

"Cool, man," Matthew said.

"It's moving," Ricky added nonchalantly.

"*What's* moving?" Matthew asked, visibly confused.

"The dragon," Ricky replied. "It's *moving*."

Matthew turned his head to see Ricky's dragon, still as a statue.

"It's coming to life," the boy insisted.

"Ricky, are you *on* something?" Matthew asked.

"Yeah," he replied.

"What are you on?"

"Purple microdot."

Matthew could only smirk. He had dabbled in light drug use himself—mostly by joining Ricky at the loading docks to smoke a joint—but he had never taken hallucinogens, let alone *in class*. That was a special kind of risky. Truth be told, Matthew thought it was kind of cool. During lunch, the two would often walk across the football field to the loading docks, smoke pot, walk back, and listen to the music teachers play Beatles records.

"We had a sit-out one time," Matthew recalls fondly. "Could you imagine a junior high sit-out *today*?"

As is the case with many drug users with limited resources, Ricky soon began stealing to support his habit. That same year, he broke into Northport's St. Philip Neri Roman Catholic Church and stole the cash that had been collected during the previous Sunday's service. Adding a strange element to the theft, Ricky also inexplicably took a box of communion wafers with him as he fled the church.

Once he realized no one was onto him, Ricky started bragging about the theft to his friends at school. Some who were tired of being dragged to mass every Sunday were enchanted by this. Others were left impressed by Ricky not getting caught. The next school year, Ricky decided to take petty crime to the next level by breaking into a Northport home with five other friends. In the winter of 1980, the group chose the house of a schoolmate they knew would be on vacation with his family.

"There was a newspaper back then called the *Northport Journal*," retired Northport Police Officer Gene Roemer recalls. "We used to call it the 'Criminal's Best Friend' because they would announce when locals would be going on vacation and how long they'd be gone for."

Unfortunately for Ricky and his friends, whatever luck he'd had at St. Philip Neri had since evaporated. After helping themselves to the family's booze and some silver, they were caught, arrested, and charged with burglary. When Dick and Lynn were notified, they reacted somewhat calmly to the news. Dick, as it happened, did not have much of a moral leg to stand on. When he was a twenty-one-year-old senior at Colgate University, he and two friends were arrested for stealing wheels, hubcaps, and tires from parked cars in Oneonta, New York. Decades later, he figured Ricky was just "sowing a few wild oats," as he later told a reporter. After speaking with the police, Dick and Lynn went upstairs to search Ricky's bedroom for any items that might have been taken from anywhere else he might have burglarized.

Instead they found a bong.

The two distressed parents sought immediate drug counseling for their son. Dick and Lynn approached the Place, a nonprofit organization on Main Street, which had been formed in the wake of tragedy. In 1968 two teenagers had been killed in a car wreck while high on marijuana. Shaken by the incident, the Northport Village Council held a community meeting, which led concerned resident Joan Ayer to create Concepts for Narcotics

Prevention, Inc., in the hope of combating the area's drug problem. Shortly after, Northport's First Presbyterian Church leased the empty clergy home next door to house the new agency.

Early on, Concepts turned the home into an active "drop-in" center, and local kids began showing up in droves. With little to do in the village after school, Concepts offered a safe place for Northport's teenagers to socialize, play games, listen to records, have something to eat, or talk privately with a counselor in an upstairs office. This warm and welcoming environment became popular, with more and more kids stopping into "the place downtown" every day. Soon, it became known simply as "the Place."

The nickname stuck.

It was in one of the Place's upstairs offices that Ricky and his mother found themselves sitting across from Tom Fazio, one of the agency's counselors. Alerted by the thirteen-year-old's demeanor, Fazio suspected that Ricky had arrived high on marijuana.

"It doesn't seem like you're trying to get off drugs, or even want to," Fazio told him.

"You're right," Ricky replied. "I *like* what I'm doing."

After walking out of this disastrous session, Ricky never attended another meeting with Fazio. However, Dick and Lynn started attending weekly meetings at the Place with a focus on helping parents cope with troubled children. They eventually found a psychiatrist for their son, but little hope was offered. After one visit, Ricky returned to his mother's car and boldly declared, "You just threw away another seventy-five bucks. This counselor's a jerk, but if you want me to, I'll play the game."

After four more visits, the psychiatrist dismissed Ricky from his practice, telling his parents that he was "uncooperative" and deliberately "sabotaging the sessions." Desperation began to creep in for Lynn Kasso. Before her very eyes, her son—her own firstborn child—was vanishing, and there seemed to be little hope of reaching him.

As the days wore on, it became impossible for Dick and Lynn to have any kind of a positive relationship with Ricky. Today, no one can agree on whether he was thrown out or ran away, but either way, by Christmas 1980, Ricky Kasso was no longer living at home. Cold and hungry with nowhere else to go, he hitchhiked nearly two hundred and thirty miles from Northport to the little red cabin up in Argyle.

Along with him was a new friend—another troubled teenager named Jimmy Troiano.

Chapter 7

"I ALWAYS SAW THE BETTER-LOOKING KIDS GETTING adopted while I was passed over," Jimmy Troiano once told an acquaintance.

Memories like these are some of his earliest.

Placed in an upstate New York orphanage shortly after his birth on December 10, 1965, Jimmy wouldn't be adopted until he was nearly five years old. The couple who decided to bring young Jimmy into their lives were Vincent Troiano, a forty-six-year-old Manhattan art director, and his wife, Mary. Twelve years her husband's junior, Mary Troiano worked as a registered nurse in the psychiatric ward at Huntington Hospital.

Jimmy's problems were immediately apparent. There was the incident on the playground where his face became horribly scarred, and Jimmy's behavior continued to be increasingly erratic after that. His grades at Dickinson Avenue Elementary

School soon tanked due to him being a slow learner and refusing to do his homework. When he could not get the positive attention that he sought, Jimmy lashed out, settling for negative.

"He would always be the kid with the 'I'm going to get you before you get me' mentality," Beth Brewer, who grew up in the same neighborhood as the Troianos, recalls. "It was like, 'If you're not going to like me, you're going to be scared of me,' or something. He was always a bit of an odd kid. He was a loner—definitely didn't have a lot of friends. I always felt kind of bad for him. One day, you'd talk to him and he was the sweetest kid. The next, you'd turn around thinking he's nuts. There were obvious mental health issues there. He wasn't a particularly big kid, but he was a *strong* kid. I remember these guys were doing construction at the school and they were picking on Jimmy because of the scars on his face. He picked up a rock and threw it down at them while they were steam-cleaning cesspools, and they beat the shit out of him. Jimmy was just sort of a poor lost soul—even from the beginning. He was just one of those kids that didn't fit in. . . ."

Sometime during elementary school, Jimmy began wandering out of his home at 2 Barry Drive in East Northport and into the living rooms and kitchens of his neighbors. Back at the orphanage, if Jimmy ever needed something to eat or drink, he could just leave his bedroom and grab some food from the kitchen. At first Jimmy didn't realize what he was doing was wrong. For him, it was merely an extension of how things worked upstate. If he was hungry for something that wasn't in Vincent and Mary's refrigerator, he would simply walk over to a neighbor's home and help himself to whatever they had.

The Troianos' neighbors eventually began to discover Jimmy in their living rooms and kitchens. Understanding his background, they chose to leave the police out of it, opting to call his parents instead. That was, at least, until more than just food started going missing from their homes. Jimmy Troiano, like a lot of his friends in the village, had moved up to burglaries. He now had money to buy drugs from the kids at the loading docks.

When Jimmy wasn't breaking into local homes or smoking pot with friends, he was back at school, brawling with his classmates. Whereas Gary bent over backward trying to get his enemies to like him, Jimmy couldn't be bothered. If someone gave him hell, he gave it right back to them.

"Jimmy Troiano was psychotic," Richard Schock recalls. "He used to throw firecrackers at people. I was always a pretty tough kid, but I never bothered anyone or picked on anybody. One day Jimmy and I were arguing about something at the top of the stairs in junior high school. He grabbed me around the waist and tried to throw me down the stairwell. Two of my friends grabbed him and stopped him. Once I got loose, we ended up having a big fight. Troiano was a tough motherfucker. Don't let me kid you—that kid would fight until he was hamburger."

Disturbed by their son's behavior in and outside of school, the Troianos followed the same route as the Kassos by taking Jimmy to the Place. Mary Troiano had become acquainted with Tony Ruggi, the organization's senior counselor, while he was completing his internship in the psychiatric ward of Huntington Hospital, where she worked. While Ruggi had developed a rapport with local kids—many of whom affectionately called him "the guy with the ponytail"—he quickly realized Jimmy Troiano was not your average troubled child.

"Jimmy concerned me because, to put it simply, he had a problem seeing the difference between right and wrong," Ruggi recalls. "He was pleasant enough, but when it came to talking about making mistakes, he just saw them as things he did, and didn't understand why his parents would get upset over it."

Ruggi advised Vincent and Mary to seek further psychological testing for their son. "After that," Ruggi says, "Jimmy stopped seeing me, and I don't know if the parents followed up with anything."

Hoping to provide a positive outlet for his brute strength, those around Jimmy encouraged him to try out for the Northport Junior High football and wrestling teams. He made the cut for both. It was on these teams that Jimmy first met a seventh grader named Ricky Kasso—the boy who would forever alter the course of his life.

"Jimmy then was a hero in Ricky's eyes," Dick Kasso later told the *New York Daily News*. "He was an eighth grader playing football and wrestling; an outstanding athlete."

He was a hero to Ricky for another reason—Jimmy Troiano was one of the few Northport Junior High athletes who, like himself, smoked pot and dropped acid.

"Jimmy was nuts," Ricky's friend Dave Johnson recalls. "I

was on the football team with him and Ricky. He wasn't scared of anything. You could say to him, 'I want you to put your head down and go run through that wall as fast as you can—left foot first,' and he would do it. I remember Coach Harper yelling at him, saying, 'Take that center and carry him down the field if you have to!' Jimmy went out there and carried this big-ass center *thirty yards*. He and Ricky used to play *hard*."

Some of Ricky's drug friends from the loading docks started turning on him around this time. They saw Ricky engaging in conservative activities like football, basketball, and wrestling as a betrayal of their more carefree lifestyle. A few even turned up at games just to heckle him from the bleachers, hollering, "Nice play, Ricky, you jock!" Ricky would look at Jimmy, shake his head, and say, "I hate this game. . . . I hate this game. . . ."

During one game, Ricky became so frustrated that he deliberately knocked out the other team's quarterback.

"It was an illegal hit, but he did it," Jimmy later told an interviewer. "He got kicked out of the game for it. He hated football. I remember his dad was on the sideline, pissed."

Ricky's coach, David Harper, took pity on the scrawny kid, who was able enough to play as both an offensive and defense end. Still, Harper could not reconcile Ricky's talents with the castaways he chose as his friends. He clearly saw the tug-of-war happening in Ricky's life. On one end, there was the life Dick Kasso wanted for his only son—a life of athletic achievement. On the other, there was the life Ricky wanted for himself—an existence devoid of pressure, but filled with music, drugs, and good times.

Any teacher with half a brain could see which side was going to win.

As their friendship blossomed, Ricky and Jimmy often rushed off the football field after practice to smoke a joint or drop acid together. Eventually, Ricky's constant drug use began to affect his athletic performance and his grades. During a wrestling meet, Ricky was badly beaten by an opponent. Incensed, Dick Kasso started berating the referee for allegedly making unfair calls. Finally, Dick's screaming got him ejected from the gymnasium.

"Can you imagine how *embarrassing* it was to be Ricky that night?" Wendy Kasso says.

Trying to cope with their troubles, Ricky and Jimmy continued to bond through smoke and chemicals. Their respective family squabbles, coupled with athletic and academic pressures, soon resulted in the two running away to the Kasso family's cabin up in Argyle during the winter of 1980, not long after Ricky's burglary arrest. It was far from Northport, but it had a roof, heat, and furniture, which made being separated from home considerably easier. However, their stay did not last long. Ricky and Jimmy were soon picked up by the police, who called Dick Kasso, telling him to retrieve his son. The boys returned to the village, but the fractures within their families failed to mend.

A period of intermittent homelessness that would last nearly four years had just begun.

Chapter 8

LACES ROLLER RINK ON ROUTE 25A WAS, FOR A TIME, the place to be if you were a Northport teenager. With great music, a good skate floor, and decent food, Laces offered a fun and seemingly safe environment for kids in the village. So safe, in fact, that dozens of local parents didn't think twice when their children asked to be dropped off for an overnight skate party. What they didn't know was how easy it was for their kids to sneak out, grab a bottle of liquor, and reenter the building during one of these skate-a-thons.

Johnny Hayward was one of the many teens smuggling booze into Laces. Hayward would often bring bottles of whiskey and rum through the back door and skate into the bathroom to chug them down with friends before returning to the skate floor. Hayward had a natural talent for roller skating, sober or drunk. He considered himself one of the best—if not *the* best—out of everyone at the rink.

One night in 1981, a short blond teenager walked into Laces, threw on a pair of skates, and proved that Johnny Hayward was not without competition. For the first time, Johnny saw someone on the floor with as much speed, grace, and skill as himself. Instead of giving in to jealousy, Johnny made his way over to the boy and introduced himself.

"Hey," he said. "I'm Johnny."

"Gary," the boy replied. "Gary Lauwers."

The two left the floor and joined their mutual friend Danny for a drink in the boys' bathroom. In between swigs of Wild Turkey, the three made small talk, leading Johnny and Gary to realize they had a lot in common. From that moment on, the two became a staple at Laces.

"We were the guys who everyone at the rink wanted to be," Hayward declares. "We had all the girls and could skate better than anyone. We skated every day for two years."

Gary's newfound friendship with Johnny certainly came with a bonus—Johnny was a brawler.

"I was so crazy when I was a kid," Hayward recalls. "I went out every night to get drunk, get laid, and get into a fight—and it didn't matter what order. If I didn't get all three, I woke up in a bad mood the next day—and that is *not* a joke."

As soon as Johnny found out bullies were tormenting Gary at school, he put the word out: "If you fuck with Gary Lauwers, I'm gonna fuck with you."

It wasn't long before Johnny Hayward got a chance to prove his loyalty.

One night, after a shift waiting tables at a local restaurant, Johnny went straight to Laces to blow off some steam. Still in his work clothes, he walked through the door and was immediately told by a few friends that Gary was being jumped behind Foodtown. Without skipping a beat, Johnny burst back outside and raced across 25A straight to the supermarket. Not wanting to soil his work clothes with blood and dirt, Johnny stripped down to his underwear and lunged at the two kids pummeling Gary. To his own surprise, Johnny single-handedly fended off his friend's attackers.

"I think it may have been the shock of seeing me come out of nowhere in my underwear," Hayward muses, "but it didn't matter—I beat the shit out of them both."

The two assailants fled into the night, leaving a bruised Gary and a nearly-nude Johnny standing behind Foodtown. The two looked at each other and burst into a fit of laughter that could be heard for blocks.

"We're either gonna be dead or in jail by the time we're eighteen," Gary quipped as they walked away.

One night, after a double date in Greenlawn, Gary and Johnny found themselves at a railroad station near Harborfields High School, trying to get back to Northport. While they waited, Gary and Johnny lit cigarettes and talked about how well their night had gone. At one point, Gary looked Johnny in the eye and said, "Hey, man, we'll be brothers forever."

"Sure," Johnny replied, almost dismissively.

Gary hopped down from the rail he was perched on, removed

the cigarette from his lips, and said, "Put your cigarette out on your arm. I'll put one out in the same exact spot on my arm, and we'll have the same exact scar all our lives!"

Johnny smiled, and as insects danced around the light hanging above them, the two closed their eyes, braced themselves, and pressed the cigarettes against their flesh. The smoldering embers left small, circular burns that soon faded into dark scars.

"To this day, I still got my scar," Johnny now says with a hint of wistful pride.

Around this time, Gary started hanging out with two older kids named Timmy and Edwin. One night in 1982, they both asked Gary to join them for a drug deal in Huntington, where they knew someone selling purple microdots in large quantities. Hoping to make another drug connection, Gary agreed.

When the trio arrived at the meeting place, a dead-end street at the top of a hill, Timmy and Edwin told Gary to walk up to the dealer, collect a bag of one hundred purple microdots, and run. When the man handed the drugs to Gary, Timmy and Edwin leaped out from the shadows. The tall, imposing teenagers stood in front of the dealer, looked him in the eye, and said, "What do you think you're gonna do about it?" as Gary raced off into the night.

After getting his share of the microdots from Timmy and Edwin, Gary, still bursting with adrenaline, put a few into his mouth and swallowed. Within a few minutes he was uncontrollably giggling at a barrage of mild hallucinations. The feeling was incredible—more intense than any pot high he had ever experienced. He needed to tell someone. Someone *had* to know how great a trip this was. Gary raced toward the Hayward house on Tanager Lane.

Gary fought hard to keep his composure as he navigated past Mr. and Mrs. Hayward, but once he got to Johnny's bedroom, he let loose.

"Johnny! Johnny! Johnny!" he shouted, extending his hand. "Here! Here!"

In his palm were two purple microdots.

"Eat these, man! You're gonna *love* 'em! Eat 'em!"

Johnny stood there, bemused. Here was his best friend, jumping around his bedroom like a lunatic, asking him to eat some strange tablets. In the end, this was not enough to weaken his trust in Gary. Johnny took the microdots and tossed them into his mouth.

"I gotta go!" Gary said unexpectedly. "Whatever you do, *don't scream*, and you'll be fine tomorrow morning! Nothing will be real!"

Before Johnny could reply, Gary ran out of his room and back into the street. At first Johnny felt extreme anxiety. He was virtually trapped in his bedroom, waiting for a drug he had never ingested before to take effect.

The dread didn't last long.

Johnny lay down on his bed, staring at the model warplanes hanging from his ceiling by fishing line. To his amazement, the planes came alive and started flying around his room. Then suddenly Johnny's closet door slammed open, and a whole platoon of soldiers marched out. He quickly pulled the bedsheets over his head, laughing wildly as the soldiers marched on top of him. By the time the hallucinations faded, it was time for Johnny to go to class at Northport High School.

As soon as he got there, he found Gary and said, "I need eighteen more hits. . . ."

Chapter 9

LONG BEFORE GARY AND JOHNNY BEGAN THEIR LOVE affair with hallucinogens, Ricky Kasso had already turned them into his cash crop. Even after his parents found his bong, Ricky still hung around the loading docks to sell pot, LSD, and purple microdots. For a time, he successfully kept these activities a secret from his mother and father, who had recently allowed him back home. After all, in Dick Kasso's mind, as long as Ricky performed well on the football team and kept his grades above a C average, he was succeeding as a parent.

That all came crashing down the moment Ricky told his father he planned to quit playing sports.

"You have to be on *something*, Ricky!" Dick ordered. "Football! Wrestling! *Anything!*"

"But I don't want to do *any* of that!" his son replied.

Wendy Kasso overheard the argument from the hallway. She

walked into Ricky's bedroom and asked, "Why does he *have* to if he doesn't *want* to?"

Dick and Ricky turned to face Wendy. Both were shocked by her standing up to her father. For Dick, the surprise quickly turned to anger. Gritting his teeth, he screamed, "*GET OUT!*" to his youngest child, who ran off. Ricky realized he would have to keep his head down and comply if he wanted to avoid his father's wrath. Denied a say in his own life, a rage seethed inside him.

After the fight, Dick walked downstairs and into the kitchen, where Wendy was sitting. He turned toward a small shelf on the wall featuring a display of five porcelain ducks—a mama duck and her four babies following in a row. Dick took the last baby duck on the end and turned it away from the mother and the three other ducklings. Looking Wendy square in the eye, Dick told her, "That one is *Ricky*. . . ."

When eighth grade ended for Ricky in the spring of 1981, the fourteen-year-old had spent most of the year avoiding his family. He continued to smoke pot and trip on LSD with friends, selling both when he needed cash, but made sure to stay below his father's radar. His reputation as a drug dealer might have been steadily solidifying in Northport, but as long as Dick Kasso heard no word of it, he was safe at home.

On the last day of school that year, the Kassos packed up their cars and headed upstate for another summer of relaxation in Argyle. Kelly and Jody rode with Dick, while Ricky opted to ride with Wendy and his mother. As soon as they hit I-87, Lynn would let Ricky pop a cassette tape into the car stereo. The Who's *The Kids Are Alright* soundtrack was a favorite of Ricky's, along with *Joe's Garage* by Frank Zappa. Counting down the miles, Ricky would sing along with the tape. Zappa's nostalgic song about teenagers forming their first rock band spoke to Ricky's soul. He had a cheap acoustic guitar he would strum in his bedroom, surrounded by the Led Zeppelin and Yes posters he had taped to the wall. He hoped to one day leave Northport for California, and maybe even make it as a musician there. But for now, he was stuck in New York with a family he was growing to hate and friends he feared were only using him for his drugs. Coasting up the highway on this hot June afternoon, Ricky Kasso let the music and his dreams carry him up to Argyle.

Once there, the summer of 1981 began like the previous ones. The Kassos reunited with the Sterlings and the Mallorys, and their kids split off to have fun. On most days, the Kasso and Sterling kids would all flock to the edge of Lake Cossayuna to catch turtles. One afternoon, Ricky grabbed his fishing pole and went down alone. To his surprise, he caught a northern copperhead—a mildly poisonous species of snake. Ricky brought it back to the cabin to show his friends. When his sisters saw the snake, they ran inside to tell their father. Dick—who had always made a point not to lose his temper in the company of the other Argyle families—went through the roof, screaming at his son for being so careless. While Ricky, Bruce, and Sue stood on the lawn, stunned, Dick grabbed his shotgun and blasted the snake's head off. The kids all moved closer to get a better look, but Dick brushed them aside.

"Stay *away* from it!" he warned. "The head is still alive. It won't die until after the sun goes down. Then it won't be able to bite you. . . ."

Once tensions died down, Ricky went outside to confide in Sue.

"My dad wants me to do *this* and wants me to do *that*," he told her. "I just don't like it. I don't know why my dad wants me to do these things, because I'm not that type of person."

Sue was still shocked by Dick's behavior.

"Dick and Lynn had to have their reputations on a pedestal," Sue recalls. "They were both schoolteachers. He was a football coach. They didn't want anybody to think they weren't a perfect family. He was just like any other normal kid, ya know? He wanted to go swimming and hang with his friends."

That summer proved to be another turning point in Ricky's short life. He now realized that even in upstate Argyle, far away from the pot and LSD of Northport, he still could do no right in his father's eyes. Kelly and Jody were becoming outstanding athletes, and with Ricky now showing zero interest in Dick's dreams for him, he stood little chance of regaining the affection his father had once shown him. The burglary arrest and discovery of his bong only further cemented Dick's growing opinion of his son as a perpetual fuck-up.

"That was the root of Ricky's major insecurities and him beginning to look for attention in other places," recalls Ricky's childhood friend Grant Koerner. "There was a sternness displayed toward Ricky at a young age. He just had different interests than what his parents expected, unfortunately, and they started throwing him out very early. That's when we noticed Kelly and Jody playing sports in the neighborhood instead of Ricky. I would hate to say it all stemmed from there, but it definitely *did*. His sisters—who had a very antagonistic relationship with Ricky—then started getting all the attention."

"Kelly and Jody didn't like Ricky because they feared their father," Dave Johnson adds. "They knew Ricky was on their father's shit list. That was programmed into them—'Don't be a fuck-up like your brother; he's a piece of shit!' He was drilling that into their heads."

"They were athletes and Dick could relate to them," Koerner continues. "He was a tough father and part of that 1950s *man* generation. I stayed away from Mr. Kasso because, as a kid, why would I want to be around *that*?"

Sue Sterling agrees.

"Ricky wanted his father's approval and he did not get it," she says. "Dick wanted him to be a whole different type of person."

The person Ricky Kasso was about to become could not have been any further from what his father wanted.

Part Three

CHILDHOOD'S END

Heard of some grave sites, out by the highway
A place where nobody knows . . .
—Talking Heads,
"Life During Wartime"

Chapter 10

NORTHPORT'S COW HARBOR PARK SITS JUST SOUTH of where Main Street ends and Woodbine Avenue begins. Directly adjacent to the marina, the park features a basketball court, a children's playground, and a small wooden gazebo covering two stone chess tables. The park was constructed by the town of Huntington in late 1976 as a proud addition to downtown Northport—despite the village board of trustees objecting to it. As far as they were concerned, there already was a wonderful place for outdoor recreational activity: Northport Village Park on Bayview Avenue, only two hundred feet from the planned location of the new park. Huntington, however, was not fazed.

"The new Park is potentially one of the most successful and beautiful the Town has to offer," Huntington Town Supervisor Kenneth C. Butterfield boasted during an October 1976 interview with the *Long-Islander* newspaper. "It will combine a gazebo, paths, and many other playground facilities with the scenic beauty of the harbor."

Despite Butterfield's optimism, Cow Harbor Park would become a living nightmare for the citizens of Northport in less than five years.

What the town of Huntington failed to consider was that Northport was completely unable to effectively patrol the new park, thanks to a statute preventing the village from making laws on property they did not own. To further complicate things, Huntington could not step in and offer any assistance, as they were legally prevented from policing any property outside the town border.

The result was that Cow Harbor Park became a veritable no-man's-land for local law enforcement. As time went on, the park eventually found its place as the new haven for the booze-chugging, pot-smoking, and acid-dropping kids who felt they had outgrown Laces.

One night in December 1981, a young man walked into Cow Harbor Park clutching a curious item—a stillborn goat fetus stolen from a local farm. Homeless and hungry, the man dumped the fetus onto one of the stone chess tables, arranged several matchbooks around it, and lit the strange assortment on fire in a failed attempt to cook a meal. When the charred carcass was discovered the next morning, the village suspected the goat had been killed and burned by a demonic cult. For years, farm animals and small pets had been vanishing from the area, inspiring rumors regarding Satanic sacrifices, but because no remains had ever been found, the possibility of the animals simply running away couldn't be ruled out. The burnt goat fetus in the gazebo, however, changed everything.

Soon after, Northport Police Chief Robert Howard received a misguided tip claiming the incident was possibly related to an organized group of a dozen or so teenage boys from East Northport. Howard's informant said they were known by an unsettling name: the Knights of the Black Circle. The informant said the Knights were easy to spot, as most of them wore denim jackets with inverted pentagrams painted on the backs. While the group may not have been responsible for the burnt goat fetus, they did exist, having formed as an offshoot of a previous group of misfit kids.

"We were the absolute last of the hippies," says Jonathan McCuller, a member of the group. "This was around 1977 or 1978. We were about peace, love, and harmony."

Despite the group's supposed peaceful nature, their presence made the residents of Northport and East Northport uneasy. They began calling the teens "Circus"—short for "Circus Freaks."

"I guess it was because we were all a bunch of outcasts," McCuller says.

With such a nickname, it wasn't long before the rumor mill took off.

"I remember being out on Eatons Neck with this group of kids when I was nine or ten years old," one Northport resident recalls. "We were walking through the woods, trying to find the swampy parts so we could look for turtles or frogs, or whatever. They were like, 'If you hear anything, just freeze, because it could be the Circus Gang!' I didn't know what that was. They explained to me that it was this violent group of kids who went around kidnapping people's pets and nailing them to trees. I never encountered them, but I was told to be afraid of them."

Jonathan McCuller disputes such lurid tales.

"We were completely nonviolent," he says, "but we had *big* masses. I mean, we would come into the park a hundred-fifty strong, but no one was coming to hurt somebody. Circus never had issues with the law, besides 'The park's closed, you gotta leave.' That sort of thing. We never even carried weapons. It wasn't about that. It was more *peace and love*. We listened to stuff like Crosby, Stills, Nash & Young. We were more like a family. Ninety percent of us came from broken homes, so we made our own family. Some of us didn't have fathers, but we had each other. It helped us through some tough times."

McCuller had an especially rough time growing up in East Northport. The son of a black father and a white mother, McCuller was often ridiculed in a community that was then—and still is today—more than 90 percent white. Some kids took to calling Jonathan and his siblings "the McNiggers."

Toward the end of the 1970s, McCuller, who was in his early teens, began hanging out in Cow Harbor Park with the rest of the Circus.

"That's where we sold our pot," he says. "We would hang out behind the gazebo and put a couple of spotters up front and in the middle. We would literally take a pound of pot, and ten of us would roll two thousand joints out of a guitar case. When one of the spotters would whistle, we would shut the guitar case and start playing guitar. The cops never knew the difference."

While selling pot out of Cow Harbor Park did earn the Circus kids some money, it also attracted attention that was even more undesirable than cops snooping around the gazebo. Rival dealers from neighboring towns soon descended onto Northport, jumping each member of the Circus one by one until they had stolen all their marijuana. This caused most of the Circus to dissipate.

One day McCuller and some close friends ventured into the woods to come up with a plan to end the beatings. Standing beside a makeshift table fashioned from a large wooden cable spool that had been painted black, McCuller looked to his buddies and said, "Look, this is what we're gonna do—from now on we're all in this *together*. We never go anywhere alone. We always go no less than four."

Paul McBride, a friend of McCuller's, agreed with the plan but felt it needed something *more*—something with a little imagery to instill fear in those who wished to harm them.

"Let's make a brotherhood," McBride said. "We'll be like the Knights of the Round Table." Pointing to the black cable spool he and his friends had gathered around, he declared, "This is our Round Table! We'll call ourselves 'The Knights of the Black Circle'!"

The group saw he was onto something.

"We called Paul 'King' as a reference to King Arthur," McCuller recalls. "We all had names. My name in the Knights was 'Lancelot.'

I was King's number two. He painted all the jackets for us."

The jackets became the highlight of a brotherhood that soon terrified their former tormentors. McBride took each Knight's denim jacket and painted the back-side black, adding white pentagrams, along with other Satanic imagery that varied for each member.

"The colors of our jackets were demonic and that was to freak people out," McCuller says. "It had nothing to do with Satan; we just did that to repulse people, which we accomplished. People were too scared to even approach us when we were wearing our painted jackets. Not only did we *not* get accosted, but business *boomed*."

Despite McCuller insisting the Knights of the Black Circle never engaged in violence, others disagree.

The Northport police suspected the group of violently assaulting a teenager before throwing him from a car. To this day, some current and former Northport residents recall hearing lurid tales of the Knights torturing and even killing animals like goats and cats. While almost all maintain that they never *personally* witnessed the Knights hurting animals, some say they *did* see another occult-obsessed teenager do similar things: Ricky Kasso.

Chapter 11

NO ONE KNOWS THE EXACT MOMENT THAT RICKY Kasso became obsessed with Satanism, but Dick Kasso believed this change occurred when his son found a book on the occult during an innocent visit to the Northport–East Northport Public Library.

"The really bizarre, really deviant behavior, started in the seventh grade," Kasso later told the *New York Post*. "We learned that he was very deeply involved in Satan, along with a number of other boys. He would go to the library and read about witchcraft and devil worship."

Ironically, only ten years before his son's arrest for allegedly sacrificing a friend to Satan, Dick Kasso, then-president of the Cold Spring Harbor Teachers Association, had publicly spoken out in defense of the Cold Spring Harbor Central School District Board of Education after they allowed an occult expert to visit one of the high school's English classes to discuss the history of witchcraft.

"Education without free inquiry is indoctrination rather than the pursuit of knowledge," he told the *Long-Islander* in a published letter to the editor. "We join with the Board of Education and the District Administration in the continuing defense of this vital principle."

Books on the occult still adorn the Northport–East Northport Public Library's shelves today, and it is certainly possible that Ricky spent his afternoons flipping through their pages. However, those who knew Ricky well say a moment like this would have been far from extraordinary.

"The books that were never available in the elementary school library were the books on witches and werewolves and all those," Grant Koerner recalls. "You could never get those because they were *always* being checked out. For me, that was normal in fifth grade. You know, I read the *Necronomicon* too! I'm sure if I told someone that back then, it would have ended up in the *National Enquirer*, but it was nothing different than anyone else in the neighborhood. My next-door neighbors and I played Dungeons & Dragons. That's the real irony: from the perspective of what was going on in the neighborhood, what Ricky was doing was really no different than what anybody else was. . . ."

No matter where Ricky first made his connection with Satan, by the fall of 1981, it was solidified. Friends remember him showing up in Cow Harbor Park after school, preaching about the devil. Most paid him no mind. At the time, several popular rock acts like Ozzy Osbourne, Judas Priest, and Iron Maiden were using morbid imagery during their live shows and on their record sleeves, so a stoned teenager occasionally rambling about Lucifer didn't surprise many Northport teenagers.

When Ricky first started hanging out in Cow Harbor Park—now dubbed "the New Park"—he tried fitting in by bringing his guitar along. Some of the older teens would sit in the gazebo they nicknamed "the roundhouse," playing Jethro Tull and Led Zeppelin songs on their acoustics. Like Ricky, these kids were outcasts themselves. Many were separated from their families and living in Merrie Schaller's house on West Scudder Place. A kindhearted woman in her early thirties, Merrie took in local runaways, giving them a safe and stable place to stay while they pieced their lives back together. Some locals joked, "Some women collect stray cats; Merrie collects stray kids." Ricky, however, never found himself fully integrated into the group, despite his efforts.

"Ricky messed around on the guitar a little bit, but nothing like our caliber," Glen Wolf, who was one of the New Park kids, says. "I was a really good guitarist at the time."

Ricky's sister Wendy also recalls her brother's limited musical ability.

"He just made stuff up on the guitar," she says. "I never heard him play any other way."

Ricky eventually sought other forms of attention. One day he walked into the roundhouse clutching a pocketknife and started carving something into one of the wooden beams. A few of the other teens walked over to see what he was doing. Ricky walked away, revealing what he had written—*SATIN*. Ricky's poor spelling caused the kids to burst into laughter. Further adding to his frustration and alienation, some began poking fun at him for it.

"Ricky was an idiot," Glen Wolf says. "He was saying all this Satan stuff, but we would tease him because he spelled 'Satan' wrong. We just thought he was trying to act out, or act tough, or whatever. He was just pretending to do stuff to have an audience; to get laid, maybe, or to make people look up to him, or fear him. You know—like a *tyrant*."

For a while, Gary Lauwers, who had also started hanging out with the New Park guitar kids, tried to balance out Ricky's dark graffiti by painting peace signs wherever he could. However, the hippie musicians soon tired of the "Satin" references piling up in the roundhouse. One day Glen Wolf approached Ricky.

"Look," Glen told him, "I'm not the graffiti patrol, and we really don't give a shit what you write, but it's all going to come back on *us*. The cops are gonna see it and they're gonna run us out of here, so why don't you go carve something else up?"

Ricky merely laughed in Glen's face and walked away.

He may have been playing the role of a rock 'n' roll rebel without a care, but Ricky's frustration over his growing social isolation soon manifested itself back at Northport High School. He was failing most of his classes and lashing out at anyone who he felt had crossed him. Matters were worsened during the winter when Jimmy Troiano, one of Ricky's few friends at school, dropped out. Then, in March 1982, Ricky was suspended five times in less than a month for brawling with his classmates. The final straw came when he was arrested for swiping a checkbook from a teacher's desk drawer.

In response, Dick and Lynn Kasso approached the Northport–East Northport Union Free School District's Committee on the Handicapped. Their plea was simple—save Ricky's scholastic career by declaring him disabled so he could attend a private school. The committee agreed to evaluate Ricky, and in April 1982 found him to be "emotionally handicapped." The Kassos could now search for a school specially equipped to handle their son's issues.

Dick and Lynn eventually found a private boarding school that seemed promising—the Camelot Campus of St. Francis Academy, just outside Lake Placid in upstate New York. High up among the Adirondack Mountains, three hundred miles away from Northport, Camelot specialized in educating students with a clear history of violence, substance abuse, and problems with authority. It seemed to be the perfect fit for Ricky. However, on the day of his admissions interview, Ricky ran away from home before Dick and Lynn could get him in the car. They would not see their son again for seventeen days. By the time he reappeared, Camelot had already decided not to accept Ricky for admission, telling his father, "We will only accept a child who is willing to give us a chance."

For a short while, Ricky was allowed back in the house while Dick and Lynn searched for another school. Sometimes Jimmy Troiano would come over to hang out with Ricky in his bedroom. On most days, the two would chat while listening to cassette tapes, usually *Who's Next* or an Ozzy album. Other times Ricky would show Jimmy songs he had been writing on his guitar. One such song dealt with his Satanic fantasies. Strumming the few simple chords he knew, Ricky would sing:

We were all up in Aztakea,
And along came the devil.
He pointed at me and said,
"You, my son, are a child of the beast . . ."

"A big part of Ricky's life was Aztakea Woods," Richard Shock, Ricky's friend from Little League, recalls. "He used to tell me, 'You've got to come up to Aztakea, man! You drop acid and trees start talking to you! They start waving, man!' Aztakea wasn't too far from the road, but it was *vast*. Ricky basically started living there. There were a lot of structures in there, so that's where he would hang out and hide out."

"Very deep in the woods, there was a foundation," Johnny Hayward says. "The story was it was an old church. I don't know if it really was or not; there was only a foundation left of whatever it was. The path into Aztakea was only about three feet wide. It went straight and then curved to the left. When you were at the foundation, you were deep enough into the woods where you could build a three- or four-foot fire without it being seen. Everyone used to go out there to drink and smoke and do drugs. It was a nice, safe place where the cops wouldn't chase you."

If the weather was too unpleasant to hang out in Aztakea,

Ricky would invite Jimmy over to share a joint in his bedroom. As Jimmy started showing up more, Lynn Kasso began to feel uneasy about her occasional houseguest. In April, while she and Dick were trying to get the school district to evaluate Ricky, Jimmy Troiano was arrested in Northport for third-degree criminal trespassing. He would be arrested three more times over the next two months, each time for burglarizing homes in Huntington. The last of these three arrests led to a conviction, and Jimmy was sentenced to five years' probation.

While this understandably made Lynn uncomfortable, she chose to remain quiet, hoping to keep her home peaceful. Her husband, however, was far from happy. Between Ricky inviting criminals into his home and arranging drug deals over the family telephone, Dick had finally had enough. He confronted Ricky and an argument ensued. What happened next would be remembered down Seaview Avenue for years to come.

"Victor Puccio and I were playing touch football in his backyard," recalls Richard Schock. "We heard this big commotion. Dick Kasso was screaming like a maniac."

Schock and Puccio ran three houses down to the Kasso's backyard fence. Almost as soon as they arrived, they saw Dick throw Ricky through the screen door and onto the ground.

"I don't want you around here anymore!" Dick screamed as he came outside. "Don't come back! I don't feel safe with you around here!"

Ricky quickly scrambled to his feet and ran off.

"Dick Kasso had no business being a father," Dave Johnson

says. "I put everything that happened to Ricky one hundred percent on his dad. I've said it for years. If Ricky missed football practice, his dad would be waiting for him with a broomstick, and beat the shit out of him when he came in. His dad was *brutal*. He was physically violent with Ricky on a regular basis. Me and Ricky would come in the house and Dick would say, 'Dave, you need to go.' Later, Ricky would show me the bruises and say, 'Yeah, he whooped my ass. . . .' He was a real jerkoff."

"If he tried that today, he would be in jail," Schock says. "Ricky and his father didn't get along—I saw that with my own eyes—but I think Ricky's sisters also may have been one of the issues between them. They were the real athletes of the family, and I think his father kind of dumped that on him because his daughters turned into the athletes that he wanted Ricky to be. What made Ricky into the person he became was his dad. . . ."

Chapter 12

FOR MOST OF NORTHPORT'S RESIDENTS, THE FIRST snow of the year means the end of fishing, sailing, and the rest of the fun to be had in the marina. For Johnny Hayward and Gary Lauwers, however, this meant *business*. Beginning in early December 1981, Johnny and Gary would both drop whatever they were doing at the first sight of snow and race down to the harbor to meet each other. There, the two would watch as hundreds of people moored their boats to the docks in anticipation of the harbor freezing. At dusk, armed with flashlights and backpacks, Johnny and Gary made their move.

"When it would snow, there would be five hundred boats and nobody else there," Hayward recalls. "Some of these boats were *houses*, you know? So, we would just go and raid all the liquor and take whatever we wanted. We had a boat we would always hang out at, and we'd open up the liquor and watch TV."

Once Johnny and Gary were finished drinking and watching television, they would fill their backpacks with whatever valuables were in sight and stash their haul on a nearby abandoned boat before fleeing. Sometimes they would grab flare guns from belowdecks and run around the docks, firing at each other.

While Johnny and Gary certainly had a lot of fun burglarizing the boats, excitement wasn't their only motive. Unemployed and craving drugs, the two struck a deal with their dealers—free pot and microdots in exchange for bottles of booze, CB radios, car stereos, or anything else worth a decent buck. Johnny and Gary found this offer hard to resist.

"There were lots of ways to make money," Hayward says. "Gary and I would pull 'Midnight Auto'—breaking into cars. We'd call some friends and say, 'Hey, you want to buy some stereos? Give me three hundred hits of mescaline and I'll give you five car stereos,' or 'How about I give you this CB radio and some walkie-talkies for a half ounce of coke?' If that didn't work, I would just go downtown and buy acid from Ricky. If you wanted acid, you went to the Acid King. . . ."

By then Ricky had moved on from the loading docks and set up shop in Cow Harbor Park. There, teenagers like Ricky Kasso and Gary Lauwers often found a mini-Woodstock waiting for them, with circles of nearly a hundred people as young as twelve and as old as sixty, drinking, smoking pot, and dropping acid. Northport Police officers would occasionally walk through but almost never intervened in any illegal activity. The patrolmen were infamous for not saying a word to anyone, as long as their hand wasn't touching the beer between their legs.

"One time, I was hanging out in the little gazebo in the New Park," Ricky's friend Matthew Carpenter recalls. "One of my friends was messed up on drugs, and was just following this woman who was walking her dog. A cop walked by us, and said to us directly, 'Don't step on my toes, and I won't step on yours. . . .' I mean, the cops would buy weed sometimes. There were no drug tests back then, you know?"

One day a Northport Village police officer decided to take a stroll through the New Park. Johnny Hayward and Ricky Kasso were standing on the south side of the park, tripping on acid. Johnny looked up and saw the officer walking on the sidewalk beyond a row of bushes. A taste for mischief suddenly came over him. Acting quickly, he grabbed Ricky, and with all his might, swung the lanky teenager through the bushes and into the officer, who was knocked to the ground by the impact. The officer immediately leaped to his feet and started screaming at Johnny while Ricky sat on the sidewalk, trying to process what had just happened. As the officer continued his tirade, Ricky noticed the eight-point police cap on the ground and decided to join in on the fun. He quickly scooped up the cap, placed it over his mop of wavy hair, and ran wildly around the park.

"It was fucking hysterical," Hayward recalls. "The cop said, 'Knock this shit off!' and walked on by. He didn't do *anything*. You could have a joint burning in your hand in the park and they still would not say anything—they'd just walk on by. So, if you have that kind of environment, all of the dregs of society are going to hang out there."

One of the New Park "dregs" Ricky Kasso soon became acquainted with was a strange man named Pat Toussaint. While Toussaint was only in his late thirties, his worn face and prematurely gray hair made him appear nearly twice his age.

"We used to call him Father Time," says Richard Schock. "He was this skinny, scraggly old fuck from the Veterans Affairs hospital who had long, gray hair and always wore a bandanna. Northport had a very bad heroin problem in the 1970s because a lot of veterans were coming home hooked on it."

Johnny Hayward also recalls Toussaint and his assortment of nicknames.

"We called him Father Time, Ghost of Christmas Past, Grandpa Dirt, and Pagan Pat," he says.

Toussaint earned the latter nickname due to his interest in metaphysics and the occult—a passion he shared with Ricky. Hayward remembers Toussaint often wearing a silver pentagram necklace while carrying a copy of Anton LaVey's 1969 bestseller *The Satanic Bible*. Those who hung out in the New Park recall Toussaint often sharing his insight into the world of Satanism with Ricky.

Macabre lectures, however, were far from the only thing Pat shared with Ricky and the other teenagers gathered downtown. Toussaint had been prescribed Librium by his doctors at the Veterans Affairs hospital in Northport. Librium, a habit-forming psychotropic drug with hypnotic and sedating effects, is often prescribed to treat anxiety and alcohol dependency. Toussaint, a longtime alcoholic, often sold his prescriptions for extra cash to supplement his monthly Social Security Insurance checks.

"Pagan Pat would get his Librium prescription from the VA hospital," Johnny Hayward recalls. "Then he would come into the park and say, 'Here; have some Librium, man! You won't have to drink as much beer!' or 'I'll trade you some Librium for some pot! I'll trade you twenty Libriums for a joint!' We used to get Librium from him all the time. If it was two in the afternoon and you wanted to get drunk and do some drugs, Pagan Pat was over there. So, we'd go sit down and talk with him for a couple hours while we got fucked up. We'd sit there, laughing at people all day long. We didn't want to go home. We stayed out all the time, and here was this old man. I mean, he's *living*. He's *old*. He's been doing this *all his life*. So, hell, we figured there was nothing wrong with this."

"Old Man Pat was a Vietnam veteran who suffered from advanced alcoholism," says Anthony Zenkus, a friend and peer of the New Park musicians. "He had post-traumatic stress disorder and was pretty out of it. There was trauma in this man's life. Post-traumatic stress disorder is highly correlated with addiction. The Centers for Disease Control says that adverse traumatic experiences are the single biggest leading causes of addiction—not genetics. PTSD and advanced alcoholism damage the frontal cortex of the brain. Advanced thinking, judgment, and impulse control are all compromised severely. This was a guy who was not capable of much more than scoring his next fix."

"Toussaint was never playing with a full deck, if you know what I mean," retired Northport Police Officer Gene Roemer recalls. "He drifted in and out of reality during most of my interactions with him. He had some very accurate moments, but they did not last long. I would say that, during one of his drifting reality periods, he possibly influenced Kasso's Satanic interests. That would be a good conclusion."

"Pat was a little stir-crazy," Dorothy, a friend of Ricky's, recalls. "He rambled a lot about how people were evil and how the government was evil. He liked to talk about the Vietnam War and death, but Pat was of use to Ricky. He always had money at the beginning of the month. He would get his Social Security check, cash it, and get drunk. Then Ricky, Gary, and Albert would roll him for money. Sometimes they would trip him, and when he was down or his back was turned, they would steal his money. Other times, Ricky would ask Pat for a few bucks, and he would give him a dollar. Ricky would then reach over, take the bundle, and give him back the single."

While Dorothy seemed to understand their dynamic, Ricky's friendship with Pagan Pat confused others. Toussaint's rough appearance made their twenty-three-year age difference seem decades wider. Most of Ricky's friends understood him wanting to hang out with a fellow drug peddler—after all, he *was* the Acid King—but their relationship seemed to be rooted in something deeper. Some chalked it up to their shared interest in Satanism, while others had darker suspicions.

"The kids were creeped out by this Father Time guy because he was kind of a lecher," Richard Shock says. "I think he was hanging around Ricky because he was trying to get young pussy. Maybe he thought Ricky and his friends would look up to him—like he was the leader of their *coven* or something. . . ."

"Maybe he and Ricky simply gave themselves friendship, comfort, and some sort of companionship," Anthony Zenkus counters. "People who are damaged *do* gravitate toward each other."

Wherever the true strength of their bond was, Ricky felt emboldened by the gained knowledge that came with his uncanny friendship with Pat Toussaint. He often spent his days hanging out in the roundhouse, preaching to his peers about the devil. If a friend showed up to the New Park wearing a crucifix, he would tell them, "It should be upside down!" If someone mentioned God, Ricky would focus his bright blue eyes on them, calmly chanting, "Satan . . . Satan . . . Satan . . ."

Through his newfound devotion to Lucifer, Ricky Kasso had finally gained a sense of power in his life. If someone hurt, challenged, or annoyed him, he could strike back at them through intimidation by professing his love for the devil.

One Sunday morning, while mass was letting out at St. Philip Neri Roman Catholic Church, parishioners were shocked to find Ricky and Jimmy—both high on LSD—shouting at them about Satan from across the street. Ricky proudly displayed his upside-down cross necklace as the crowd made their way back to their cars, trying to ignore him. Sometime later, the two walked farther down Main Street and saw the sidewalk facing St. Paul's United Methodist Church being replaced. As the wet concrete was drying, Ricky grabbed a stick and wrote, *SETH IS SATIN*, leaving a devilish in-joke about a friend to dry in the sidewalk.

The inscription still survives.

Other Northport residents recall Ricky often walking around downtown, speaking what sounded to them like Latin. Ricky's chants may have, in fact, been a series of mantras detailed in *The Satanic Bible* called the Enochian Keys. The Enochian language, purported to be the language of angels, was first popularized in the sixteenth century by John Dee, an English mathematician and occult philosopher, and Edward Kelly, a self-described "spiritual medium." Another possibility is that Ricky was training himself to speak backward, a practice advocated by Aleister Crowley in his 1929 book *Magick in Theory and Practice*. Incidentally, one of Ricky's favorite musicians, Ozzy Osbourne, sang of the occultist in his 1980 song "Mr. Crowley."

Again, this sort of behavior displayed by Ricky went largely ignored. To most people in Northport, Ricky was just another stoned teen rebelling through fear and intimidation. However, one of Ricky's later boasts frightened and disturbed his peers far more than his previous ones ever had.

"He bragged about sacrificing animals to Satan or something, but we didn't know if it was bullshit or not," Glen Wolf recalls. "We never confirmed or saw anything, and it wasn't like we'd go check on it. It was just more bullshit coming out of his mouth. We would just move to another part of the park if Kasso was around and pulling that stuff."

Others believe Ricky's tales of killing animals were heavily exaggerated.

"Ricky was never mean to me," Jean Wells says, "but he did some fucked-up things like putting cats in the water so he could watch them freak out. Stupid shit like that bothered me."

While friends like Jean and Glen were incensed by Ricky's rants and deeds, others insist they could see through them.

"Ricky played Satan jokingly," Johnny Hayward says. "We'd all be tripping out and he'd be running through the park like a crazy person, throwing his arms in the air, screaming, 'I AM SATAN!'"

Still, between the increasing obsession with the occult and his constant homelessness, some of Ricky's friends sincerely believed he needed professional help. At first Ricky resisted, citing his experiences with the private psychiatrist and Tom Fazio at the Place. Ricky's friends couldn't speak for the private psychiatrist, but Dave Johnson recommended giving the Place another chance, this time with a different counselor. Ricky's friends told him to "go see the guy with the ponytail"—Tony Ruggi.

Ruggi's good reputation was well-earned. Unlike many other traditional social workers, Ruggi would go out of his way to check in on Northport's troubled teenagers. If he had a free afternoon, Ruggi would grab one of his acoustic guitars and head down to the two parks at the end of Main Street to jam with the kids, asking how they were doing between songs. His approach was sincere and the connections he made were strong.

One afternoon Ricky finally swallowed his pride and walked over to the Place. Stepping inside the small white house at

324 Main Street, he asked to speak with "the counselor with the ponytail." Ruggi was free and invited Ricky upstairs to one of the individual counseling rooms on the second floor. Cautious and guarded, Ricky sat on a couch and broke the ice by politely asking Ruggi several questions about his background. The thirty-three-year-old counselor discussed his two master's degrees—one in creative arts therapy and the other in social work—but also spoke of his love of listening to music and playing guitar. This immediately grabbed Ricky's attention. A therapist who wasn't ashamed to admit to loving rock music and even played guitar? The idea seemed ludicrous—yet here was Tony.

Ruggi kept two acoustic guitars at the Place, a Yamaha acoustic and an Angelica twelve-string, and invited Ricky to have a look at them. They were not top-end instruments by any means, but once Ruggi opened the cases, Ricky marveled at the guitars lying inside.

"I'd like to get one like yours one day," Ricky told Ruggi.

By the time the guitar cases were closed, Ricky had decided that he trusted Ruggi. He sat back on the couch and vented about his problems at home and school. Ricky complained about his parents blaming him "for everything," and how this often led to him being kicked out. He told Ruggi about having to sleep on the streets when he couldn't find a friend's car or garage to crash in, and how others would sometimes sneak him into their parents' homes so he could take a shower and have something to eat. Ricky was particularly upset by how some of these parents said they did not want someone like himself in their house, despite knowing he was homeless.

Hearing Ricky's stories left Ruggi frustrated. Here was a polite, articulate, and likeable young man who, as far as he was concerned, couldn't catch a break. Granted, Ricky was sugarcoating a lot of his own issues, but that was typical of many teenagers. The kind and considerate kid sitting across from him was a far cry from the Acid King who wandered the streets of downtown Northport, peddling drugs and shouting praises to Satan. Still, Ruggi felt determined to help make a difference in Ricky's life.

As the impromptu session came to an end, Ricky stood and said, "You know, you're different from the other therapists."

"Well, there are a lot of different ways to do therapy," Ruggi replied. "This is the way that I do it, but if you're looking for something else, I can give you a referral."

"No," Ricky said. "I *liked* talking to you. Can I stop by again?"

Ruggi told him he could, and for the first time in months, Ricky Kasso walked back onto the streets of Northport with something to look forward to.

Chapter 13

DURING THE EARLY MONTHS OF 1983, RICKY KASSO began showing up at the Place nearly every day. While never an official client of Tony Ruggi's, Ricky still stopped in to talk, usually in the evenings. Sometimes he would bring his guitar and ask Ruggi to show him some chords. Ruggi eventually taught Ricky how to play "Stairway to Heaven" along with a few Doors songs. Once the guitars were put away, the two often talked over coffee.

One of the other people at the Place whom Ricky developed a relationship with was Ruggi's coworker Suzi Strakhov. Strakhov was an involved parent and a popular substitute teacher in the Northport–East Northport Union Free School District who attracted attention and admiration for the grace with which she moved—almost certainly a holdover from her younger days as a dancer. While Strakhov was Irish, she had totally immersed herself in the Russian heritage of her late husband, Dmitri, often demonstrating Russian folk and Cossack dances to fellow counselors at the Place.

It was Strakhov's mind, however, that won the most respect.

"Suzi had a master's degree in pastoral counseling, but her knowledge in the field of psychology was vast," Ruggi recalls. "She was always reading the latest books and articles. I think that's part of what made it easy for a lot of kids to talk to us—not only did we have knowledge of a lot of what they were talking about, but we were truly interested in learning more and hearing what they had to say."

Ricky Kasso may not have been initially interested in Suzi Strakhov and how she approached therapy—he had only seen her around the agency and had never actually spoken with her—but this soon changed. One day Ricky stopped by the Place to speak with Tony, but found he was busy with another client. Suzi, however, was free and struck up a conversation with Ricky. Once Tony Ruggi was finished with his session, he went downstairs and found the two engaged in a full-on therapy session.

Ricky noticed Tony and happily said, "I like Suzi. She's just like you."

Ruggi was pleased with Ricky's enthusiasm.

"Suzi's not just my coworker, Ricky," he told the boy. "She's also my friend. I trust her one hundred percent. If I'm not around and you need someone to talk to, you can talk to her."

Ricky now had two people in his life who seemed to genuinely care about him. After all, Tony and Suzi certainly weren't hanging around because they wanted drugs from him. They seemed to *understand* him. They commiserated with him as he spoke of his growing alienation and troubles at home and school. They laughed at his jokes and helped his guitar playing. Most importantly, though, they spoke to him like a real human being who deserved care and dignity.

"From that point on he talked freely to both Suzi and me," Ruggi recalls. "This is just a guess on my part, but because of difficulties he had with his mother and father, he may have seen Suzi and me as some sort of surrogate parents. Not only would he come to talk when he was having problems, but he would also stop in to tell us when he did well in school or if something went well at home."

As Ricky began to confide in Tony and Suzi more and more, he felt comfortable enough to discuss his ongoing drug abuse. On most days, Ricky would sit with Tony or Suzi in the living room or one of the upstairs counseling rooms, casually talking about the pot and acid he was regularly taking and selling. Like any conscientious therapist would, Tony told Ricky he was engaging in very dangerous behavior.

"Listen, Ricky," he once said. "Simply put, the drugs are not good for you."

Ricky brushed off Ruggi's concern.

"I *know* they're bad for me," he replied, "but they make me feel *good*."

"What about the long-term damage they could be doing to you?" Ruggi pressed.

"Look," Ricky said, "I know I'm not going to live past twenty, so I'm just going to have fun while I'm here."

The problems in the Kasso home soon returned. Ricky had recently been attending nearby Commack High School's special section for troubled students, but he soon started cutting classes. The school eventually expelled him for his repeated absences. As always, once word of this got back to Dick Kasso, tempers flared. Dick demanded that Ricky start taking his education seriously. After all, this was the second school he and Lynn had to approach after their son was expelled from Northport High. Ricky, however, remained belligerent.

"You know, Dad," Ricky fumed, "you expect me to be perfect just because you're a teacher and a coach!"

Dick was not falling for his son's sob story.

"No, I don't," he countered, "I expect you to *pass*."

Dick agreed to look yet again for another school that would accept his son, but he was not without demands. He told Ricky he needed to cut his hair and stop wearing ratty jeans and concert tees. Ricky refused. Enraged, Dick grabbed a pair of scissors from a kitchen drawer and chased his son throughout the house. Ricky ran out the front door and his father followed behind, pursuing his son down Seaview Avenue. However, the forty-four-year-old football coach was no match for his six-foot-tall son's long legs. Winded, Dick gave up and watched Ricky flee into the woods behind Grove Street. Still fuming, he returned home, grabbed a pile of Ricky's clothes, cut them into shreds, and tossed the remains into the street while his neighbors watched.

Time passed and things eventually cooled down. Ricky returned home—this time with a pocketknife he had purchased at a Main Street store called the Midway. The knife was cheap, a Pakistani knockoff of the Buck 110 hunting knife, sporting a shiny black plastic handle. The four-inch-long blade bore the word FLASHER in gold letters. The knife was typical of the items sold at the Midway: cheap, tacky, and containing an element of danger—though this had not always been the case. When Ricky was a child, the Midway was a nondescript stationery store that sold school supplies, candy, and comic books. However, as Ricky and his peers grew older, the Midway turned into a full-fledged head shop, selling bongs, knives, rolling papers, and other drug paraphernalia.

This ruffled more than a few feathers in upper-middle-class Northport.

Many citizens tried to get the store shut down. When it became clear that operating a head shop wasn't enough to get it booted from the village, residents hoped to penalize the owners of the Midway by complaining about the trash piling up behind the store. The concerned parties cited Northport's "Unsightly Building and Lands" law at village council meetings, but it was of little use. In the end, no matter how hard its detractors tried, the Midway would remain in Northport for decades to come.

While Ricky had no real need for his newly bought weapon, he made little effort to hide it from his family once he returned home. This, coupled with antagonistic behavior like loudly playing his self-composed songs about Satan, left Ricky's parents annoyed and fearful. At their wits' end, Dick and Lynn approached the Northport Village Police Department, asking for help getting Ricky committed to a rehabilitation facility. They told Chief Robert Howard about their son's drug use, his obsession with the devil, and the threats he had supposedly made toward his sisters—though Wendy Kasso disputes the latter.

"He never threatened me," she insists. "He hated my sisters and they hated him, but as far as I know, if he threatened them, it was sibling-rivalry-type shit."

Rivalry or no rivalry, Chief Howard agreed to help the Kassos, and on March 22, 1983, Ricky was involuntarily committed to the South Oaks Hospital in Amityville. South Oaks, formerly known as the Amityville Asylum, specialized in mental health care, along with substance abuse problems—all at a rate of three hundred and twenty dollars per day. Using their health insurance and life savings, the Kassos were able to afford this treatment, and hoped it would be the answer to their prayers for Ricky's well-being.

Chapter 14

WHILE RICKY KASSO WAS SLOWLY DETOXING IN SOUTH Oaks, Gary Lauwers was doubling down on the habits that eventually led to his murder.

Sometime in 1983 Gary decided to break into his friend Barbara's house. There, he stole over four thousand dollars in cash. Desperate for affection and approval, Gary grabbed two friends, Joe and Danny, and asked if they wanted to go buy some motorcycles. Surprised by the offer, the two agreed. Gary called a cab, and the three headed down to the nearest place that sold Honda mini-bikes. Once there, Gary bribed the taxi driver to come inside the store with him and pretend he was their father. In the end, the ruse worked, and Gary paid two thousand dollars of the stolen money for three dirt bikes. He gave Joe and Danny one each, and kept the last for himself. The trio smiled as they stuffed the bikes into the back of the taxi before driving away.

Later Gary bought a three-hundred-dollar boom box and a pretty gold chain that he planned to give to his ex-girlfriend Chrissy. The two had recently broken up, but Gary hoped this shimmering token of affection would once again win her heart. Unfortunately for him, Chrissy wasn't impressed and turned him down. Heartbroken, he threw the brand-new boom box to the ground, kicking it in frustration. Leaving the broken pieces behind, Gary walked away defeated, and headed to his old hangout—Laces Roller Rink.

On the way there, Gary ran into another friend and handed him five hundred dollars, saying, "Here; have fun tonight. . . ."

When he got to Laces, Gary dug into his pocket, pulled out another thousand dollars, and tossed the wad into the air. He stood back and smiled as the bills floated into the hands of the surprised skaters below.

Gary had good reason for wanting to butter up his peers. Recently a Northport teenager named Albert Quinones had taken a dislike to him.

"Albert would beat the shit out of Gary because Albert was an asshole who liked to beat people up," says Johnny Hayward. "He was a pretty tough guy back then. He was like the featherweight boxing champion of Long Island, or some crap like that, and he liked to start fights."

One day, while Johnny and his friend Mike were walking on "the Path," a wooded dirt road between Northport's First Presbyterian Church and the Place, Albert showed up, saying he was "going to go kick Gary's ass." Johnny warned Albert not to lay a finger on his best friend or he would get his own ass kicked. Angered by this, Albert lunged at Johnny and the two began to brawl. They soon rolled all the way down the hill, punching each other as they passed through a patch of rosebushes, before Mike broke up the scuffle.

From that day on, whenever Albert Quinones and Johnny Hayward saw each other, they fought. While Johnny's intentions were honorable, he could only protect his best friend for so long—and from so many people. The Northport Village Police Department eventually caught wind of Gary's burglary habit and arrested him. None of the officers cared about Gary trying to be Northport's own Robin Hood.

Another person Gary couldn't be protected from was his own father. Cut from a similar cloth as Dick Kasso, Herbert Lauwers was shocked by his son's burglary arrest. After all, he had come from next to nothing, working his way up from modest Antwerp shipping clerk to respectable Manhattan banker—and he had not worked this hard for his son to become a common criminal.

"My dad was *European-strict*, even with me," recalls Gary's sister, Nicole Lauwers-Law. "We tried get out of the house before Dad got home. Otherwise, we were not going *anywhere*. He commuted into the city, so he usually didn't get home from work until around seven thirty p.m. So, I would have dinner before he came home and go to Long Beach Island."

As for Gary, he and his father rarely saw each other, but when they did, there was never any heavy conflict. This all changed when Gary was arrested. Herbert was personally insulted by his son's actions and didn't shy away from voicing his displeasure.

One night Gary had his friend Colm Clark over to the house. While the two were leaving to hang out downtown, Herbert Lauwers made a snide remark to his son. Infuriated at being embarrassed in front of a friend, Gary began screaming at his father. The argument quickly escalated, and punches were thrown. Gary broke free and raced out to the driveway, grabbed a rock, and pelted it through the back window of the family station wagon before storming off.

After this, Gary avoided going home for two weeks. At first he slept in doorways or in an abandoned building inside the Axinn & Sons lumberyard, before his friend, Scott Travia, let him sleep in the back seat of his Ford Fairlane. Gary finally caught a break when he ran into his friend Corey Quinn. Gary and Corey had met while hanging out at Laces in April and had since enjoyed a flirtatious friendship. However, when the two crossed paths on this day, Corey found a sullen Gary. This was an unfamiliar sight. She had not known him for long, but the Gary she saw was always upbeat. If he knew anyone around him to be depressed, Gary would walk over with a smile, telling them to "Be butch!" Yet here was Gary Lauwers, tired and broken.

When Gary told Corey that he was living in a friend's car, she felt compelled to help him out in some way. While she couldn't invite him to stay in her house—her mother would never approve, as Corey was only twelve years old—she did have one solution. In her backyard was an old chicken coop that had been converted into a clubhouse for Corey and her friends. It was no Ritz-Carlton—or even Motel 6—but it did have a couch Gary could sleep on. He took Corey up on her offer and spent several nights there.

Eventually, Gary reconnected with his family and decided to return home. When he did, his parents asked that he go to therapy with them and his siblings. They feared if he continued down the path he was on, Gary would end up like the undesirable street kids who were influencing him—the "dirtbags," as locals referred to them. Gary agreed, and the Lauwers family started going to counseling once a week. During the sessions, Gary chalked up his recent behavior to the problems he was having with some of his peers.

"Gary had trouble with people picking on him and getting angry over it," Nicole Lauwers-Law recalls. "He was not an aggressive person. Gary tried to be tough, but he really wasn't. I think the issues he had stemmed from these friends."

Some nights after therapy, Gary would go visit Johnny Hayward at an ice cream parlor in Huntington where he worked. Serving cold desserts five nights a week drastically cut into his social life, but it paid enough to buy pot, purple microdots, or whatever else he wanted. When Gary would stop by, Johnny would invite him down to the parlor's cellar to get high by sucking nitrous oxide gas out of whipped cream cans. The dangerous process, known as "Whip-Its," gave Gary and Johnny a brief sense of light-headed euphoria, coupled with the sensation of floating. "We'd sit down there and suck the nitrous oxide out of all the canisters," Hayward recalls. "I mean, like, two hundred of 'em. We'd talk funny and goof off. It was wild times."

While it may be true that Gary's friends influenced some of his poor decisions, they were, at the end of the day, the only friends he had.

Chapter 15

RICKY KASSO'S TIME IN SOUTH OAKS WAS TUMULTUOUS. A week into his stay, he celebrated his sixteenth birthday with zero fanfare. Later, he tried to hang himself with a sweater in the shower. He was discovered unconscious, but alive, and cut down. Doctors who evaluated Ricky afterward felt he had done it for attention and did not sincerely wish to die. They diagnosed him as a manic depressive and he was prescribed Lithium, a mood stabilizer. To top it off, Ricky ran away at least five times during the eleven weeks he was a patient. On each occasion, he was found by Suffolk County police officers and returned to the rehabilitation center.

During one such escape, Ricky fled to a nearby store and stole a box of hair dye before venturing into the woods behind Dickinson Avenue Elementary School. There, with the help of Dave Johnson, Ricky dyed his wavy brown locks a bright shade of blond, hoping to throw the cops off his trail. Afterward, he bumped into Beth Brewer, his former schoolmate, at the East Northport train station.

"What's going on, Ricky?" Beth asked as she approached him.

A very jittery Ricky replied that his parents had put him in a hospital against his will, and that he had recently broken out.

"No way are they gonna lock me up," he insisted. "I'm *not* crazy."

"I never said you were crazy," she replied, "but *maybe* you need help with drugs."

This remark set Ricky off. Rapidly seesawing between drug-free South Oaks and the acid-filled streets of Northport had left him paranoid and hostile.

"I do not!" he screamed.

Ricky moved closer to Beth with every syllable. She kept her cool and deescalated the situation by speaking calmly to him before he got onto his train.

Later that week, despite his L'Oréal disguise, Ricky was again picked up by Suffolk County police officers and returned to South Oaks. Desperate to leave the facility once and for all, Ricky decided on another tactic—simply telling his doctors what they wanted to hear. He approached his therapy sessions relaxed, calmly insisting he would return to school and that he no longer worshipped the devil.

The ruse worked, and Ricky was formally released from South Oaks during the last week of May 1983. He returned home, and for a while, things were quiet. Lynn dyed Ricky's hair back to brown and bought him new clothes. However, Ricky soon found life at home just as restricting as the hospital. Dick and Lynn had once again asked him to cut his hair and wear respectable clothes, and they gave him a strict curfew—nine p.m.

Resentful of these rules, Ricky decided to take his frustrations out on his mother one day in early June. While Lynn was preoccupied with housework, Ricky snuck into the kitchen, grabbed a bottle of ketchup, and darted back up to his room. When he heard Lynn walking nearby, he smeared some of the condiment onto his wrists and stood at the top of the stairwell, hollering, *"Mom! Mom!"* Lynn rushed past Wendy, who was walking out of the bathroom near the stairwell, and stood at the bottom of the steps. Before she could ask what was wrong, Ricky held up his arms, both dripping with crimson gore, and boasted, "Look what I did!" Lynn screamed in horror. Ricky laughed and licked his wrists.

"It's ketchup!" he cackled.

Tired of her son's antics, Lynn threw Ricky's clothes onto the front lawn and told him to get out of her house. He made no effort to change her mind, and again walked away to a life on the streets of Northport.

That same spring, Gary Lauwers dropped out of Northport High, shortly after his sixteenth birthday.

"He had a few classes that he enjoyed, like photography," Nicole Lauwers-Law recalls, "but he didn't want to go back to school. My parents weren't happy that he dropped out, but they didn't give him a hard time."

Gary tried to gain sympathy from his parents by telling them he'd dropped out because of kids bullying him. However, those closest to Gary dispute this.

"He just wanted to hang out and get fucked up more," Johnny Hayward insists. "Everyone knew Gary was my best friend. I would have known if there were issues between him and others. I beat up everyone who messed with us."

Gary's friends also recall Ricky Kasso reconnecting with Jimmy Troiano around this time, and the two renting a small apartment together on Cherry Street. Most of their time inside the small dwelling was spent smoking pot, but friends would later claim that séances with a Ouija board were conducted, with Gary Lauwers occasionally stopping by.

Another resident of Cherry Street was nine-year-old Brendan Brown. One warm day in June, Brown and a friend decided to grab their BMX bicycles and head to a nearby park. As Brown coasted down his parents' driveway and onto the street, he saw three older kids—Ricky, Jimmy, and a girlfriend—walking in his direction. He turned his head for a moment, thinking little of the trio headed his way. Suddenly Brown heard his friend shout *"Holy shit!"* as Ricky, Jimmy, and the girl started racing toward them. Terrified, the two turned their bikes around and headed back up Brown's driveway.

"I think they were probably going to steal our bikes," Brown says today. "I had seen Kasso around, but this was the first time I had interacted with him. I didn't know he was the 'Acid King' or any of that stuff—he was just an older high school kid who was scary."

Ricky's days of messing with kids on Cherry Street would be short-lived. Soon after, Jimmy was arrested for violating his probation when he and a friend drove down to Florida to pick up more drugs. He was brought back to Long Island and sentenced to one year in the Suffolk County Sheriff's Office Correctional Facility in Riverhead. With his best friend now in jail, Ricky's life lost direction. He gave up on the apartment and left before the second month's rent was due.

One afternoon in the middle of June, Ricky walked over to the Midway with a pocketful of dope money and decided to get his ear pierced. There, he a met a pretty, young brunette—Gary's friend Corey Quinn. The two immediately hit it off, casually flirting despite Corey being nearly four years Ricky's junior. Behind Ricky's confident exterior, however, Corey could see a sadness lingering under the surface. At one point, a mutual friend told her that Ricky was homeless, just like Gary had been a couple months before. While she felt sorry for him, Corey didn't immediately offer Ricky a place to stay in her clubhouse. After all, the two had only just met.

The next day Corey walked into her backyard. There, she found Ricky sleeping inside the clubhouse. She woke her uninvited guest and asked how he had learned where she lived. Apparently, Corey's friend Kim had told Ricky he could stay there for the night. Corey wanted to be angry, but she could only laugh at her friend's meddling. After all, Ricky was cute and had been sweet to her at the Midway. She told Ricky to wait in the clubhouse and went back inside to cook him a quick breakfast. When she returned with the food, Ricky thanked her, and the two chatted while they ate. The conversation was initially mundane, but soon turned to the grief in Ricky's life. He told Corey of the troubles with his parents and sisters, his failures at school, and the lack of connection he felt with his peers.

Just like they had with Gary, Corey's protective instincts kicked in, and she told Ricky he could sleep in her clubhouse whenever he wanted. For a while, he did stay, often talking with Corey late into the night. Ricky felt like he could trust her as much as Tony and Suzi from the Place—maybe even more. Corey was not interested in Ricky's drugs and she didn't ask him to rob houses with her, as other friends had in the past. Unlike his parents, she never asked him to change how he dressed or how he wore his hair. Just like Tony and Suzi, Corey accepted him for who he was and listened to his problems. This gave Ricky a much-needed boost in confidence. By the last week of June 1983, Ricky was ready to return home and mend relationships. He showed up at the front door of his parents' house just in time to join them on their annual summer trip to Argyle.

It would be their last vacation together as a complete family.

Chapter 16

ON THE EVENING OF AUGUST 11, 1983, WHILE RICKY Kasso was upstate relaxing with family, two young boys, Christopher Barber and Sean Dentrone, were riding their bicycles over by East Northport's Dickinson Avenue Elementary School. When it began to rain, the boys sought shelter under one of the school's outside overhangs and waited for the weather to clear up. Just as the quick shower stopped, a figure exited the small patch of woods to the east of the school and began walking toward the boys. As he got closer, he pulled a gun from the waist of his pants and pointed it at them.

"You're under arrest!" he yelled. "I'm a cop!"

Considering this "cop" had long hair and wore jeans and a T-shirt, he was obviously lying. However, the sight of the pistol was enough to frighten the boys.

"What for?" Christopher asked.

"For vandalizing the school!" he replied. "Give me your names and phone numbers! *Now!*"

Christopher told him his name and part of his phone number.

Suddenly the young gunslinger noticed Sean crying and focused his attention on the twelve-year-old.

"Give me your name!" he ordered.

Sean just stood there, silently weeping.

"Tell me your name and number!" he demanded, pushing the gun against the boy's head.

Before Sean could answer, another teenager pulled up on a ten-speed.

"Hey!" he called out. "You got my two bucks?!"

The blond gunman turned away from Christopher and Sean and began arguing with the other boy. In the middle of the squabble, the boy on the bike grabbed the gun from the teenager. He opened a compartment, spilling a cache of small metal pellets onto the soaked pavement—the weapon had been a BB gun all along. The boy then looked at Christopher and Sean and told them to go home. The two grabbed their bicycles and quickly fled to Christopher's house on Catherine Street.

When they got inside, Christopher told his parents, William and Linda, who called the police. Several Suffolk County officers arrived and took statements from the boys and Christopher's father. Using Sean and Christopher's description of their assailant, the officers briefly searched the area but had no luck. They returned to the Barber residence, promising to investigate further. After the squad cars pulled away, Sean looked at his friend's father and said, "Mr. Barber, I was afraid to mention it, but I'm pretty sure it was Gary Lauwers. . . ."

A few days later the Kassos returned home from Argyle. Despite having Ricky in tow, the trip had been quiet and uneventful, thanks mostly to his lack of drug connections upstate. While most of the family was anxious having Ricky around, Wendy loved having her brother along for the trip, and now back at home.

One evening during the third week of August 1983, Wendy was sitting in Ricky's bedroom and noticed a Sucrets tin on his drawing table. Curious to see what was inside, she reached for the tin, but was stopped by Ricky.

"Don't look in there," he told her.

"Okay, sorry," Wendy replied.

"It's fine," Ricky said. "I'm gonna go take a shower. You can hang in here, if you want."

Wendy decided to stay while Ricky grabbed a change of clothes and left for the bathroom. After a few minutes, Wendy's curiosity got the best of her, and she decided to open the Sucrets tin, despite her brother's wishes. Inside, she found several joints. Being ten years old and naive about Ricky's drug use, Wendy assumed they were cigarettes and put the tin back on the table. After Ricky showered, he went back into his room and saw the Sucrets tin had been moved.

"Did you look in there?" he asked.

"Yes," Wendy replied.

"What did you see?"

"Cigarettes."

"Okay, good," Ricky said, relieved.

Wendy left to see if dinner was ready yet. When she returned to tell Ricky that it was time to eat, she found his room vacant. His window was open and his blue New York Giants comforter was missing from his bed. She looked outside and saw the comforter lying on the lawn. Wendy looked to her right and saw her brother already halfway down the block, fading into the distance. He had used the comforter to brace his landing.

Racing down the stairs, Wendy shouted, "Mom! Dad! Ricky's gone! He went out the window!"

Dick, who was already seated at the dinner table, turned to Wendy and wondered aloud, "Why didn't he just go out the front door?"

Chapter 17

DURING THE FINAL DAYS OF AUGUST 1983, WILLIAM Barber kept himself busy trying to find the teenager who had pointed a pellet gun at his son. He asked several neighborhood kids, and a few answered, "It was probably Gary Lauwers."

Gary had rightfully earned his newfound reputation for violent mischief. He had recently shocked several of his peers by attacking a former friend, Mike Muxie. Coincidentally, the pellet gun used to terrorize Christopher Barber and Sean Dentrone had belonged to Mike, who had only given it to Gary after nearly an hour of pestering.

A few days after that incident, Gary was hanging out behind the 7-Eleven uptown with Mike, Colm Clark, and their friend Steve. At one point Steve said, "Hey, Gary! Let's give Muxie a bowl burn!" Panicking, Mike ran across the street, but Steve and Gary chased him down. Steve grabbed Mike, put him in a headlock, and started punching him in the chest, laughing wildly as he delivered the blows. Gary then took a pot pipe and started heating one end with a cigarette lighter.

"That's sick!" Colm yelled. "Don't do that to him!"

High on power, Gary ignored Colm and pushed the hot end of the pipe against Mike's skin, instantly searing it. Mike cried out in pain, but Gary was far from finished. Before Mike was finally freed from Steve's headlock, Gary had burned him nearly a dozen more times.

Soon after, Gary was arrested for this and spent a night in the county jail. A very unhappy Herbert Lauwers bailed his son out the next morning. At his hearing, Gary's lawyer, Eileen Evans Newmark, succeeded in getting Gary only five years' probation, as opposed to the five years in jail the prosecutor had sought. During a later interview, Newmark attempted to downplay the assault, telling *Newsday* that Gary had merely been "acting out."

Around the same time, William Barber finally tracked down Gary and confronted him about the pellet gun incident. Gary immediately owned up to it and apologized, insisting it was a stupid joke, and Barber briefly considered letting the matter pass. However, his wife insisted that he press charges, and Barber relented. On September 15, 1983, Gary was arrested by the Suffolk County Police Department, who charged him with criminal menacing. Gary pleaded guilty and was given one year's probation.

One autumn morning, Harry Schock—Gary's and Ricky's old Little League coach—was walking through the woods behind his Grove Street house on his way to work. When Schock wasn't coaching, he made his living as an employee with the United States Postal Service. Since the Northport post office was close to home, Schock chose to walk through the woods to work instead of driving. That morning he found Ricky Kasso sleeping in the woods. A large tree had recently collapsed, and its roots were pulled clean from the earth, leaving a large indentation in the dirt. Ricky had filled the hole with fallen leaves, crawled in, and covered himself with the foliage to keep warm. Schock woke the boy, telling him, "Come on, let's get you some warm clothes and something to eat." Ricky followed him back to Grove Street. Once inside, Schock woke his wife, Yvette, and told her what had happened. Stunned at the idea of a neighborhood kid sleeping outside in a hole in the dirt, Yvette grabbed some of her son's clothing from the laundry and brought it to Ricky.

"Here, go put these on," she said, handing him some jeans and a shirt. "I'm going to wash your clothes and make you some food."

Ricky thanked her and went to go change out of the grimy army jacket he was wearing. Shortly after, Richard Schock awoke and walked downstairs to find Ricky heading to the bathroom, carrying a pile of his own clothes.

"He had leaves in his hair and dirt on him," Schock recalls. "He had been wearing beat-to-shit army surplus crap because it was dirt cheap. It wasn't even to be *cool*; it was because you could buy a used Vietnam-era GI shirt for like fifty cents. He had been through so much with his family and his drug addiction."

Ricky's hunger was temporarily eased when Yvette gave him a plate of food for breakfast while Harry went to call the Kassos. Dick answered.

"Hi, Dick. It's Harry Schock," he said. "Sorry to bother you, but I just found Ricky sleeping in the woods behind our house. Do you think you could come pick him up?"

"We can't have him in the house," Dick replied. "He's using dope."

"What?" Schock said. "Listen, pal, you can't just throw your kid out!"

Dick was unmoved.

"Mind your own fuckin' business!" he growled into the receiver. "He's a monster!"

To Harry Schock's surprise, the line then went dead.

"I think in Dick Kasso's fucked-up mind, he thought, 'Ricky's got to pull himself up by his bootstraps! What he needs is a dose of reality!'" Richard Schock says. "That works *sometimes*, but most of the time, it doesn't. That whole 'tough love' stuff doesn't work when people have alcohol problems or narcotics problems. They need professional help. He had a legitimate reason to be concerned—the boy was unstable—but the way he handled it was one hundred percent *wrong*. Also, you have to understand that, unless you were literally beating your kid with a bat, the cops would say, 'Hey, mind your business; it's his son, not yours.' Things were different back then."

After he hung up the phone, Harry Schock decided to let Ricky stay in his home—but mindful of Dick's revelation of Ricky's drug use, Schock asked his son to stay near his mother while he was at work.

"It wasn't that he thought Ricky was going to *rape* her or anything," Richard Schock says, "but my father didn't know what he was capable of. My mother and father were normal, blue-collar people. When they asked someone a question, they expected a normal answer, but Ricky was *strange*. He would say crazy shit like, 'Oh man, the trees are talking to me! I can see faces. . . .' They would have him lay down and my father just wouldn't go to sleep. He would not let a young boy freeze to death in the woods, but he wasn't going to go to sleep with a drugged, deranged weirdo in the house, either."

After a few nights, Ricky thanked the Schock family for their kindness and left, despite having nowhere else to go. Sometimes he would break into an unlocked car and sleep in the back seat. On rainy nights, when he couldn't find a car, Ricky resorted to sleeping in the public bathroom down at Scudder Beach, only a short walk from Aztakea Woods. The small brick building wasn't much, with its cold tile floors and the awful odor coming from the nearby sewage treatment plant, but at least it was dry. When all else failed, he would return to the crater left by the dead tree in the woods behind the Schock house.

One day in mid-October, Harry and Richard Schock were raking leaves in their backyard when they heard a commotion in the woods. Dropping their rakes, they ran in the direction of the screaming and found Dick Kasso beating his son to the ground in the middle of the small forest. Harry Schock pulled Ricky away from his father and brought him back to his house. He sat Ricky in a chair on the back porch and helped him clean up before going back into his house and fixing Ricky a few sandwiches. Before returning outside, Harry Schock turned to his son and said, "One of these days, I'm gonna find him hanging from a tree. . . ."

Chapter 18

AUTUMN 1983 LATER PROVED TO BE A TURNING POINT leading up to the tragedies of the following year. In October, while Northport's younger children were getting ready for Halloween, the older kids were hosting several drinking parties across the village. One such party was held at the home of sixteen-year-old Randy Guethler. There, Randy met an older kid named Gordon. Over beers, the two talked about popular hangouts in the village, with Gordon volunteering that he liked spending time in local cemeteries. Such a revelation might have creeped out other teens, but in Northport, this was common.

"Graveyards are very wonderful places because there's nobody there except for dead people," Johnny Hayward says. "When we were kids, we'd grab some girls and some beer, and go out to the back corner of the graveyard and drink. Hell, the dead people don't mind, you know?"

At some point during the conversation, Randy mentioned he had heard that a real human skull could fetch five hundred dollars in New York City. Some former Northport residents recall "Pagan Pat" Toussaint as the source of this rumor. No matter where the information came from, Gordon was down for this venture. In fact, he even knew just the place to pull it off—Northport Rural Cemetery, just outside of town on Sandy Hollow Road. There, Gordon knew of a stone mausoleum that would be easy to access, due to a flimsy wooden panel covering one of its windows.

One week later, shortly before midnight, Randy and Gordon ventured into Northport Rural Cemetery carrying a crowbar and a sack taken from Gordon's garage. Gordon led Randy over to a crypt marked MORRELL. The two pried the wooden panel from the rear of the tomb, and Gordon climbed inside while Randy stood watch. Inside, Gordon used the crowbar to smash the marble top of a stone sarcophagus, revealing the wooden casket of Joseph B. Morrell.

In life, Morrell had been a well-accomplished man, serving as the president of the Northport Trust Company, the YMCA of Nassau and Suffolk Counties, the Methodist Episcopal Social Union, the Brooklyn–Long Island Church Society, and the Northport Yacht Club, before dying in 1930 at the age of seventy.

Once the top was smashed, Randy climbed into the mausoleum and opened the lid of Morrell's casket. Randy pulled out a cigarette lighter so he and Gordon could see the body lying inside. Fifty-three years after his death, Morrell's body had decomposed to the point of near-skeletonization. A thin layer of what looked like ash covered Morrell's burial suit, and his leather shoes had completely disintegrated, leaving only rubber soles behind. While Randy kept the tomb illuminated, Gordon reached down and twisted off Morrell's skull. Afterward, he removed a small brass plaque from the coffin that read JOSEPH B. MORRELL, 1859–1930.

Randy decided he wanted a souvenir for himself and asked Gordon to retrieve something for him. Gordon grabbed Morrell's right hand and snapped it off with a loud crack. The two then bagged up the grisly remains, put the marble slabs back in place, and climbed out of the crypt. Last, they covered the window with the wooden panel and fled.

After Gordon dropped him off at home, Randy went into his kitchen, grabbed a brown paper lunch bag, and placed the hand inside. He then took the bag and hid it on the side of his house under a pile of leaves.

The next morning, in an incredibly daring move, Randy brought Morrell's hand to Northport High School, stashing it in his locker. Over the next two weeks, Randy showed the grim relic to Johnny Hayward, three more friends, and finally, Ricky Kasso, who showed up one day to say hi to friends.

"I call him 'Joe,'" Randy laughed as he pulled the hand from the bag.

"Why 'Joe'?" Ricky asked.

"That's the name of the guy we stole it from," Randy replied. "At least, I think it is. That was the name on his grave. Anyway, Gordon's got the guy's skull in his van."

"Why?" Ricky asked. "What are you going to do with it?"

"Make it into a mug and sell it in the city," Randy said. "I hear we can get five or six hundred bucks for it there."

On the surface, Ricky didn't react any differently from the other boys Randy had shown the hand to, all of whom displayed the adolescent mix of curiosity and enthusiasm that comes with being let in on a dark secret.

Eventually, word got back to Gordon that Randy had loose lips. He told Randy he needed to give him Morrell's hand.

"You can't be trusted!" the older boy scolded.

Randy reluctantly agreed and gave it to him. Once Gordon's van pulled away, Randy never saw "Joe" again.

This, however, would not be the last time a group of Northport teenagers gathered to view rotting human remains out of some misguided sense of morbid curiosity. Next time, it would be one of their own.

Chapter 19

THE PARALLELS BETWEEN RICKY'S AND GARY'S LIVES continued through the end of 1983 and the beginning of 1984. Ricky was still homeless when winter arrived, and he soon began sleeping in an abandoned building inside the Axinn & Sons lumberyard, just as Gary had months before. He braved the cold nights alone, surviving on white bread and cheap bologna—the only food he could afford. At one point, he dragged an old discarded couch into the building to sleep on, using his prized leather biker jacket to keep warm. When he couldn't sleep there any longer, Ricky brought the couch up to Aztakea Woods.

Aztakea wasn't any warmer than the other places Ricky had been sleeping, but it offered a relative degree of security. The land was private property, as it belonged to Northport resident and former New York state senator Bernard C. Smith, so the police couldn't legally enter without a warrant. Even when the cops occasionally ignored this law, they were easily evaded.

"The cops could never catch us in Aztakea," Richard Schock recalls. "We could run like deer, and we knew places to hide. A friend and I hid up a tree once. You think a cop is gonna look up a *tree*? There we were, forty feet up in the air, quiet as mice, just looking down at them—like that fuckin' *Predator* alien."

Ricky survived in Aztakea by keeping the couch close to a campfire as he slept. One night, however, a bad winter storm blew through, soaking the area. Ricky's firewood supply was now useless. Stuck in the forest with no other options, he set the couch on fire and slept on the cold, wet ground. The next day he left Aztakea and returned to the patch of woods behind the Schock residence on Grove Street.

While walking his dogs one evening, Harry Schock saw the distant light of a campfire in his woods. After letting the dogs back inside, Schock went in search of the source. He wasn't surprised when he found Ricky trying to sleep beneath a grove of rhododendron trees. Schock invited Ricky back into his home, and again erred on the side of caution by staying up all night.

The next morning Ricky awoke with a harsh cough that alarmed the Schock family. Harry immediately dialed the Kasso home. Again, Dick answered.

"Hey, Dick, it's Harry Schock," he said. "You need to come down here and get your kid. He's sick."

"Harry, I'm not coming to get him," a groggy Dick Kasso told him. "He is not welcome here."

"I don't want to hear your bullshit," Schock said. "The kid is *sick*. He's hacking his guts up. Now, don't fuck around—get your ass down here and get him to a hospital, or I'm calling an ambulance."

"Look, Harry," Dick said, audibly annoyed. "You just woke me and my wife up, and—"

"I don't give a *fuck* about you or your wife!" Schock interrupted. He was now late for work and tired of Dick Kasso's tough-love games. "I care about your *kid*. Just get your ass to my house, get him into your car, and get him down to Huntington Hospital. He's *sick*."

Dick again hung up on Harry Schock, leaving his neighbor to solve his son's problems. Before the Schocks could intervene any further, Ricky thanked them and left. He decided to walk downtown to find a friend to crash with, stopping first at the Place. Walking through the front door, Ricky saw Tony Ruggi and asked, "Is it okay if I hang out in here? I'm waiting for some friends to get home. If not, I can wait outside."

Ruggi said it was fine, and the two sat down to chat over coffee. Ricky told Ruggi everything: his homelessness, lack of direction, and inability to repair his relationship with his family.

After discussing these issues at length, Ricky said he was ready to get his life together. He was tired of living in the woods, sick of numbing himself with pot, booze, and hallucinogens, and wanted a future.

"I want to go back to Northport High," he told Ruggi. "I want to graduate, get a job, a car, and my own apartment. Maybe a girlfriend to watch TV with after work, too."

Ruggi was inspired by this sudden burst of motivation coming from Ricky, and asked if he wanted the Place to reach out to his parents in the hopes of making peace. Ricky said yes, and Tony placed a call to Dick Kasso. After a very tense conversation where Ruggi related Ricky's goals to his father, Dick finally agreed to let Ricky come back home under the condition that he cut his hair, wear "decent" clothes, and stop cursing in the house. Ricky agreed and left the Place that day in January 1984, giving Tony Ruggi and Suzi Strakhov hope for the boy.

Once Ricky returned home, his parents immediately noticed his cough and brought him to see a doctor. He was diagnosed with a bronchial infection, almost certainly the result of sleeping outside in the winter, and prescribed medication. While Ricky recovered, Dick approached Northport High School, asking if his son could be readmitted. Dick hoped his clout as a teacher would sway the decision in his favor, but much to his embarrassment, his pleas fell on deaf ears. Northport High School had not forgotten or forgiven Ricky's prior violent behavior or theft and refused to have him back.

Dick swallowed his pride and used some of his connections to get Ricky enrolled in the Washington Learning Center in nearby Deer Park. Initially things went well, until Ricky left early one day to hang with friends. When his teachers found out, they suspended him. As always, a fight erupted in the Kasso home. Ricky argued that he had merely left early that day and had not actually skipped school, but it was to no avail. Frustrated with his inability to get through to his infuriated parents, Ricky went upstairs to his room and packed a small bag of belongings. Walking out the front door, he shouted *"Fuck this!"* and again returned to life on the streets.

He would never attend school again.

Desperate for someone to talk to, Ricky walked downtown to vent his frustrations to Tony Ruggi.

"Why didn't you come to us first?" Ruggi asked. "We might have been able to intervene."

"I know," Ricky replied. "I fucked up, Tony."

"I can give your father a call, if you'd like," Ruggi offered.

"No," Ricky said. "No one can reason with my dad. He doesn't care about me at all. He just wants me out of the house. Would it be okay if I left my things here overnight?"

"Of course," Ruggi said.

Ricky thanked Ruggi for his help and got up to leave. On his way out, he saw a friend who was hard to miss. His long, flowing hair and strong, angular face had earned him the nickname "Lion." No one bothered to call him by his real name. Lion had just gotten out of a family counseling session with his mother and stepfather. The two chatted for a moment, with Ricky slightly stretching the truth by saying he had been "kicked out" of his house. After shooting the breeze a little while longer, Ricky and Lion walked next door and caught a movie. While sitting in the theater, Ricky pulled a small paper packet out of his pocket and looked at his friend.

"You gotta try this dust I got, man. It's *fantastic*. . . ."

Chapter 20

MUCH LIKE HIS FASCINATION WITH THE OCCULT, NO one is exactly sure when Ricky Kasso became hooked on angel dust. Some say it was Jimmy Troiano who got the Acid King to switch from LSD to PCP sometime in 1983, while others maintain that it was a friend from nearby Kings Park. Whoever is correct, one fact remains true—by January 1984, Ricky wasn't just hooked on the drug, but he was also taking very dangerous trips into places like the South Bronx to buy large quantities to sell.

Phencyclidine—also called "PCP" and "angel dust" on the street—was first discovered in 1956 by Dr. Victor H. Maddox, a chemist for the Michigan-based Parke-Davis pharmaceutical company, while researching synthetic painkillers. While Maddox's discovery was purely accidental, it was not without proposed scientific merit. Within a year, phencyclidine was being tested as a surgical anesthetic. It was eventually approved for use and marketed under the name "Sernyl." However, problems soon arose. Patients began experiencing delirium, hallucinations, and other dissociative effects after being administered the anesthetic intravenously. In 1965 the drug was discontinued, and by 1967, it was strictly limited to use during veterinary surgery.

That same year, during the so-called Summer of Love, phencyclidine hit the Haight-Ashbury district of San Francisco, where it was immediately embraced by the hippie community due to the drug's mind-altering effects. Phencyclidine was now being sold on the streets in capsules called "**P**ea**C**e **P**ills," and later as "angel dust" when offered in its pure form, a white crystalline powder. It would be another decade before the United States government took notice and declared PCP an illegal Schedule II controlled substance. As is often the case, the legal classification did little to curb recreational use.

PCP may not have caught on with the counterculture of the late 1960s in the same way marijuana and LSD had, but by 1984, the drug was making a strong comeback. For Ricky, selling PCP was quickly becoming a significant source of income. The residents of Northport and Kings Park rarely, if ever, had access to the drug, leading to sizeable curiosity and demand. Ricky and a small group of friends took advantage of this, traveling into the city to buy their stock. He had been making similar trips to buy purple microdots during the past three years, and by this time, he had become a seasoned pro.

In early 1984 the South Bronx resembled a bombed-out war zone more than a habitable community. Twenty years earlier, a combination of white residents leaving the borough for cushy suburbs like Northport, steadily decreasing property values, and the construction of the Cross Bronx Expressway, which destroyed entire neighborhoods and uprooted thousands of people, set off a chain reaction that completely gutted the South Bronx. Ricky and his friends, however, didn't mind driving into an area like this to score. In later years, many Northport residents projected the collective sins of the local youth onto Ricky, portraying him as the village's sole teenage drug peddler, but he was merely one of the many aimless Suffolk County kids selling hallucinogens for pocket cash.

"These guys were *heavily* into dope," Richard Schock says. "Those neighborhoods were *death traps*. Let's be honest—if you're white, eyeballs are going to be clicking the second you walk into that neighborhood for two reasons: one, you're looking to buy; and two, they know you're not living there. They're going to try and rip you off, if they can. They'll either give you rat poison or just kill you and take your money. You really had to be *desperate* crawling in there."

Desperate or not, Ricky always made it safely back to Suffolk County, where he could unload. While Ricky was starting this new venture, Gary Lauwers was finally making a little money of his own.

Earlier that winter, he, Johnny Hayward, and their mutual friend Mark Florimonte found work washing dishes at the Australian Country Inn & Gardens on Fort Salonga Road. The three had a great time working at the restaurant, often blasting music to sing along with before and after the dinner rush. During the week, the crew usually worked until eleven p.m., allowing Johnny and Mark to get a full night's rest before school. On weekends, however, the three usually didn't get out until after four a.m., and they often sat outside drinking until the sun came up.

While the Australian Country Inn & Gardens was providing Gary with a steady paycheck, he still failed to curb some of his old habits.

"Gary and I used to steal cases of Foster's Lager," Johnny Hayward says. "The restaurant didn't take inventory at all. We took *lots* of cases of Foster's."

One night Johnny and Gary took things a step further when they grabbed two kegs of beer and pushed them out the window above the dishwashing station. Below was a table the two had set up in the hopes of catching the kegs. Instead they bounced right off the table and rolled clear across Fort Salonga Road. Watching out the window, Johnny and Gary couldn't help but laugh.

Sometimes Gary's sister, Nicole, would pick him up from work and give him a ride home. She hoped Gary would eventually quit the job and go back to school, but when her brother wasn't stealing cases of beer or breaking into parked cars, he was hanging out with Ricky Kasso. The two hadn't been close in recent years, but once Ricky became a big-time drug dealer in Northport, Gary started tagging along with his old schoolmate more often, sometimes dropping acid with him in Aztakea.

Soon Gary began joining Ricky on other adventures. As Ricky got more and more into dust, he started spending his evenings in cemeteries, particularly the Crabmeadow Burying Ground off Waterside Avenue. Inside the woods that now make up the Henry Ingraham Nature Preserve, a graveyard resides on a small hill bordered on all sides by large pine trees. For years, local teenagers referred to it as "the Indian cemetery" due to the Native American settlement that had occupied the area centuries before. Despite its nickname, the graveyard is not an "ancient Indian burial ground," but the final resting place of more than 150 Long Island residents interred there between 1738 and 1892.

As 1983 came to an end, Ricky began leading friends like Gary Lauwers and Rich Barton onto the hill, where they would smoke PCP, take purple microdots, and listen to him discuss Satanism. Ricky's words, coupled with the eerie surroundings, provided a special thrill to his cohorts. Sometimes Ricky would bring a boom box, sit next to a grave, and record himself chanting, "Satan . . . Satan . . . Satan . . ." To everyone's shock and surprise, the tapes, when played back, seemed to contain a series of unrecognizable and otherworldly voices in the background.

Ricky and his friends soon became convinced the devil himself had possessed these cassette tapes.

"It got dark after he started doing all the angel dust," Johnny Hayward says. "Dust makes you fucking crazy. That's when you lose yourself. If you eat ten hits of mescaline, and then you smoke ten bags of dust, you are *done*. If you can even *get up* to walk, you are going to walk like a zombie with a big ol' shit in its pants. Your arms are probably going to float up in the air all by themselves, and you're going to have to remember to put them down. LSD, mushrooms, or any other hallucinogenics, have to go with your *mood*. You don't want to do anything like that when you're really depressed because it's going to make it *worse*. If you smoke a joint of angel dust and read *The Satanic Bible*, it will amplify the feelings you presently have. You only want to do that shit when life is good—and I think you could call this a pretty *dark* time. . . ."

Gary Lauwers also started reading *The Satanic Bible* around this time, though most of his friends insist he only did so to fit in with people like Ricky. On a couple occasions when Gary accompanied Ricky to the Crabmeadow Burying Ground, Ricky suggested digging up a body. The first few times, Ricky's friends said no, and the subject was changed.

However, one chilly night in March 1984, they all said yes.

Grabbing a shovel he had hidden behind a tree, Ricky started digging into the grave of Ruth Harriet Scudder, who had died nearly one hundred and seventy years before at the age of twenty-three. Scudder's grave sat on the back side of the hill, just out of view of anyone who might wander into the cemetery. Gary, along with Rich Barton, Albert Quinones, and their friend J. P., all watched as Ricky hurled heaps of cold dirt onto the ground. The four stood pensively, waiting for Ricky's shovel to make a loud thud as it hit the lid of a coffin—or perhaps the shrill crack of it slicing into bone.

Surprisingly, none came.

Ricky dug seven feet into Scudder's grave without finding any hint of prior occupation. Tired and disappointed, he gave up and the group left.

In later years, people often confused Ricky's motives with Randy Guethler's reason for stealing parts of Joseph Morrell's body—money. The truth was far more sinister. One day Ricky and his friend Richard Schock were hanging out in the woods behind Grove Street. Usually, their discussions focused on cars or music, with Ricky being particularly fascinated with the mystery of Jim Morrison's missing Shelby GT500 Mustang. However, on this afternoon in early April, the conversation quickly turned dark.

"I'm trying to get a skull," Ricky said, out of the blue. "Do you know where I can get a skull?"

"How the fuck would I know where to get a *skull*, Ricky?" Richard replied, angered by this ridiculous question.

Ricky was oblivious to Richard's contempt.

"We went to the Crabmeadow Burying Ground," he continued. "We dug, and we dug, and we *dug*, but we didn't find shit!"

"Ricky, those graves are from the 1740s," Richard replied. "Those skulls probably decayed a long time ago. Bones rot *too*, ya know!"

"I'm just gonna go try a mausoleum," Ricky said, recalling Randy's and Gordon's efforts. "Pagan Pat says we gotta get a skull so we can go to the Amityville Horror house."

Nearly ten years earlier, during the early morning hours of November 13, 1974, Ronald "Butch" DeFeo Jr. took a rifle and systematically murdered his parents, Ronald Sr. and Louise, along with his four siblings, Dawn, Allison, Marc, and John Matthew, while they slept inside their Amityville home. DeFeo was later arrested and charged with six counts of second-degree murder. He was found guilty one year later and sentenced to life in prison.

Twenty-eight days after Ronald Jr.'s conviction, George and Kathleen Lutz moved into the former DeFeo home at 112 Ocean Avenue with their three children. The family later claimed they were terrorized by supernatural forces within the house, eventually fleeing after only four weeks spent there.

Two years later, in September 1977, Jay Anson's book *The Amityville Horror* was published, bringing the Lutz story to a national audience. Suddenly the small Long Island village of fewer than nine thousand residents was catapulted to stardom. The book was an instant bestseller, leading to a hit Hollywood movie that had, by 1984, birthed two sequels. For most in Suffolk County, the whole saga was a blight on the community, leading to an unwelcome horde of reporters, thrill seekers, and filmmakers.

For others, like Ricky Kasso and Pat Toussaint, it was a strange piece of local history to be worn as a badge of honor.

"Their plan was to dig this skull up," Richard Schock recalls, "and that would get Ricky and Father Time in touch with their main man, 'Satin.' They would then go to the Amityville Horror house to invoke 'Satin' and demons by reading incantations on the lawn. I guess they were reading from *The Satanic Bible*, or whatever. He was a kid who was tripping out of his mind and was probably barely literate. He probably thought Ozzy was into this, or some bullshit like that. . . ."

Bullshit or not, the Suffolk County Police Department was about to become very familiar with what was happening inside their local cemeteries.

Chapter 21

SOMETIME IN EARLY APRIL 1984, A NORTHPORT resident reported the grave-digging and vandalism to the Suffolk County Police Department, which immediately opened an investigation. Around the same time, Northport Village Police Officer Anthony Iannone received a tip from a confidential informant that Randy Guethler might have been behind the incident, as several teenagers had seen him with a skeletal hand in the halls of Northport High School. Iannone immediately passed this information on to Suffolk County Detectives Douglas J. Varley and Joseph Saukas, who, on April 8, 1984, decided to confront Guethler directly at his home on Woodbine Avenue.

Randy was very intimidated by this visit, due to his friendship with Detective Varley's son, Robert. After a brief conversation, Randy broke down and confessed—but not to the crime Varley and Saukas were there to investigate. After all, he and

Gordon had robbed the Morrell mausoleum in Northport Rural Cemetery, *not* Crabmeadow Burying Ground. This revelation momentarily confused the detectives, but they remained silent. Randy told Varley and Saukas everything, and even rode with them to Northport Rural to point out the crypt. Later, the two had Randy sign a written confession and placed him under arrest, charging the sixteen-year-old with felony body stealing.

Varley and Saukas were happy solving a crime they didn't even know had occurred, but this still left the Crabmeadow case to be closed. While Varley and Saukas continued their investigation, and Randy Guethler prepared for his upcoming court appearance, life carried on as usual for the rest of Northport. As it got warmer, the local youth returned downtown to stake their usual claim in the New Park. Despite the playground—known to locals as "the wood forest"—originally having been built for young children, very few kids under the age of ten dared to go anywhere near it.

"As soon as I began riding my bike downtown when I was around nine or ten years old, I knew from the get-go that Cow Harbor Park was completely dominated by very dangerous teenagers," recalls Brendan Brown, the boy chased by Ricky on Cherry Street. "By that point, I had already been told, 'Don't you ever go into that park.' It definitely wasn't a place where even *adults* in this quaint, pretty little town could bring their kids. That general air of full-blown violence at the drop of a hat was *very* real. It was like *Lord of the Flies.*"

The New Park teenagers also enjoyed stealing anything in the area that wasn't literally nailed to the ground. Johnny Hayward and his friends often broke into liquor stores to steal cases of vodka. Sometimes they would sneak into local bars while they were open, quietly rolling kegs of beer out the back door. On other occasions, the young bandits would return after the bar had closed for the night and steal the cash registers. As they were leaving, Hayward would rip the telephones out of the wall, later selling or trading them for drugs. If they ran out of stolen booze to drink, Johnny would steal from the Budweiser delivery trucks when they came to town.

Stealing had become sport for the New Park teenagers, and Johnny Hayward's antics were quickly becoming legendary. Unfortunately, his best friend was about to commit a theft that would alter the lives of every single man, woman, and child in Northport forever.

Chapter 22

ON THE CLOUDY, WINDSWEPT EVENING OF APRIL 21, 1984, a few of the New Park kids walked to Dave Johnson's house for a party in his basement. Ricky Kasso was there, and he brought Gary Lauwers along with him. Ricky also brought a special treat—several bags of angel dust he had just picked up from the South Bronx. Stuffed inside Ricky's leather jacket pocket was a bundle of little manila packets containing crushed mint leaves sprayed with liquid PCP. Each packet was stamped SUDDEN IMPACT in red ink—a crimson testament to the drug's potency.

After entertaining himself by playing a few Black Sabbath and Iron Maiden records backward to look for demonic messages, Ricky sat on a couch and got high with his friends. Earlier that evening Gary had asked his friend Ellie Love if she wanted to buy some pot with him, as he only had three dollars. Love gave Gary seven bucks and said she would wait for him to return. He never did. Instead Gary bought the weed and walked downtown to sell some to Ricky, who bought a bag, completely unaware that Gary had ripped off a mutual friend to get it.

Later, Ricky rolled a large joint, mixing in some of the PCP-laced mint leaves when Dave wasn't looking, as his friend didn't approve of harder drug use in his home. Ricky smoked the "super joint" and eventually passed out while the party continued around him. Gary saw this as a golden opportunity and reached into his friend's pocket, swiping ten bags of dust. If sold to the right person, the packets could bring him ten bucks apiece. Considering Ricky had passed out around several of his friends, Gary figured he would never get caught. He left the party, stolen packets in tow, and walked over to a friend's house. There, he smoked a bag of Ricky's PCP but didn't enjoy the high. He gave away four of the little envelopes and walked home. The next morning, Easter Sunday, Gary woke up, got dressed, and walked downtown to the New Park with the remaining five bags of dust in his pocket.

He didn't make it past the parking lot.

Ricky was there waiting and immediately confronted Gary about the theft. He made little effort to conceal his guilt. Searching Gary's pockets, Ricky found the five envelopes. With one swift punch, he told Gary he had two weeks to pay him back. Gary ran off, leaving Ricky in the parking lot, fuming. For Ricky, this was the ultimate betrayal. After all, he and Gary had known each other since second grade and even played on the same Little League team together—and *this* was how he chose to honor that bond?

A few moments later a van pulled into the parking lot. Inside were two Cherry Street families who had bought ice cream from a Main Street shop and drove to the New Park to sit and eat. Just as the van entered the lot, Ricky jumped onto its running boards. Filled with anger, he took his frustration out on the two families by pushing his upper body through the front passenger window and hissing at the van's occupants. Brendan Brown, who was sitting in the back seat, was shocked by the reappearance of the teen who had chased him for his bike.

"His eyes were *tremendous*," Brown recalls. "I remember how he just didn't care at all that he was in somebody else's car."

Sitting in the passenger seat, one of Brown's neighbors pushed Ricky as hard as she could, trying to get the boy out of her van. She quickly realized she wasn't strong enough to move him, but Ricky soon gave up. He jumped off the van and walked back to his friends, cackling with each loping step his lanky legs took. Much to the surprise and disgust of the van's occupants, Ricky's friends joined in with his menacing laughter. Brown's neighbors quickly turned the van around and headed back to Cherry Street, far away from the dirtbag kids of the New Park.

In the days following Gary's theft of the dust, Ricky seemed to be waging an internal war. On one hand, he was still trying to better himself by stopping into the Place to speak with Tony Ruggi and Suzi Strakhov, but on the other, Ricky was feeding his darker obsessions by continuing to read about Satanism and the occult. On April 24 both worlds collided when Ricky found a list of "the dignitaries in Hell" inside a book at the Northport Library and decided to show it to Tony. He made a photocopy of the page in question, stuffed it into his pocket, and walked over to Main Street. After playing guitar together for a few minutes, Ricky pulled the folded list out of his pocket and laid it before Tony.

"What do you think of this?" Ricky asked.

"What is it?" Tony replied.

"It's a list of the most powerful demons in Hell," Ricky said. "I found it in a book."

Tony pushed the sheet of paper back in Ricky's direction.

"Don't you want to know who's on there?" Ricky asked.

"Nah," Tony replied. "There might be someone I know on that list."

Ricky laughed—something Tony was always happy to hear.

"Do you think it's true?" he asked sincerely.

"Ricky," Tony replied, "just consider who's supposedly in Hell to see these people and then *came back* to write that list."

"So, this is all bullshit, then?" Ricky asked. "I guess people will believe anything—especially if it scares them. . . ."

Ricky left the Place and walked half a mile up Main Street to the Midway. Also heading there were Detectives Varley and Saukas of the Suffolk County Police Department. Word had finally reached them regarding who was behind the grave-digging inside the Crabmeadow Burying Ground. They had been searching for Ricky, having first stopped at his parents' house to arrest him. When Varley pulled up to the Kasso house on Seaview Avenue, he was immediately greeted on the front lawn by Dick Kasso.

"Mr. Kasso," the forty-four-year-old detective began, "I'm Detective Varley with the Suffolk County Police Department. Do you know why I'm here today?"

"Yeah," Dick answered. "You're here because my son's a piece of shit."

Despite Kasso's soured view of Ricky, he was ill-prepared for what Varley was about to tell him.

"Mr. Kasso," Varley continued, "I'm here today because we have reason to believe your son is responsible for robbing a grave over by 25A."

Kasso was stunned. Drugs? High school rebellion? Theft? These were all unsavory, yet common things among teenagers—but *grave robbing*? Dick Kasso couldn't think of a more disgusting label for his son—his own namesake. Once Ricky was caught, it would certainly make the newspapers, and every Suffolk County citizen with a *Newsday* subscription would see the name "Richard Kasso" associated with the act of desecrating someone's final resting place. How would this affect him as an educator? Sure, he could write off having a rebellious punk of a kid to his coworkers and students, but how would they react to reading about what Ricky had done in the Crabmeadow Burial Ground?

Varley left the Kasso residence feeling sorry for Dick.

"It appeared to me at the time that Mr. Kasso was a man frustrated about Ricky's troubles with the police and was fed up with it all," Varley says.

Later that day Varley and Saukas finally caught up with Ricky at the Midway and arrested him. While searching his pockets for identification or weapons, Varley found Ricky's photocopied list of demons.

"I pulled that stuff out of his wallet," Varley recalls. "It was Satanist material. Beelzebub was on there. So was Baal, along with a little session on how to call all these demons up. Shit you'd get out of the library if you looked hard enough. He told me all about who was who and their ranking in Hell."

Back at the station, Ricky made the surprise move of immediately confessing to the allegations against him. He told Varley and Saukas that he was a Satanist and had planned to use any remains he would have dug up in an occult ceremony.

"His attitude was odd," Varley says. "He thought little of being arrested and was mostly sneering through the process. I remember Ricky telling me and Joe about some cult of devil worshippers in the city who drank beer from skulls and used bones for their rituals. I think he liked the idea that he was impressing us with how weird he was. I remember getting the feeling that this was a totally lost kid."

Since there was no evidence to suggest Ricky had stolen anything from the grave, the detectives gave him the lesser charge of violating the public health law. This was only a misdemeanor compared to the felony charge levied against Randy Guethler. Ricky was given a court date of June 18 and was released from custody.

"Shortly afterward, I was interviewed on a radio show regarding the grave robbing," Varley recalls. "As soon as it aired, I was getting calls from all sorts of crackpots. One called me from

England, offering to conduct cleansing rituals in Northport. Finally, my supervisors said, 'Enough, Dougie . . .'"

To this day, Doug Varley is convinced that Ricky and Randy robbed more graves than the ones they were caught for. However, with his superiors telling him to back off due to the negative press Northport was receiving, no one can ever be sure.

Word of Ricky's arrest eventually made it to *Inside Newsday*, the fledgling broadcast television branch of one of New York's biggest newspapers. The story caught the eye of Rex Smith, a thirty-two-year-old reporter who had been with *Newsday* for three years before moving from the newsroom to their new TV division.

"At the time, it just seemed like one of those weird Long Island stories," Smith recalls. "A teenage grave robber? *Really?*"

Smith assembled a three-man camera crew and traveled to Northport in search of Ricky, using an old yearbook photo as a guide. After several failed attempts, Smith finally called the Northport Village Police Department and asked Chief Howard where he might find the accused grave robber.

"Probably at the Midway," Howard told Smith. "You can always find him there."

Smith and his crew then drove to the infamous head shop on the hill, and sure enough, they saw Ricky walking out of the Midway just as they were parking.

"Hey, Ricky!" Smith hollered as he jumped out of the car. "You got just a minute?"

"Whatever," he replied nonchalantly as he walked over to Smith.

Smith's crew set up, aiming the camera at Ricky, with the Midway displayed prominently behind him. During the brief interview, Ricky brushed off the arrest.

"I went through a phase a little while ago where I was into devil-worshipping," he told Smith. "I was into drugs and stuff."

Surprisingly, Ricky didn't boast of his supposed connections to Satanic cults who drank beer from human skulls, as he had to the Suffolk County Police. In fact, he backpedaled when pressed on the issue.

"The cops exaggerated the Satanic stuff because they found a picture of the devil in my wallet," Ricky claimed.

When the interview ended, and the equipment was packed up, Smith left Northport empathizing with Ricky.

"He seemed to be one of those forgotten suburban kids," Smith says. "He was probably wearing the same clothes all week, eating donuts and chips, and living off the goodness of other kids' parents. He didn't exude any evil sensibility to me at all. He was more like a stoner, actually. Later, I was told that when he was high on PCP, he got frenetic and vicious, but this was just a normal teenage pothead, in my view—a kid who probably would have managed to get himself straightened out before his life got into big trouble. . . ."

Despite what Ricky told Rex Smith, his Satanic "phase" was far from over. On the night of Monday, April 30, 1984—while Gary Lauwers was celebrating his final birthday alive—Ricky and Pagan Pat traveled twenty miles outside of Northport to the Amityville Horror house, hoping to have a celebration of their own. It was Walpurgis Night, an evening Bram Stoker once described as being a time when "according to the belief of millions of people, the devil was abroad—when the graves were opened and the dead came forth and walked. When all evil things of earth and air and water held revel. . . ."

Much to their disappointment, however, Ricky and Pat would have to revel in this macabre holiday sans human skull. And while a few sleepy-eyed residents of Ocean Avenue may have been inconvenienced by the duo's hooting and hollering on the front lawn, no members of the DeFeo family rose from the grave to walk the earth. Nor did Satan—or *"Satin"*—make an appearance.

After a few minutes, Ricky and Pat gave up and returned to the pedestrian streets of Northport.

Chapter 23

THURSDAY, MAY 3, 1984

"DAD, I'M SICK. I THINK I HAVE PNEUMONIA. CAN I COME home?"

Dick Kasso gripped the telephone in his hand and thought long and hard about what Ricky was asking. He wasn't eager to have his drug-dealing, knife-carrying, grave-robbing son back in the house, but Ricky's illness might lend itself well to a possible recovery plan.

"You can come home," Dick said, "but *only* if you check yourself into a psychiatric hospital and get some help."

Ricky, tired of sleeping on a pile of trash behind the Midway, agreed, and walked back home. He arrived hoping to lie down on a bed for the first time in months. However, when he went upstairs to relax, he discovered his parents had given his bedroom to Kelly, who had previously shared one with Jody. Dick and Lynn told their son he could have the couch in the basement playroom. Ricky didn't put up a fight and went downstairs to stretch out, his cough growing worse.

Once Dick was confident that Ricky was out of earshot, he turned to his wife and said, "You know, I think he's finally going to get his act together."

Normally, Lynn would have been surprised by Dick's sudden display of optimism regarding their son, but by now, she was worn out.

"Don't expect this to be permanent," she told her husband. "He's going to do this again."

"No, no," Dick replied. "I think this is going to be *it*. He even agreed to go into a mental hospital."

"No, Dick," Lynn insisted. "*Please*. I've watched it. He is going to do this again and again and again. . . ."

Despite her skepticism, Lynn called Huntington Hospital and asked if her son could be admitted into the psychiatric ward once he was brought in to be treated for a possible case of pneumonia. Lynn was told Ricky could only be admitted if a psychiatrist approved. She was given the phone number of a highly recommended doctor, whom Lynn called, asking if she could bring Ricky over for an evaluation. She told the psychiatrist about her son's recent grave-robbing arrest, his obsession with Satan, daily hallucinogenic use, and his habit of carrying a knife around the house.

"You *cannot* bring him here," the psychiatrist replied firmly. "In fact, you shouldn't even bring him to Huntington. You have a desperately dangerous situation on your hands, and

Huntington Hospital is simply not equipped to handle it."

The psychiatrist recommended Long Island Jewish Medical Center's Schneider Children's Hospital in New Hyde Park, thirty minutes away. Once Dick and Lynn drove Ricky there, the emergency room doctors confirmed that Ricky had pneumonia and admitted him. Over the next three days, Ricky was given two psychiatric evaluations. During both, he was asked if he was considering harming himself or others. Ricky mentioned the pending charges against him and said that if he were convicted and sent to jail, he would kill himself.

After Ricky made this comment, one of the two psychiatrists immediately suspected the hospitalization was a ruse on his behalf to gain sympathy from the judge presiding over his grave-digging case—never mind the fact that Ricky was clearly suffering from pneumonia, and the psychiatric evaluation had been requested by Dick and Lynn, not Ricky.

Despite this, the damage was done. The doctors made note of Ricky's suicide remark but observed no psychosis, delusions, or hallucinations exhibited by him. With his history of drug abuse in mind, they asked Ricky if he wanted to sign himself into the psychiatric ward. Now realizing he had a say in the matter, Ricky had a sudden change of heart. He declined to be committed, leaving the doctors with no choice but to write him a prescription for antibiotics and send him on his way.

On Saturday, May 5, 1984, the hospital told Dick and Lynn that their son was ready to be discharged. Shocked by this decision, Lynn quickly reminded the psychiatrists of her son's drug use, criminal history, and his alleged suicide attempt in South Oaks. The doctors, however, were not swayed.

"We carefully reviewed your son's case," one of the psychiatrists told Ricky's parents, "and we do not feel that he is a danger to himself or society at this time."

"But we're *afraid* of him!" Lynn told him. "Can't you see that?! We just *know* he's going to do something!"

"I understand your frustration, Mrs. Kasso," the psychiatrist replied. "Your son most likely has an antisocial personality disorder of some kind, leading to his difficulty adhering to a structured environment. However, he has exhibited no psychotic behavior to us. He's not presently hallucinating, nor is he delusional. The hospital simply *cannot* commit him against his will without the approval of two psychiatrists, and we just don't find him to be a threat right now. In the meantime, his pneumonia can be treated at home."

With this, Dick and Lynn were now at the end of their rope. They had no further options to explore, other than bringing Ricky home and hoping for the best.

The same day Ricky was discharged from the hospital, a young woman leaving her job at Abraxas Hair Salon in Huntington noticed something peculiar lying under a nearby mailbox. At first glance, the strange, rust-colored object appeared to be a dirty toy ball. As she bent down for a closer look, the stylist found the rotting visage of Joseph B. Morrell staring back at her.

The Suffolk County Police Department was called, and

Detective Doug Varley raced to the shopping center on East Main Street. When he arrived, Varley figured Morrell's skull had been placed under the mailbox only after the perpetrator had already dropped the hand inside and subsequently realized the head would not fit through the slot. Varley's hunch paid off. When the mailbox was opened, he found Morrell's hand waiting inside.

While evidence technicians went to work dusting the mailbox for fingerprints, Varley went inside the salon to interview the stylist and her coworkers. When a shopkeeper from an adjoining store asked who the head belonged to, the detective smiled.

"Some guy from upstate is waiting back at the precinct for it," Varley chuckled. "He rode up on a black horse, wearing a cape and swinging a sword. . . ."

Chapter 24

AS ALWAYS, RICKY'S FIRST FEW DAYS BACK HOME WENT well enough. Things were quiet, and he often hung out with Jimmy, who had recently been released from prison, or with Wendy. The two often watched movies together, usually *The Man with Two Brains*, or one of the Pink Panther films Ricky had loved as a child. These few tranquil days gave Dick some measure of hope, but after a short while, the two started butting heads again, and Ricky was out of the house.

It would be the last time he ever lived at home.

Ricky's brief hospital stay bought Gary some time to come up with the money he owed, but by the second week of May 1984, the Acid King was back on the streets of Northport, looking to collect. This was bad news for Gary, who had recently lost his new job as a dishwasher at Feed & Grain, a classy restaurant on Main Street. The owner had fired the boy for dyeing his hair pink, leaving him significantly short on cash. One day Ricky and Jimmy found Gary downtown in the New Park.

"When are you gonna have my money?" Ricky asked.

"Saturday," Gary replied.

This wasn't good enough.

Ricky balled up his fist and punched Gary in the face, giving him a black eye. Gary tried to run, but Ricky jumped off one of the gazebo walls, landed on him, and started ripping up Gary's faux leather jacket with his bare hands. Gary took a few more punches from Ricky before he was finally able to slip away.

He didn't make it far.

As Gary tried to flee, Jimmy tackled him, landing a few punches of his own. Once confident that he had adequately defended his friend's honor, Jimmy released Gary from his grip and let him run off.

Later that night a party was held in Corey Quinn's backyard clubhouse. Just like he had at Dave Johnson's house, Ricky passed out after a few hours of smoking and drinking. Gary Lauwers wasn't there to take any drugs from his pocket, but Johnny Hayward was.

"Everyone please note this," Johnny said in a deliberate and measured tone. "I am going to take two hits of mesc from Ricky and pay him tomorrow. I am *not* stealing, as I am telling everyone here and now what I am planning on doing."

As Johnny went to reach into Ricky's jacket, Albert Quinones grabbed his hand.

"No!" Albert said. "*That* is why Gary is in the shits with Ricky. You will *not* be doing the same thing."

Albert released his grip.

"Uh, sure . . . ," Johnny replied, slightly taken aback.

The once jovial mood of the party evaporated. Johnny said his good-byes and left.

As spring 1984 dragged on, Ricky sank deeper into drug use and his dark obsessions. By now he was making several trips a week into the South Bronx to get angel dust. He was also praising Satan to nearly anyone who crossed his path. One night, while riding around with some friends in Kings Park, Ricky's devotion to the devil nearly caused a violent confrontation. Ricky's friend Roy Jackson was riding in the back seat with him, along with their mutual friend Ursula. Roy started talking about a recent motorcycle accident that had nearly taken his life, and at one point he pulled out a pocket Bible, claiming his faith in God had saved his life. Ricky turned to Roy and said, "You should burn it."

Roy lashed back at Ricky, emphasizing that the Bible had saved him physically *and* spiritually, calling Ricky a few choice words in the process. Ricky didn't care. Bent on taunting his friend, Ricky began chanting, "Satan . . . Satan . . . Satan . . ." Finally Ursula intervened and broke up the fight before it got out of hand. However, despite the unsettling nature of Ricky's mocking, she wasn't afraid.

"Ricky was just *high*," she insists. "I don't believe he meant it outside of the common adolescent '666' focus that was popular then. The Satan hype was, unfortunately, big and regarded as 'cool' at the time. 'Shout at the Devil,' 'Hells Bells,' et cetera. One of the guys I knew self-tattooed '666' behind his ear. Ricky wasn't *Charles Manson* or anything. . . ."

Ricky's antics were not limited only to his social circle. One afternoon in mid-May, a group of parishioners from the Northport Baptist Church on Elwood Road ventured downtown to hand out pamphlets. One of them, a college student named Jim Edwards, saw Ricky and his friends on Main Street and thought they looked like prime candidates to hear the good word. When Edwards handed Ricky one of the tracts, Ricky looked at it, raised his arms, and screamed, *"I am Satan! God will burn!"*

Edwards soon realized Ricky was a lost cause, and left.

One of the few people to challenge Ricky on his self-professed belief in Satanism was his friend Corey Quinn.

Ricky approached Corey one night while high on PCP and tried to sell her on the idea of devil worship. Corey might have been young, but she was not falling for it. She ignored Ricky, telling him to go away. The next day, after Ricky's high wore off, she confronted her friend.

"Ricky, do you really, *truly* worship Satan?" she asked.

"Yeah!" Ricky confidently replied.

Corey was still unconvinced.

"Ricky, c'mon," she implored him. "Where does Satan come from?"

"I don't know," he answered.

"Well, why do you worship Satan?" Corey asked.

"I don't know," he repeated.

Corey later told others that Ricky eventually said he didn't worship Satan—or even believe in God, for that matter—despite his actions suggesting otherwise.

On May 17, 1984, tensions between the New Park teenagers and the residents of Northport finally came to a head. That night forty citizens crammed into the tiny Northport Village Hall to make their concerns known. One resident, Dorothy Luckas, spoke passionately, saying, "What the town created was a *monster*! The park has been a disaster at night, and if we stand a chance at having this corrected, we should do it!"

Another resident, Thomas Gaines, concurred.

"The park creates a very unsafe situation for younger children playing there after dark," he said.

Luckas and Gaines seemed to be gaining momentum in their mission to have the park figuratively and literally cleaned up, but the meeting was suddenly hijacked by a few other residents who were more concerned with the unpaved parking lot at the end of Main Street.

"Why are we allowing valuable waterfront to be used for *parking*?" fifty-year-old Jacqueline Ingham demanded.

Before attention could be returned to the problem facing the New Park, other residents began arguing over the lack of available boat slips in the marina. While Northport had nearly three hundred slips, more than nine hundred were people on the waiting list—with some having been on the list for almost a decade.

It soon became obvious to Luckas and Gaines that nothing was going to be done about the juvenile delinquents and vagrants destroying the park. The village council felt there were more pressing matters to attend to, and everyone was just going to have to deal with the rowdy teens for the time being.

This included Larry Decker, who owned Village Books on Main Street. One early morning, only a few weeks after the meeting, Decker went to open his shop and found the front door covered in what looked like blood. He suspected this was retaliation from the handful of teenagers who had stopped by the store over the past nineteen months in search of *The Satanic Bible* only to find that Decker no longer stocked it. Before Decker bought the business in 1982, it was known as Avatar New Age Books and Records and catered to the occult crowd in town. Once Decker took over, however, he decided to focus on stocking bestsellers and popular magazines.

Decker called the village police, who filed a brief report, but in the end they told him there was nothing they could do.

The problems with Northport's teenagers would only continue to escalate from there.

Chapter 25

"WHERE'S MY MONEY, GARY?!"

Ricky barreled toward the boy with his fist clenched. It collided with Gary's face, and a large pewter skull ring that Ricky had recently bought from the Midway sliced open his eyebrow. Gary fell to the ground, but Ricky kept after him, hammering his face with one savage blow after another. Finally Gary managed to roll away and reach his hand into his pocket. He pulled out his wallet and handed Ricky a wad of bills.

"Here!" Gary said, wiping the blood from his eye and nose.

Ricky counted the cash, quickly discovering Gary had only given him thirty dollars.

"There's only thirty bucks here!" Ricky screamed.

"I know, I know!" Gary said. "It's all I got! I'll get you the rest soon, I promise!"

Ricky grabbed Gary by his jacket.

"Next time, I'm coming back for more—and it's not gonna be just a *black eye*."

Ricky then threw him to the ground and walked back down the path leading to Main Street. Gary waited for a few minutes before heading in the same direction. When he got up, he found Johnny Hayward, along with their friend Jane Allen, sitting on the large stone war memorial in front of the First Presbyterian Church. Johnny saw the fresh cuts and bruises on Gary's face and told him, "You *need* to pay that motherfucker back."

Gary wasn't happy to hear his best friend defending Ricky and continued walking up the hill, farther away from downtown. Johnny turned to Jane and said, "Gary's a good friend of mine, but he ripped Ricky off. . . ."

Gary walked up to the Midway, where he bought a knife to protect himself. There, he ran into one of his girlfriends, Michelle DeVeau.

"Oh my God!" Michelle exclaimed. "What happened to you?!"

"Ricky," Gary replied, spitting a wad of blood-tinged spit onto the ground. "He's an asshole."

Michelle reached into her pocketbook and pulled out a few Band-Aids and some bacitracin ointment.

"I'm leaving," Gary told Michelle as she wiped his wounds. "I'm getting out of Northport. This town sucks. I'm sick and tired of this."

Michelle understood why.

"*All* of us just wanted to get out of there," she recalls. "I wanted to leave East Northport and move to Woodstock. We all just wanted to find our place in life. We all wanted to be somebody and have someone acknowledge us as people. If our families weren't going to, we wanted other people to. I kind of relate us to *The Outsiders*. We were all just *there*."

Outsider or not, Gary got out of *there* as quickly as he could. For the next couple of weeks, he avoided going downtown completely, spending his days hiding out in his bedroom or sneaking off to Kings Park. With Gary's marked absence around Northport, Ricky grew more and more impatient for the money he was owed.

One afternoon in early June, Yvonne Lauwers found a very agitated Ricky Kasso knocking on her front door.

"Hello, Richard," she said, stepping out onto the front porch. "Can I help you?"

"Is Gary home?" Ricky asked.

"No, he's not here right now," she replied, sensing tension in his voice. "Is there something *I* could help you with?"

"Well," Ricky said, "Gary took something from me. He owes me some money."

Yvonne wasn't terribly surprised. After all, Gary had been in serious trouble before for stealing. She invited Ricky into her home, where they continued their conversation in the living room.

"How much does Gary owe you?" she asked.

"Well," Ricky replied, "he owes me fifty bucks."

He didn't bother mentioning that Gary had already paid him thirty dollars.

Yvonne trusted what Ricky told her and reached for her purse.

"We'd known this kid since he was in grade school," Nicole Lauwers-Law says. "So, my mother turned around and gave him fifty bucks."

Handing Ricky the money, Yvonne looked him in the eyes and said, "Can you just let bygones be bygones and be friends?"

Ricky said okay, pocketed the cash, and left. Walking away from West Scudder Place, he enjoyed a moment of satisfaction, knowing he had just made thirty bucks profit off Gary. The feeling quickly dissipated, however. Street logic got the best of Ricky. Mrs. Lauwers hadn't stolen the dust from him; *Gary* had—yet here was his mother covering for him. The thought angered Ricky. No one was helping *him* solve his problems, so why should anyone help Gary?

"Just let bygones be bygones"?

No way.

There *had* to be some sort of retribution.

Ricky needed revenge.

Chapter 26

DURING THE EARLY DAYS OF JUNE 1984, RICKY KASSO was having serious trouble finding a place to stay. Sometimes he and Jimmy would sleep in a friend's station wagon when they were wheeling and dealing in Kings Park. If he couldn't find a ride there, he would sleep in a public bathroom or behind the Midway. While the newspaper and TV coverage of Ricky's grave-digging escapades brought him a kind of macabre street cred, he now found his friends reluctant to let him sleep on their couch. Their parents simply wouldn't allow it.

Ricky eventually found an abandoned home on Grove Street to squat in. Coincidentally, the house was only a few doors down from the Schock family.

"One of our neighbors, a lovely old lady, used to check on Ricky when he'd crash there," Richard Schock recalls. "She'd say to him, 'Is everything okay? Can I give you some food?' and he would scare the living shit out of her so bad she would call the police. She was a sweet, eighty-year-old woman and he would scare the fuck out of her. That was the point where I lost all respect for that kid. . . ."

After the cops chased Ricky out of the abandoned home, he stayed with Pagan Pat inside an old houseboat he had commandeered out by Scudder Beach. An elderly sea captain once owned the vessel, but after he had fallen ill and died, it sat abandoned until Pagan Pat began occasionally living in it. Around this time, something happened between Ricky and Pagan Pat that permanently destroyed their friendship. No one is certain what occurred between the two, but rumors quickly flourished and still abound to this day.

"I don't know if he made *advances* toward Ricky one night or something," Richard Schock recalls, "but somebody told me that they kind of broke up after that."

Whatever the case might have been, Ricky and Pat's friendship ended with a violent confrontation one June afternoon on Bayview Avenue, near Northport Village Park, now called "the Old Park." While no one heard the words exchanged between the two, several people saw the punches thrown when Ricky knocked Pagan Pat to the ground. As a small group of stoned teenagers quickly approached the commotion, Ricky looked at the silver pentagram around Pat's neck. Clutching the necklace in his hand, Ricky yanked it off and fled, leaving a bloody pulp behind. As Pat writhed on the ground, bleeding profusely from his face, the teenagers descended upon him, giggling wildly. High on LSD, they began shouting, "HALF-FACE!" convinced his injuries were a ghoulishly hilarious hallucination.

Once Pat pulled himself up off the ground, he hobbled over to the Northport Village Police Station to report the mugging. He told the officers about his pentagram necklace and some cash being stolen and how his face was pummeled until it bled. It is currently unknown if Pat told the police who was behind the assault and theft, but considering Ricky—an ever-present character downtown—was never arrested and charged with what he had done, it's likely Pat never did. After all, even if the cops *did* bust him, it wasn't like Ricky would be going away for *life*. He would have gotten a slap on the wrist and been back on the streets in no time.

In any case, Pagan Pat was never seen with the Acid King again.

Ricky's friends were finally becoming concerned for his well-being. It was easy to write off his earlier hijinks by blaming them on the drugs or acting out for attention. His pals even dismissed the grave-digging episode—Randy Guethler had done *worse* and no one seemed to mind. But now there was a darkness surrounding Ricky that made people uncomfortable. A rage that had been building for years was finally seeping out, and no one knew how to help him control it. Some of his friends wondered if something truly sinister had happened between Ricky and Pagan Pat, or worse—at home. Like many teenagers do, Ricky's friends whispered gossip behind his back, but most neglected to offer him any real assistance or advice, simply ignoring his behavior and hoping it would go away. Others gave up without even trying, assuming he was already too far gone.

One day Ricky showed up to the New Park wielding a baseball bat and began striking the roundhouse's support posts—while his friends sat inside.

"I wanna kill someone . . . ," he muttered in between each vicious swing. "I wanna fucking kill somebody. . . ."

Ellie Love, who was sitting in the roundhouse, yelled, "Ricky! You're too close to us! You're gonna hurt us!"

Suddenly a switch seemed to flip inside Ricky's mind. He lowered the bat, turned to Ellie, and said, "I would never, *ever* hurt you."

"He was walking around town like that for at least a week," Ellie recalls. "Just murmuring with his shoulders hunched. We just thought it was the drugs speaking, not him. He was emaciated and looked like a zombie. Ricky was a walking drug by that point. . . ."

Ellie had good reason to believe her friend looked like a zombie. In the last month, he had lost nearly forty pounds, almost certainly the result of sleeping in the woods and going without eating for long stretches of time. Most of Ricky's drug profits were going toward buying more stock for business and personal use. Spending nearly every hour of every day high on either LSD or angel dust, Ricky found little desire or opportunity to eat a decent meal.

One weekend when Dick and Lynn were out of town, Ricky

called home to see if Wendy would let him in to take a shower. She told him the coast was clear and that he could walk over. After Ricky took a long, hot shower, he went downstairs to the basement playroom to grab a few things that might make living in the woods a little easier. He didn't see much in the way of camping or survival equipment, but he did find an old red-checkered tablecloth that looked to be of some use. The tablecloth was made from durable vinyl, and Ricky figured if he draped it over a lean-to made from a few wooden shipping pallets he had up there, it would keep most of the rain out. Many years earlier his mother had laid it out on the kitchen table for his childhood birthday parties. Now this old tablecloth would be the only barrier between him and the elements as he slept on the wet dirt of Aztakea Woods. He put it under his arm and walked back upstairs.

There, Wendy was waiting for him in the living room. As Ricky went to leave, she stopped him and held out a few dollar bills—the only money she had to her name at eleven years old.

"Here," she said. "In case you need it."

This was the first time in a long while that someone in his family had done something for him out of love, instead of obligation.

"I . . ." Ricky struggled to find the words. "I can't take your money, Wendy."

He gave his sister a hug and, like so many times before, left his parents' home facing an uncertain future.

Chapter 27

MATTHEW CARPENTER HAD BEEN AWAY FOR A LONG time. His parents had pulled him out of Northport High School three years earlier, when his drinking and drug use had gotten out of hand, and enrolled him in a private boarding school. By eleventh grade, however, Matthew's behavior had not improved, and he was expelled. Luckily, his mother convinced Northport High to take him back, but wanted him out of the house as often as possible during the summer. She was going through difficult times of her own, having recently divorced her husband, and didn't want to deal with Matthew's problems. After leaving her home and moving into a rented house on Bayview Avenue, Matthew's mother asked him to go out and find a summer job.

Walking down Main Street, Matthew saw a familiar face staring into the window of Village Books—Ricky Kasso. As Matthew headed over to say hi, he noticed Ricky making a series of bizarre faces and gestures at his own reflection in the glass.

"What are you doing, Ricky?" Matthew asked with a laugh. "What are you on?"

"Drugs," he replied.

"By then, Ricky would only say 'drugs' if you asked him what he was on," Matthew recalls. "He would never be specific. I hadn't seen him since junior high school, but the first thing I noticed that day was that he and I were both dressed very similarly. Ricky was wearing a black leather jacket, a concert T-shirt, a pentagram necklace, black jeans, and biker boots."

The two stood outside Village Books catching up. Despite his issues at home, Matthew was in a jovial mood. It was a beautiful day, and he was enchanted by the vivid shades of green foliage swaying in the gentle June wind. He was also happy to run into his old buddy downtown. Ricky, however, seemed sullen and forlorn.

"So, where are you headed?" Matthew asked, trying to keep the conversation light.

"Oh, I don't know," Ricky replied. "I don't really have anywhere to go. My parents kicked me out."

Matthew pitied his childhood friend. Granted, he didn't have much to offer Ricky, other than a couch to sleep on inside his tiny bedroom—but it was better than sleeping on the street.

"Hey," Matthew said, "why don't you come hang out with me?"

Back at the rented house on Bayview Avenue, Matthew showed Ricky the outside door that led straight to his room and pointed to the red velour couch he could use as a bed. The couch wasn't very long, which was problematic for Ricky, but he figured he could always stretch out on Matthew's black linoleum floor if he got too uncomfortable. Ricky took off his leather jacket and asked if he could take a bath.

"Sure," Matthew replied. "No problem. Go ahead."

While he cleaned up, Matthew took Ricky's clothes and put them in the wash. The dirt stains on his jeans made it obvious that his friend had been sleeping in the woods. Once Ricky's shirt and jeans were dry, Matthew handed them back to Ricky, who gave him his wet towel in return. The two didn't know it yet, but Ricky had just given Matthew scabies.

Later that night, Ricky crashed on the couch, using his leather jacket as a blanket, as Matthew didn't have a spare. Ricky figured he would just sneak back into his parents' house and grab one, along with a few of his things, sometime later that week. Unfortunately for him, he was about to discover that he had very few possessions left in the world. While hanging out with a girlfriend, Ricky received word that his parents were having a spring cleaning yard sale and several of his belongings were being sold. Ricky quickly rushed to a phone and called his parents. His mother picked up.

"Did you have a garage sale?" Ricky asked.

"Yes," Lynn replied.

"What did you sell?"

"Your stuff."

Ricky couldn't believe his ears. Sure, his parents had been kicking him out for the last three years, but they always eventually let him back in. Even when he was sleeping in the basement, Dick and Lynn usually left his things alone. Now they were trying to erase any hint of his former presence. To add insult to injury, they were now *profiting* from his absence.

"Did you sell *all* of it?" Ricky finally got up the nerve to ask.

"Not all of it," Lynn replied.

"Can I come over and get it?" he asked.

"It'll be waiting outside," Lynn said coldly before hanging up.

Soon after, Ricky arrived, gathered his things from the front lawn, and returned to Matthew's house. For the next two weeks, the boys spent nearly every day together, usually smoking weed and discussing music. Sometimes Ricky would talk about the problems he had with his parents. He told Matthew about the ketchup incident, his clothes being thrown out on the lawn, and his time in South Oaks. When Satan would come up in conversation, Matthew would openly wonder why Ricky had developed such a dark interest while he was away.

"Why would you knowingly choose evil over good?" Matthew asked

"To gain power," Ricky replied. "Drugs make me feel closer to evil. They give these . . . *abilities*."

"What kind of abilities, Ricky?" Matthew asked.

Ricky thought for a moment.

"When I'm on them," he replied, "I can *see* evil. . . ."

Matthew didn't press the issue any further. He didn't mind Ricky's ramblings about the devil too much. When the topic came up, Ricky never tried to "convert" him, and Matthew paid Ricky the same respect by not trying to sell him on Christ. Ricky's habit of giving Matthew free drugs in gratitude for a place to sleep also helped his friend look the other way.

Jimmy Troiano and Albert Quinones didn't mind either. The two would sometimes show up to Matthew's house, ready to party. The teens were afforded a relative amount of privacy due to Matthew's mother's work schedule, and they often sat in the bedroom, smoking pot and blasting Black Sabbath.

One night the group invited a few girls back to Matthew's house. One of them, a friend named Tina, entertained everyone by repeatedly claiming she could conjure the spirits of dead people. While Tina carried on about her supposed supernatural abilities, a ceramic coffee cup used as a makeshift ashtray began to emit smoke. A small flame soon rose from the mug; the result of too many cigarette butts being placed inside.

"Aha!" someone cried out. "Satan is here! Welcome! Welcome!"

Everyone laughed at the joke, put out the fire, and resumed drinking.

None of the kids sitting on Matthew Carpenter's front porch that night could have had any clue that "Satan" wouldn't be a laughing matter for long.

Chapter 28

BY THE TIME THE THIRD WEEK OF JUNE 1984 ROLLED around, Ricky Kasso still hadn't let go of his grudge against Gary Lauwers—despite having already made his money back, plus extra, thanks to Mrs. Lauwers. All that mattered was that Gary still owed him twenty dollars. One of the few times Gary dared to show his face downtown, Ricky quickly found him and beat the boy to the ground.

Johnny Hayward was nearby, and while he saw Ricky's point, he couldn't stand watching his best friend getting hurt.

"Hey!" Johnny shouted as he pulled Ricky off Gary. "Don't *ever* touch Gary in front of me or I'll stomp your ass! He deserves to get his ass whipped because he ripped you off, but I ain't gonna let you do it in front of *me*."

"All right, man," Ricky replied. "I can respect that."

Ricky left Gary with a reminder to pay up and walked away.

Later that night Gary and Johnny pulled Midnight Auto again, stealing a handful of car stereos. Johnny left the haul with Gary, who planned to sell them to one of his connections, and said he would be back for his share of the money in a few days. Gary quickly sold the stereos, but instead of setting Johnny's cut of the cash aside, he spent all of it.

On Sunday, June 17, Johnny caught up with Gary at the Phase II pizzeria on Main Street. When he asked for his cut of the money, Gary told him it was gone. Johnny was at a loss for words. First, Gary had been stupid enough to steal from Ricky, but now he was stealing from his own *best friend*? The two teenage thieves had always lived by an unspoken code: *You steal from people you do not know or from companies that can afford it; you do not steal from your family.* Gary had already broken that rule with Ricky, and now he was breaking it with him. The feelings of utter disappointment and frustration festering inside Johnny quickly reached a boiling point. He lashed out and punched Gary hard, throwing him against one of Phase II's arcade games.

"Fuck you, you *prick*!" he screamed. "You *stole* from me!"

Before Gary could reply, Johnny stormed out of the pizzeria.

The two best friends would never see each other again.

Down the street, Ricky Kasso stood at a pay phone, high on angel dust. Over the past few hours, he had called home three times. During each call, he repeated the same sentence in a groggy, slurred voice: "You know, you got to go to court with me tomorrow. . . ."

The fourth time that Ricky called, Lynn answered.

"Ricky, are you all right?" she asked. "Are you high or something?"

"No, no," he lied. "I'm straight. Just really tired."

Ricky hung up and walked to the rear of the Midway, where he fell asleep against a bag of trash. Early the next morning, he made the mile-long walk to the Kasso home, arriving around seven thirty. When Lynn opened the front door, she was horrified by what she saw. Her son was shockingly underweight, his hair was greasy, and his clothes were full of holes. Lynn hollered for Wendy, asking her to grab some shampoo. Wendy ran to the upstairs bathroom, grabbed a bottle of Gee, Your Hair Smells Terrific, and gave it to her brother, who quickly washed his hair in the sink. Once he was somewhat presentable, Ricky hopped into the passenger seat of his father's Corvette and slept the whole way to the courthouse.

"I'm surprised my dad let anyone ride in that car," Wendy Kasso says. "I rode in it once and he screamed at me for rolling my window down. It was a '77. He just came home with it one day. He never discussed it with my mom. She was pissed. We couldn't afford it and he knew it."

Ricky's court appearance was brief. Despite his confession to Detective Varley and his appearance on *Inside Newsday*, Ricky pleaded not guilty and the judge referred him to legal aid. A subsequent court date was set, and Ricky was permitted to leave. On the way back to Northport, Ricky asked Dick to drop him off at the Midway. When they pulled up to the head shop, Ricky checked his pockets and realized he was broke.

"Can I have a quarter?" Ricky asked.

"No," Dick replied.

"I just want a quarter so I can get a bagel from the deli," Ricky insisted. "I haven't eaten in three days, Dad."

"No."

Ricky was furious and desperate. The two began screaming at each other while Ricky's friends stood in front of the Midway, watching intently. Finally Ricky stormed out of the car and kicked the door, much to the chagrin of Dick, who sped off in a cloud of exhaust. Twenty minutes later Dick returned, rolled down his window, and motioned Ricky over to the car. He threw two dollars at him and said, "Don't call me. Don't come to the house. Don't ask for *anything*. Don't talk to your mother or your sisters ever again. Just leave me alone—I never want to see you again."

Ricky bent down to collect the dollar bills from the ground as his father pulled away.

"What was that all about?" a friend asked.

"Nothing," a humiliated Ricky replied. "Asshole just wants me out of his life."

Ricky tried to shrug off the ordeal and headed inside the deli next door to the Midway to buy his bagel. Later he walked down the side of 25A with his thumb out, trying to hitch a ride to Kings Park. There, he planned to meet Jimmy and score some microdots and dust to sell. Ironically, the one car that pulled over was driven by none other than Tony Ruggi from the Place. Just like Lynn Kasso, Ruggi was shaken by Ricky's appearance as he got into the car. Aside from his dramatic weight loss, Ricky also smelled horrible and looked gravely ill.

"Ricky," Ruggi said, "you really should stop by the agency this week. Suzi and I can help you work on a plan to get your life back on track."

"I would," Ricky mumbled, "but I'm too busy now. . . ."

"What's wrong?" Ruggi asked.

"My parents kicked me out again," Ricky replied. "I've been staying with Jimmy in a station wagon in Kings Park. Do you know Jimmy?"

"Yeah, I know Jimmy," Ruggi replied. "I feel sorry for him. He's had problems all his life."

Ruggi paused.

"You know," he finally said, "I heard about you getting picked up for grave robbing."

"Don't believe everything you read," Ricky snapped back. "That was *Randy*, not me. He was trying to get back at me for shit. He's such a waste. He shouldn't even be alive."

"Ricky, you're talking nonsense," Ruggi replied. "Besides, what about that interview you gave in front of the Midway?"

"It was fun!" Ricky boasted. "I was a *star!* They *wanted* to hear some of those things, anyway!"

"That was a really dumb thing to do if you were joking," Ruggi said. "People are going to take it at face value."

"It'll all come out when it goes to trial," Ricky replied confidently. "You'll see it wasn't half as bad as people make it."

"Ricky, you really need to get clean." Ruggi meant this both figuratively and literally.

"Why?" Ricky asked. "What's the use? No one *loves* me.

Why bother? The universe *wants* me like this. . . ."

Ruggi realized he wasn't reaching Ricky and decided not to press that matter any further. He dropped Ricky off at the 7-Eleven in Kings Park, where Jimmy was waiting, and promised himself he would find a way to help Ricky. He drove back to the Place and talked to Suzi Strakhov about how concerned he was about Ricky's health and behavior. The two discussed the possibility of getting him emergency housing and into a local rehab if they could get his parents involved. Ruggi got on the phone and called Dick Kasso.

"Unfortunately, the dealings with his father were very difficult," he recalls. "He was very strict and demanding. Whenever we tried to talk to him about Ricky, he had all the answers that he needed—that Ricky was just a waste. . . ."

Once again, Tony was out of options. He and Suzi seemed to be the only people left in the world who believed in Ricky. Despite his many transgressions and failures, they always saw the good in him, holding on to their faith that with the right tools and opportunities, Ricky could become a happy and productive member of society.

That night Tony Ruggi locked up the Place and went home, completely unaware that any hope of salvation for Ricky would vanish the next day.

Chapter 29

THE EVENING OF JUNE 19, 1984, BEGAN ON A HIGH note. The school year was ending, and the New Park kids all headed downtown to hang out. There were beers to be chugged, pot to be smoked, acid to be taken, and laughs to be had. Meanwhile, Johnny Hayward was uptown at the local Sizzler steakhouse. He sat in his seat, impatiently fidgeting as he chewed his dinner. Flanked by his parents, he thought about his friends and the fun they were having. Johnny appreciated the meal, of course, but he would rather be downtown.

There was also the tension at the table. The last time the Hayward family went out to eat, Johnny had just been released from the hospital after a surprise allergic reaction to the caramel coloring in Johnnie Walker Red Label Scotch Whisky. When Johnny's parents met him at the hospital, they found their son in such an animated state that the doctors warned of transferring him to the psychiatric ward. Upon hearing this, Johnny's father gave his son one good punch upside the head, knocking him out cold.

As time went on, Johnny grew to appreciate that punch.

A few weeks had passed, and Johnny had agreed to his father's order to "swear off the red stuff." He had other vices, after all. Tonight he was going to see the Acid King. Ricky would have drugs, and maybe he would see Gary so the two could bury the hatchet. Enough time had gone by for Johnny to forgive him.

Gary was certainly looking for forgiveness that night. It was time to make everything right with the world. Nearly two months after reaching into his friend's jacket pocket, Gary was finally going to pay Ricky the remaining twenty bucks for the stolen PCP. Granted, the money he was carrying was technically owed to Johnny, but Gary was worn and wearied from the ordeal.

Convinced his life was now getting back on track, he headed downtown. For the past couple of days he had been hiding out, thinking his life over. He was set on leaving Long Island and was seriously considering joining the army. However, before all that was to be done, Gary had a movie date with his new girlfriend, Grace Schinmann, and wanted to hang out with Ricky afterward. Still driven by a raging desire to fit in, Gary desperately wanted to repair their fractured friendship—and what harm would another night or two of partying do before leaving Northport for good?

On his way downtown, Gary stopped at Merrie Schaller's house to say hi to a few people. There, he found Glen Wolf and their mutual friend Valerie MacKenna sitting in one of the bedrooms.

The three exchanged pleasantries and lit a joint as Gary sat on the floor.

"So, what are you doing tonight, Gary?" Valerie asked.

"I'm meeting up with Ricky and then I'm going to the movies with Grace," he replied.

"You know Ricky's looking to kick your ass, right?" Glen said. "The word's out, man."

"It's fine," Gary replied with a chuckle, knowing he had twenty dollars in his pocket with Ricky's name on it. "I'm all paid up."

Valerie was worried. Something seemed *off*.

"You should hang with us instead, Gary," she offered. "We're all going to chill out in the New Park and play guitar. It'll be a good time, man."

"Nah," he said. "I gotta find Ricky, then we're gonna hang out."

Glen and Valerie were silent. Gary sensed their apprehension.

"It's okay, guys," he said. "Seriously, it'll be fine."

"I still wouldn't go if I were you," Glen warned.

"I swear, it's fine," Gary said with a confident laugh.

"Well, at least walk with us downtown?" Valerie asked.

Gary agreed, and the three left Merrie's for the New Park. Glen left Gary and Valerie once they hit Main Street. Glen's girlfriend, Jane Allen, was waiting for him inside the Feed & Grain restaurant, and he told the two he would catch up with them later. When Gary arrived at the New Park, he didn't immediately see Ricky, but he did find another familiar face—his friend Liz Testerman. Liz was a few years older than Gary, but she had always been kind to him, despite the occasional problems they had.

The two stood in the far corner of the park and talked about the television shows they'd watched as children. Liz and Gary laughed as they tried to remember the lyrics to the theme songs from *Sesame Street* and *Mister Rogers' Neighborhood*. Once the duo agreed that they were recalling the words correctly, the sounds of Liz and Gary harmonizing began to drift across the harbor.

"Come and play, everything's A-OK . . ."
"It's a beautiful day in this neighborhood, a beautiful day . . ."

Up the block, Jane Allen loudly stormed out of the Feed & Grain. Her dinner date with Glen had turned into a heated argument, and she left him to go hang out in the New Park. Wiping the tears from her eyes, she avoided the group of kids hanging out inside the roundhouse and walked over to the wood forest playground to fix her makeup. She soon noticed someone approaching. It was Gary Lauwers. She was surprised to see him downtown. Everyone knew about the rift between him and Ricky, and most of Gary's friends assumed he was still hiding.

"What's wrong, Jane?" Gary asked.

"Just stupid shit with Glen," Jane replied, brushing the dark red curls away from her eyes.

"Don't worry about it," Gary said, trying to comfort her. "It'll all work out."

"I'm not worried," Jane replied. "I'm gonna go out with him again. I'm just pissed off."

Jane chatted with Gary for a few more minutes before she walked over to the roundhouse to say hi to everyone. Ricky, along with Jimmy Troiano and Albert Quinones, had just shown up. The trio were celebrating Jimmy's recent release from jail. Just a few days earlier, on June 15, he had been arrested for burglarizing a house on Main Street and was released the next day pending trial. The three noticed Jane as she walked over.

"Hey, Jane," Ricky said. "You wanna buy some mesc?"

"Nah," she replied. "I don't do mesc."

"Oh, c'mon!" Jimmy prodded, flashing a grin. "It's fun! We're on, like, ten hits each!"

The sharp-toothed salesman's pitch didn't work. Ricky quickly changed the subject.

"I feel dehydrated," he said, staring off into the distance. "Do you know where the nearest pool is? I wanna go pool-hopping!"

Jane giggled. Ricky, lost in a state of euphoria, was obviously feeling the full effect of the microdots.

"The only water I know close to here is the harbor, the marina, or Scudder Beach," she replied.

Ricky didn't feel like going to any of those spots, and instead asked Jane if she would walk over to the Northport Harbor Delicatessen and buy them some orange juice. Jane, still upset about her fight with Glen, decided she could use the short walk to calm down, and agreed. Jimmy handed her a dollar and she set off for the deli. Once there, Jane grabbed the biggest carton of Tropicana orange juice she could find.

Back at the New Park, Gary noticed a small group of people

out of the corner of his eye. Seated on a bench near the park's wooden gazebo were Ricky, Jimmy, and Albert. Gary walked over, grabbed a wad of bills from his pocket, and offered Ricky a twenty. Surprisingly, Ricky refused to take the cash, instead offering Gary a seat on the bench, along with an invitation to get high with him. Ricky opened his hand to reveal a stash of purple microdots. Gary happily accepted three.

Ricky, Jimmy, and Albert were already high by the time Gary showed up, but soon he was tripping along with them. Once the microdots kicked in, Gary ran off, laughing hysterically about phantom cats and giant sharks in the harbor. Excitedly zipping through the New Park, Gary bumped into Lion, who was standing in the parking lot.

"I saw cats, man!" Gary shouted.

"Sure!" Lion laughed.

"No, man," Gary insisted. "There are *cats* all over the place!"

Gary eventually calmed down and told Lion how happy he was that he could finally show his face in Northport again.

"Well, I guess it's safe for me to come back down here now," he said. "I'm all paid off, I'm in good, it's safe. I'm gonna get some beers and get fucked up." Gary hugged Lion and walked away.

When Jane returned from the deli, Ricky, Jimmy, and Albert grew ecstatic at the sight of the large container of juice. The three hurriedly passed it around among themselves, quickly emptying the carton. Glen Wolf then ran up to the group, shouting, "Hey! There's a keg party right over there! What are you assholes sitting *here* for?! Let's everybody go!"

Ricky definitely wasn't going. It was Randy Guethler's birthday, and his friend Orville had decided to help him celebrate by ordering a few kegs for a party at his house. Ricky was still convinced it was Randy who had ratted him out to the cops, and wished him dead. Jane didn't feel like going either, since Glen would be there and she wasn't ready to forgive him. She stayed behind in the park, along with Ricky, Jimmy, Albert, and Gary—who was still excitedly racing around, vividly hallucinating. Most of the roundhouse crowd then departed for Orville's. Jane hung around for a little while longer, talking to Ricky before she was picked up by a friend.

There were only a handful of people left in the New Park now. One of them was Matthew Carpenter, who had just arrived with his boom box, cranking tunes for the few who remained. The radio had a built-in tape player and was blasting Matthew's cassette copy of Ozzy Osbourne's *Speak of the Devil* album. When Matthew approached the roundhouse, Ricky said, "Hey, we're going up to Aztakea. You wanna come?"

"I'm gonna stay behind for a bit," Matthew replied. "I'll meet you there later."

"Is it cool if we bring your box?" Ricky asked.

Matthew said it was fine, and Ricky grabbed the silver General Electric AM/FM radio off the ground.

"Well," Ricky said, "if you see any girls, tell them they should go up there if they wanna get fucked."

Matthew laughed as he watched his friend walk away.

In another section of the park, Gary was sitting with his friend Dorothy, talking about his future.

"I'm going back to school," he told her. "I got my act together. I paid my debts, I got a lot of friends, and I really care about myself. I don't need drugs anymore. I'm gonna start over."

Ricky approached the two, boom box in hand, with Jimmy and Albert following close behind. By now, Gary's high was peaking and—much to Ricky's annoyance—he began gushing about their repaired friendship.

"I'm happy we're buds again, Rick," Gary said.

"Yeah," Ricky replied. "Because 'buds' totally *steal* from each other, right?"

Gary froze.

"Hey, I'm sorry, man—I really am."

Suddenly Ricky lunged at Gary and grabbed him by the back of his neck.

Thinking quickly, Gary reached for the wad of bills in his pocket and again offered it to Ricky.

"Here, man! *Here!*"

Ricky stared at the crumpled bills in Gary's shaking hand and laughed before shoving the boy away.

"Shut up," he said with a reassuring smile.

Confused, Gary got back up to his feet. He assumed Ricky was just messing with him, and laughed along before saying good-bye to Dorothy and walking away.

Ricky, Jimmy, and Albert followed.

"Hey," Ricky said, calling out to Gary. "Let's go up to Aztakea and trip."

Gary hesitated. He had plans with Grace and didn't want to

ditch her on what was supposed to be their first date. Glen's warning also began to replay in his mind.

"I don't know, man," he replied sheepishly.

Ricky wasn't fazed.

"Come on!" he implored. "We'll go to Dunkin' and get jelly donuts. My treat!"

Gary remained quiet and Ricky quickly realized why.

"I'm well over it, dude," he assured him. "I'm not going to kick your ass."

After a brief pause, Gary smiled. He enjoyed the camaraderie that came with Ricky's newfound forgiveness. Grace would understand. After all, he wouldn't have to hide anymore. She would be happy about that.

"Yeah!" he finally said.

Like a leaf caught in a windstorm, Gary was swept away by the trio as they faded farther and farther down Woodbine Avenue.

While Ricky, Gary, Jimmy, and Albert headed off in search of pastries and cigarettes, Matthew Carpenter stayed behind in the New Park, chatting with friends. A short while later he decided he wanted his radio back and walked toward Aztakea in search of the group. When he entered the woods, he saw no fire in the distance. The only sounds Matthew heard were the distant, echoing cracks of branches being broken, accompanied by vagabond drafts of wind whistling through the trees. He soon grew unsettled. The woods seemed unnaturally dark to him. With no adequate moonlight or nearby campfire to guide him, Matthew couldn't see more than few inches in front of him, and nearly every advancing step brought a smack to his face from a dangling tree branch. The possibility of getting lost inside a pitch-black patch of unforgiving woods was quickly becoming very real. A voice inside Matthew's head began to whisper, *You shouldn't be here*. . . . He didn't need further convincing. Leaving the darkness behind him, he turned around and ran back home.

Only minutes after Matthew left, Ricky, Gary, Jimmy, and Albert exited Dunkin' Donuts, and the Acid King led his march to Aztakea. Walking out the door, Gary swallowed three more microdots given to him by Ricky. As the group made their way down the narrow trail, Ricky noticed three black crows circling overhead. He smiled, turned to his friends, and said, "Satan is with us. . . ."

Over on Tanager Lane, the Hayward family pulled into their driveway. Johnny went inside, grabbed a jacket, and walked out the front door. He made his way down Bellerose Avenue until he got a ride from a passing motorist, who dropped him off at the New Park. Johnny thanked the driver as he exited. The moon, now in its waning gibbous phase, glistened off the softly rolling sheets of pitch-black water that filled Northport Harbor. Johnny lit a smoke and scanned the park for any sight of Ricky. No luck. He did, however, see Lion.

"Hey, you seen Ricky?" Johnny asked.

"Yeah, a little bit ago," Lion replied. "He was with Jimmy, Albert, and Gary. They all went up to the Dunkin' Donuts."

"Thanks, man."

Johnny waved and set off toward 25A. It was a little over a

mile away, but he kept telling himself it would be worth the effort if he found Ricky. By the time Johnny Hayward finally made it to Dunkin' Donuts, he didn't see his friends sitting at any of the five small tables inside. His best guess was they had already left to go party at Aztakea. They were only half a mile away, so what would another ten-minute walk matter at this point? After all, he had already come this far.

Heading out the door, Johnny walked over to Franklin Street. He soon found the gravel path leading to Aztakea Woods. The road crunched with each footstep as Johnny inched farther and farther. Like Matthew Carpenter, he entered the opening trail of Aztakea expecting to quickly spot the glowing embers of a campfire in the distance. He saw nothing and called out to his friends.

"Ricky! Gary! It's Johnny! Hello?!"

Johnny started to worry. Despite his anger toward Gary, he knew his best friend was with people who might be holding even worse grudges against him. Suddenly he heard strange noises in the distance. He couldn't make out exactly what they were—to his ears, it was simply *movement*. He called out two more times, again receiving no answer. Finally Johnny decided to head back home. He had been trying to find everyone for a few hours by this point and didn't feel like sticking around to see what was lurking within the woods.

Sometime later, three shadows exited Aztakea Woods.

The shadow of Gary Lauwers was not among them.

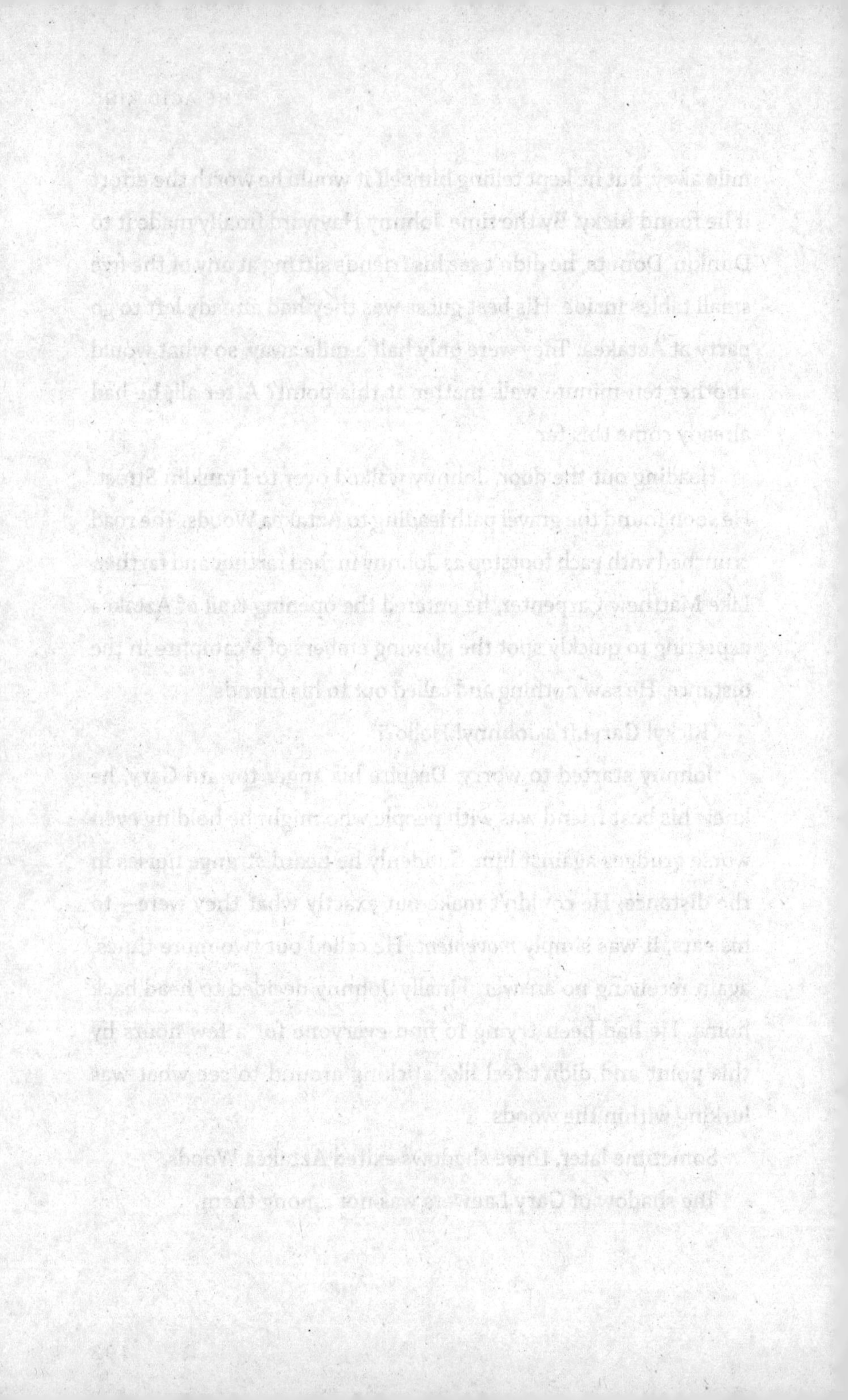

Part Four

THE DARK

This is our island. It's a good island. Until the
grownups come to fetch us we'll have fun.
—William Golding,
Lord of the Flies

Chapter 30

IT WAS QUIET. A CALM HAD SETTLED OVER THE harbor during the predawn hours, and most of the kids who had spent the previous evening partying were sitting around downtown when Ricky and Jimmy walked back.

While no one noticed Gary's absence, his friend Dorothy did pick up on something out of the ordinary—Ricky's outfit. He was still wearing the same jeans, but he had returned wearing a different shirt. Dorothy also noticed that Ricky was wet, as if he had recently taken a shower, but as she got closer to him, she realized that he still smelled of body odor.

Dorothy didn't know that Ricky was wet from washing Gary's blood off his face and chest.

After leaving Gary's body under a pile of leaves in Aztakea, Ricky, Jimmy, and Albert walked back to Albert's house on Maple Avenue to wash up. Ricky then borrowed a fresh shirt from Albert and disposed of the bloody one in a neighbor's trash can before walking back downtown with Jimmy. The two were still high on pot, microdots, and PCP when they arrived.

Ricky decided to hang out with Dorothy, who he enjoyed a friends-with-benefits relationship with, while Jimmy tried in vain to get ahold of his girlfriend, Karen. Adrenaline coursing through his veins, Ricky grabbed Dorothy and aggressively kissed her. At first Dorothy enjoyed Ricky's energetic display of affection, but this changed when Ricky bit her lip, sending blood trickling from her mouth. She quickly pushed Ricky away.

"You're an asshole!" Dorothy cried as Ricky got up and walked off.

Ricky left his friends and headed over to Corey Quinn's backyard clubhouse, about two miles away. There, he fell asleep on the couch where he and Gary had crashed so many times before.

The next morning he left the clubhouse to head back downtown. A friend of Corey's who had slept over at the house saw Ricky through the window and hollered to him. Corey overheard this and went downstairs to say hi. She immediately noticed that Ricky wasn't wearing his pentagram necklace.

"Hey, Ricky," Corey said, "where's your star?"

Ricky lifted his hand to his chest, reaching for the missing necklace. Images from the night before began to flash inside his mind. Gary must have pulled it from his neck while he was stabbing him.

"Oh," Ricky replied. "I lost it last night."

He put his hand in his pocket and clutched the blood-soaked knife.

Later that day, Albert found Ricky standing near the wooden rails at the edge of the harbor. He pulled the bloody knife from his pocket and said, "What should I do with it?"

"Throw it in the water," Albert replied.

Ricky chucked the knife into the air. Just as it hit the water, Johnny Hayward walked up to Ricky.

"What was that?" he asked.

"Ah, nothin', man," Ricky said, walking away from the dock. "It was just a rock."

Ricky's silence didn't last long. When the drugs wore off, a part of him was haunted by what he had done, but when he was high, he felt proud of having murdered Gary. He had finally struck back at someone who had harmed him, albeit superficially. Knowing Gary Lauwers was now dead because of him, Ricky Kasso was finally beginning to feel the power he had so desperately been seeking from drugs and the devil.

This sensation soon began to manifest itself in strange ways. Only a few minutes after Johnny almost caught him throwing the knife into the harbor, Ricky began spinning a bizarre yarn about murdering a man who had recently stopped to give him a ride.

"Jimmy and I were hitching back from Kings Park," he told Johnny. "This guy picks us up. We wanted his car so we could drive out to California, so I just stabbed him."

"*What?*" Johnny asked.

"Yeah," Ricky said. "He jumped back in his seat and I stabbed him like six more times, but he wouldn't get out of the car, so we just jumped out."

Johnny ignored Ricky, hoping he was just bullshitting. Later he grabbed a local newspaper to see if any murder or stabbing like the one Ricky described had been reported. To his relief, Johnny found nothing, and wrote Ricky's ramblings off as the product of a stoned imagination.

The very next day Ricky was back in the roundhouse, high on angel dust and microdots. Pacing back and forth inside the gazebo, he desperately wanted someone to brag to without having to make up another story. When Rich Barton showed up, Ricky pulled him aside.

"Rich, come here," Ricky whispered. "I gotta tell you something—*I killed Gary*."

"Bullshit!" Rich laughed.

"Come on," Ricky urged. "I'll show you the body. It's up in Aztakea. I'll take you there."

"No way," Rich said dismissively. He figured his friend was high and pulling a sick prank, and walked away.

By the next day, Rich wasn't so sure. He walked up to Ricky and said, "All right, I'll go up and see the body." He still figured Ricky was lying, but he wanted to see what was in Aztakea. Ricky told Rich, along with their friend Mark Florimonte, to follow him.

"You're really gonna see it now," Ricky told them. "I'm not joking."

Once the trio entered Aztakea, a disgusting smell met their noses.

"Rick, what the hell did you kill—a fucking *cat*?" Rich asked.

Ricky didn't answer. He just kept leading them deeper into the brush until they finally came upon a pile of leaves and broken branches lying on the ground.

"There it is," Ricky said, emotionless.

Rich and Mark moved closer to examine the mound. It seemed to be moving; almost *breathing*. Once the two were only inches away from the pile, it all became clear—the leaves were covered with thousands of squirming maggots. They jumped back once they saw bits of Gary's bloody clothing peeking out from underneath the leaves.

"Holy shit, man!" Rich screamed. "Rick, I'm getting the hell out of here! I'll meet you back downtown!"

Mark looked his friend square in the eye.

"You're *stupid*, Ricky," he said, quickly walking away. "You did the crime, now you're gonna have to pay the time!"

Rich and Mark took off, leaving Ricky with whatever remained of Gary Lauwers in the woods. Racing back downtown, Rich saw Matthew Carpenter approaching. As Rich was walking past Phase II, Matthew stopped him to say hello.

"Hey, Rich," he said. "Do you have any pot on you?"

Matthew suddenly noticed how pale his friend looked.

"Are you all right, man?" he asked.

"Ricky is really *fucked up*," Rich replied.

"What do you mean?" Matthew asked

"Ricky did something *really* fucked up," Rich said.

"Well," Matthew replied, "what did he do?"

Rich didn't answer. Instead he walked away, hypnotically

repeating the same sentence over and over like a broken record. "Ricky is fucked up. . . . Ricky is fucked up. . . . Ricky is fucked up. . . ."

Confused, Matthew let it go and walked way.

Later Ricky found Rich sitting in the New Park.

"See," Ricky said nonchalantly, "I told you."

"I think you're crazy," Rich replied. "You're gonna get caught. Why'd you do that, man?"

"For *kicks*," Ricky said sarcastically as he walked away.

Rich began to panic. He knew he couldn't tell the cops. If he did, and word got back to Ricky, he might end up dead too. Anyway, Ricky was bound to get caught. He had just shown two people the rotting corpse of the friend he had murdered—and who knew how many others had made the horrible trip to Aztakea over the last couple days? If Ricky did get caught, however, Rich's name would surely be mentioned to the authorities.

Could he go to jail just for *knowing* what had happened to Gary Lauwers?

Rich and Mark left the New Park and walked home to the Barton house on Maple Avenue. There, they discussed everything they had seen. Later they talked to Albert Quinones, who said the only option was to stay as far away from Ricky and Jimmy as possible and hope for the best. After all, no one was even looking for Gary, let alone the cops. He left home so often that his parents didn't think anything of his absence.

That would soon change.

One night during the last week of June, Yvonne Lauwers was

sitting at home when the phone rang. She picked up the receiver and heard a voice that sent chills up her spine.

"You will never see your son again because I just killed him. . . ."

The ghoulish caller hung up before Yvonne could respond. At first she thought it was a crank call and tried not to think about it. By the next morning, however, Yvonne could no longer ignore the words echoing in her mind. She picked up the phone and dialed Scott Travia, one of Gary's close friends.

"Scott, have you seen Gary?" she asked. "He hasn't been home in a while and I don't know where he is."

"I haven't seen him either, Mrs. Lauwers," Scott replied.

"Scott," Yvonne continued, "someone with a scary voice called last night and said we would never see Gary again because they *killed* him."

This chilled Scott to his core.

"Do you think they were just joking?" Scott asked, trying to hide his fear.

"Maybe," Yvonne replied. "*Hopefully* . . ."

Meanwhile, back in Aztakea, Grant Koerner was riding his bike through the BMX trails he and his friends had made throughout the woods. At one point, he rode past a strange pile of leaves.

He didn't notice the maggots.

Chapter 31

MATTHEW CARPENTER COULDN'T SLEEP.

Ricky was crashing on his couch again, as Corey Quinn's stepfather, sick of all the boys sneaking in and out of his backyard, had torn down her clubhouse a few days earlier. Matthew could hear Ricky muttering about something but couldn't make out the words. Finally he turned toward Ricky, who sat up.

"What's going on?" Matthew asked.

"There are people in here," Ricky replied fearfully. "They're coming to *get* me."

"*What* people?" Matthew demanded.

"They've *returned*," Ricky insisted, his body shaking. "They're haunting me."

"Oh, fuck off!" Matthew replied. "You're just having a bad dream. Get back to sleep!"

Ricky, however, kept talking about the people in the room

until Matthew got up and took him outside to calm down. Once Ricky relaxed, Matthew decided to strike up a conversation.

"So, why do you like Aztakea so much?" he asked.

"What do you mean?" Ricky replied.

"Remember how you invited us all up there that night?" Matthew asked.

"Yeah," Ricky replied.

"Well," Matthew said, "I was just wondering why you like it up there."

"It's just a good place to trip," Ricky insisted.

"Oh, really?" Matthew asked. "What do you see up there?"

"I don't like talking about it," Ricky replied. "People think I'm nuts."

"Try me," Matthew replied.

"Well," Ricky began, "I saw this tree one time. It just sprouted up out of the ground and grew to full size. Then it started glowing."

"Oh, wow," Matthew said.

"Yeah," Ricky replied. "Then, another time, Satan came to me in the form of a crow and started talking to me."

Matthew had no idea that Ricky was alluding to the night he killed Gary Lauwers.

"How do you know it's actually the devil who's talking to you?" Matthew asked. "I talk to God all the time through prayer. but it's not like he taps me on the shoulder and says, 'Hey, here I am,' or anything."

"He told me to do things . . . ," Ricky said.

"Like what?" Matthew asked.

"I don't want to talk about it," Ricky replied. "Like I told you, people think I'm nuts. Maybe I need to get into a rehab or something. I'm tired of living on the street."

Matthew decided to change the subject.

"Well, speaking of Aztakea," he said, "is my boom box still up there?"

Ricky didn't bother lying. He had taken Matthew's radio into the South Bronx a few days earlier and traded it for more angel dust. Either Ricky failed to see the hypocrisy in committing the same act that drove him to kill Gary, or he just didn't care. Luckily for him, Matthew was much more forgiving.

"I'm sorry, man," Ricky said. "That was wrong of me."

Ricky tried to make up for it by offering Matthew a joint laced with the angel dust he got in return for the boom box. He accepted.

When all was said and done, Matthew wanted to get high more than he wanted a radio.

The next morning he grabbed a few boxes he needed to unpack. He and his family hadn't been in the rented house on Bayview Avenue for long, and he still had some work to do. The cellophane tape on one of the boxes refused to budge.

"Ricky, hand me your knife, would ya?" Matthew asked.

"No," Ricky replied. "I don't carry a knife anymore, and you shouldn't either. You might end up hurting somebody."

Just like their conversation about Aztakea, this exchange would later come back to haunt Matthew. Later that day Ricky walked downtown to meet Jimmy and get high. There, he found an unexpected visitor—Gary's mother, Yvonne.

"Richard, I haven't seen Gary in a few days," Yvonne said. "Have you or James seen him?"

"Oh, no, Mrs. Lauwers," Ricky said before walking away, laughing hysterically. He was already high on PCP when he arrived at the New Park, and the minuscule amount of empathy he had for his victim had since faded. Yvonne was unsettled by Ricky's reaction to her question but still decided not to report her son missing. She walked back home, hoping Gary would turn up sooner rather than later.

Yvonne was not the only person wondering where her son was. Soon others among the New Park crowd began to whisper about the missing boy. The few who knew the truth were left to deal with a dark knowledge growing inside them like a cancer. They felt bad for Gary, but one slip of the tongue could mean ending up in a shallow grave next to Gary or in a jail cell next to Ricky. Even if they got away with their lives and their freedom, what good would life as a rat be in Northport? Teenagers there lived by a code—and Gary Lauwers was dead for breaking it.

"If you're a street kid doing drugs, why would you go to a cop?" says Anthony Zenkus, a friend and peer of the New Park kids. "If you don't have a good relationship with your parents, why would you tell them your friend *murdered* somebody? Many of these kids were distanced from their families as well as their community. They were looked at as *throwaways*. That's what I thought of when I heard about the things Ricky's father was saying about him—*Ricky was a throwaway*. When you don't believe you have a connection to a loving world, why should you tell *anyone* what you saw? You're more likely to worry about yourself and take care of yourself. That's what kids in abusive homes learn: 'I've got to take care of myself'—or they don't take care of themselves at all. There was no conspiracy of silence, just a bunch of disaffected kids."

Anthony was one of the few people who took Gary's absence seriously, along with a few of the kids who lived at Merrie Schaller's house.

"Gary had people looking for him," Anthony insists. "We were walking around, talking to people, saying, 'Did he run away? Is he hiding out somewhere?' He knew kids on the street, so who knows what he was doing, you know?"

Glen Wolf was also looking for Gary. A friend had recently given Glen a beat-up car that he and Gary were having fun taking apart in Merrie's driveway, and he was concerned that Gary hadn't picked up his tools or the thirty dollars Glen owed him for helping with some odd jobs around the village. Glen checked the local hospitals and jails to see if Gary had been hurt or arrested, but when he found out Gary's probation officer knew he was missing, he gave up the search. He figured if the officer didn't think much of Gary's disappearance, it would do little good to call the police.

Soon after their visit to Aztakea, Ricky started following Rich Barton home. Even when Rich successfully evaded him downtown, Ricky still made a habit of showing up at his house late at night. The back door that led downstairs to Rich's basement bedroom was often left unlocked, allowing Ricky to come and go as he pleased. Unlike Matthew Carpenter, Rich didn't have a spare couch, so Ricky would pass out on the floor, again using his leather jacket for a blanket. He usually slept until late in the afternoon, exhausted from the previous night's dust high. Wanting to stay on Ricky's good side, Rich would cook him a breakfast of hot dogs while they watched *Friday the 13th* and *Mad Max* before leaving for the New Park.

One day Ricky went downtown and got stoned on a boat that was docked in the harbor. When he was done, he tried jumping back onto the dock but fell straight into the water. Climbing out, Ricky asked a friend if he could borrow a shirt and a pair of pants. The friend ran home to grab some clothes for Ricky. He found a shirt that would soon end up on the front cover of every major newspaper in the country.

The garment in question was a bootleg AC/DC shirt sold in the parking lot of Madison Square Garden during one of the band's concerts in December 1983. It was white with long sleeves, and the front featured the silk-screened image of a green devil accompanied by the AC/DC logo in large, bloodred letters. In less than two weeks' time, the shirt would become iconic—a veritable weapon wielded by paranoid parents and tabloid journalists against hard rock acts all over the world.

Later that day Ricky took two girlfriends up to Aztakea to see Gary's body. Staring at the grisly remains, one of the girls turned to Ricky and said, "You know, you should at least have the decency to *bury* him."

Rather than take offense, Ricky thought his friend might be onto something. Not that he gave a damn about giving Gary any dignity in death, but he suddenly remembered hearing talk of a housing development that was going to be built on top of Aztakea Woods in the near future. What if some construction worker were to clear the pile of leaves, scattering Gary's bones all over the ground? Would the cops find something there to tie the murder back to him—his stolen pentagram necklace, maybe? Would the people he'd brought to watch Gary rot in the muggy summer heat rat him out?

Something had to be done.

Chapter 32

"ALBERT SAYS WE SHOULD BURN DOWN AZTAKEA. . . ."

Ricky briefly considered Jimmy's words but ultimately rejected the idea. What if someone saw them fleeing the scene? Even worse—what if the fire led the cops to Gary's body before the flames could permanently cover up their crime? It simply wasn't worth the risk. Still, the two needed to get out of Northport; there was no question about that. However, with no car, education, or income aside from sporadic drug money, their options were few and far between.

Eventually, Jimmy suggested enlisting in the navy. He figured they would be sent to boot camp somewhere outside of Long Island. Best of all, they wouldn't have to spend a dime—Uncle Sam would foot the bill. Ricky thought the idea had merit, and on June 28, he and Jimmy hitched a ride to Patchogue, about forty minutes away. There, at the US Navy Recruiting Station on

East Main Street, the two took their Armed Forces Qualification Tests. Ricky scored a 42, which would have been good enough for enlistment had he already earned his high school diploma. He had not, so the office had no choice but to turn him away. Jimmy also failed his test. However, the recruiter told them both to return soon and try again.

After finding a ride back to Northport, Ricky walked back to Rich Barton's house, where he spent the next two nights. On Saturday, June 30, Ricky awoke early and asked Rich if he would help him bury Gary's body.

"Fuck *that*, man!" Rich exclaimed. "I'm not getting near that thing! I saw it once and that's enough!"

Rich retrieved a garden shovel from his backyard and handed it to Ricky.

"Here," he said. "You can have this. You don't have to give it back to me."

Ricky took the shovel and walked down the block to the Quinones house, where he found Albert hanging out with Mark Florimonte. He asked the two if they would help him, but they also refused. Undeterred, Ricky made his way down to the New Park, where he found Jimmy sitting with two of their friends, Ronnie and Cathy. He wasted no time telling them what he had done to Gary Lauwers.

"Oh, yeah?" Ronnie said. *"Bullshit."*

Ronnie had known Ricky and Jimmy for less than a year, but he came from a tough crowd in Kings Park. He was familiar with Ricky's habit of getting stoned and babbling strange things—

mostly about Satan—and didn't believe him any more than Rich Barton or Mark Florimonte had. Ricky may have been tall, looming several inches over most other kids, but he was also terribly thin and gangly. Ronnie simply couldn't picture him killing someone.

"No, come on!" Jimmy said, visibly excited. "Drive us up to the woods! We'll show you!"

Intrigued, Ronnie and Cathy decided to play along. The four hopped into Cathy's car and drove to Franklin Street. There, they parked at the end of the cul-de-sac and followed Ricky into Aztakea. The putrid smell of decomposition hit them almost immediately. Still, Ronnie refused to believe Ricky had actually murdered Gary. He figured there was a dead animal up there—maybe a dog—and Ricky was pulling a prank. This all changed once Ricky led Ronnie and Cathy over to the pile of sticky, blackened leaves tucked away between the poison ivy plants and cedar trees. Ronnie walked up and brushed some of the foliage away with his foot, revealing Gary's denim jacket. Startled, he stumbled backward. The realization that he was staring at a murdered human being while the killer stood behind him set in rapidly.

"Gary's in Hell now because we made him say he loved Satan," Jimmy said proudly.

"Yeah," Ricky added. "We came up here to hang out. Started doing acid and we got this fire going. I made Gary burn his jacket sleeves."

"That's when he said he had a bad feeling we were gonna kill him," Jimmy laughed.

"I started kicking Gary's ass for stealing from me," Ricky continued. "There was this crow flying overhead, screeching. That was a sign from Satan. He was ordering me to kill Gary. So, I pulled out my knife and stabbed him once before he ran away. Jimmy went and dragged him back. I started stabbing him more and more until we thought he was dead. We started to drag him away from the fire when he sat straight up. I flipped out and started hacking away at his face."

Ronnie had heard enough. He grabbed Cathy, and the two left Ricky and Jimmy behind to bury Gary. As they made their way out of Aztakea, Ronnie looked at his girlfriend and said, "Oh my God, these guys are going to jail for fucking *life*. . . ."

As Ronnie and Cathy left Aztakea, Ricky and Jimmy went to work on the grave, digging a hole that was only about four feet long, two feet wide, and eighteen inches deep. After they were done, they grabbed Gary's remains by his jacket and went to drag him into the hole. When Ricky and Jimmy lifted Gary's body up off the dirt, his head gave way to decomposition and fell to the ground. In one last petty display of hatred, Ricky kicked Gary's skull into the grave before covering the bones with a thin layer of dirt, leaves, and branches. He then picked up the shovel and left Aztakea Woods for the last time.

Chapter 33

A DAY AFTER BURYING GARY, RICKY AND JIMMY SPLIT off to visit their girlfriends. Jimmy made plans to see a movie with Karen and her friend Jean Wells, while Ricky decided to hang out with Jane Allen, who had recently started hooking up with him after her fight with Glen Wolf. The two were an odd couple: Jane with her hippie clothes and peace-symbol necklaces, and Ricky with a red bandanna tied around his hair, and an inverted cross and a dagger recently self-tattooed on his arms.

On this hot July day, Jane found herself sharing a bottle of stolen wine with Ricky. As she reached for a cigarette, Ricky took a big swig, trying to drown his thoughts. The flashbacks had started up again, leaving him shaken.

"You want one, Ricky?" Jane asked, holding a cigarette in front of his face.

"Nah," he replied. "I'm gonna try not to smoke that much."

Jane lit hers and inhaled.

"I know you don't even care," she said, "but have you seen Gary? We talked to his mother, and she hasn't seen him in a while."

"No," Ricky replied, scratching his left wrist. "I haven't seen him."

Suddenly Jane noticed the blotchy red patch of blisters on Ricky's arm and immediately recognized the source—poison ivy. She took him back to her house and gave him some calamine lotion to help relieve the itching. Jane couldn't have known that Ricky got the rash while burying her friend.

Later Jimmy caught up with the two. Ricky kept complaining about the "flashbacks" he was getting, always stopping short of describing them. Jimmy was unconcerned.

"So, when are you gonna trip again?" he asked.

"I'm *never* gonna trip again," Ricky replied. "I just had a bad trip—a really *bad* trip."

"No, c'mon!" Jimmy scoffed. "If somebody threw eight hits in your face for *free*, you'd eat 'em."

Ricky stood his ground.

"Nah, Drac," he said. "I wouldn't."

"Oh, whatever, man," Jimmy replied.

Jimmy seemed to be completely oblivious to the situation he and Ricky were now both in. Little did they know that the Northport Village Police Department were onto their dark secret buried away inside Aztakea Woods—all thanks to Jimmy's loose lips.

The next morning, July 2, Ricky awoke determined to leave

Northport for good. Convinced it was only a matter of time before the cops caught up to them, he talked Jimmy into coming with him. Jimmy had virtually no reason to stay on Long Island either. Aside from helping Ricky kill Gary, Jimmy's court date for his June burglary arrest was rapidly approaching, and there was little left in the village for him to feel sentimental about.

While Northport Police Officer Gene Roemer and Police Chief Robert Howard were across town interviewing Yvonne Lauwers about her missing son, Ricky and Jimmy began planning their escape. Ricky suggested hitchhiking up to Argyle, and Jimmy agreed. The two had done this once before during the winter of 1980 and were confident they could pull it off again. From there, they could use some of their drug money to buy a used car and flee across the country to California. Ricky had always wanted to live there, spending his days playing guitar and his nights lying on the beach. He would have to settle for hiding there as a fugitive from the law.

Before leaving, the two curiously created even more loose ends by telling friends they were leaving for California—and even asked a few to come along. Ricky stopped by Rich Barton's to ask if he wanted to "go camping upstate." Rich almost went along until his mother intervened. After leaving the Barton house, Ricky walked downtown to see if Matthew Carpenter might join him and Jimmy.

Ricky arrived at Matthew's house on Bayview Avenue in the middle of the afternoon while his friend was taking a nap. Ricky knocked, and a groggy Matthew sat up in bed, noticing Ricky's silhouette against the white curtain covering the window of his bedroom door. For some reason, Matthew suddenly became very uneasy. Something told him, *Don't open the door. . . .* Ricky knocked again, and Matthew froze. After another short burst of knocking, Ricky finally gave up and left. Matthew breathed a sigh of relief and lay back down.

Ricky later caught up with Jimmy in the New Park and the two said their good-byes to a few select friends. Once they were done, they raised their thumbs and began a two-day journey hitchhiking out of Northport. They had no idea that the Northport police had just finished interviewing Jean Wells and were now on their trail.

Chapter 34

RICKY AND JIMMY SPENT THEIR FIRST NIGHT ON THE road sleeping under a highway overpass on Interstate 87. The two were used to roughing it by this point, but the sleeping bags they had brought along made a difference. In one day of hitchhiking, they had made it as far as Saratoga Springs and only had thirty miles left to go before they reached Argyle. They got a slow start the next day, stopping to sell some purple microdots, and didn't arrive until about an hour before sundown. Ricky took Jimmy over to his friend Tony Mallory's log cabin on Tall Pines Way. While en route, Ricky carefully avoided his own family, who were vacationing a mile down the road.

At eighteen years old, Tony was the polar opposite of Ricky. He was married, gainfully employed, and owned his own home. Despite Tony leading his life on the straight and narrow, Ricky trusted him and knocked on his door.

Tony walked outside to find Ricky and Jimmy standing there. The Kassos had been up in Argyle for nearly two weeks now, and with no sight of Ricky, Tony assumed he had been allowed to stay home for the summer. He didn't bother asking, but others who did were told by Dick and Lynn that Ricky chose to stay home. They were lying. Disgusted with their son's grave-robbing arrest and continuing drug use, they hadn't invited him along.

"Ricky," Tony said, surprised to see his friend. "What's up, man?"

"Hey, Tony," Ricky replied. "Can I talk to you for a little bit?"

"Sure, dude."

Tony invited Ricky and Jimmy inside and the three walked upstairs to Tony's bedroom.

"So, what's going on?" Tony asked as he closed the door.

Ricky didn't waste any time.

"I killed someone, Tony."

"What?"

"I killed someone," Ricky repeated. "I got really high in the woods back home and killed somebody, and I think the cops are after me."

Tony was stunned. Having seen Ricky only during the summertime, Tony had never witnessed him doing drugs, let alone displaying any threatening or violent tendencies. To him, Ricky was just one of the guys.

"Ricky, what the hell happened?" Tony asked.

"I don't know," Ricky said. "I was so high on mescaline. I didn't even remember doing it until some of my friends brought me back to see the body."

Jimmy knew Ricky was lying through his teeth but stayed quiet.

Strangely enough, as Ricky spoke more and more, the lie quickly faded and soon he was giving Tony a detailed account of Gary's murder.

"That kid had been ripping people off for a while," Ricky said. "It was time someone did something about it."

"Ricky," Tony replied, "if this is true, you're going to go to jail for a *very* long time."

"No way!" Ricky said. "I'm not spending the rest of my life behind bars, Tony!"

"If you did this," Tony insisted, "you're going to have to face the consequences sooner or later."

"If they ever catch me, I'll kill myself!" Ricky countered. "I'll never stay in jail! I can't live in jail!"

Despite his own panic slowly setting in, Tony tried to calm Ricky.

"What is it that *I* can do for you?" he asked.

Ricky thought for a second.

"Is it all right if Jimmy and I crash here until we figure out how we're going to get to California?'

Out of loyalty to his childhood friend, along with the fleeting hope that none of this was actually true, Tony said yes. By the next morning, however, he was ready for Ricky and Jimmy to leave. He could no longer ignore the horrifying story he had been told.

"You gotta leave," he told his old friend. "I can't have you here with what you're telling me."

Ricky nodded.

"Look, man, if this is all true," Tony continued, "they're gonna know where you're at. They're gonna come here."

"I know, I know," Ricky replied. "Can you at least help me get a car? I need a car."

"Yeah, I can get you a car," Tony said, "but man, you should have never come *here*."

The three originally planned to drive over to Vermont. Ricky knew of a place there where he could buy a cheap car, throw a paper tag on it, and drive off. However, Tony thought of a quicker plan. He knew a guy in nearby Cambridge with a car for sale and decided to drive Ricky and Jimmy there first.

When they arrived, they found the car parked on the side of the road. It was a maroon 1973 Pontiac Catalina two-door that had obviously seen better days. The grille was missing, the bumper was twisted, the tires were bald and low on air, the seats were ripped, and there was an empty hole where the radio used to be. However, it had seats and a roof that didn't leak, which was more than Ricky could say about his makeshift lean-to in Aztakea.

Ricky pulled a wad of cash from his pocket and offered Tony's friend fifty bucks for the car. He accepted, and Ricky and Jimmy threw the few worldly possessions they had—a pile of ratty clothes, the camping gear, and nearly one hundred purple microdots—into the trunk. They waved good-bye to Tony and sped off.

In an almost comical twist of fate, the two almost immediately encountered Dick Kasso, who was shocked to see Ricky behind the wheel of the Pontiac. He knew his son didn't have a driver's license and wasn't sure Ricky even knew *how* to properly drive a car.

"Ricky!" Dick shouted, rolling down the window of his Corvette. "Ricky, pull over!"

Ricky slowed down and stuck his head out of the Pontiac.

"I don't have time to see you!" he shouted, and drove away.

Dick gave up and headed back to Argyle.

A few minutes after their encounter with Ricky's father, Ricky and Jimmy pulled over and found a Chevrolet Caprice station wagon parked on the side of the road. Acting quickly, they unscrewed the rear license plate from the Chevy, bolted it onto the Pontiac so as not to attract suspicion from passing police, and headed back onto the highway. Their plan, however, immediately became flawed in its execution. The bottom of the yellow plate read OFFICIAL. Due to an almost astounding lack of judgment, Ricky and Jimmy were now driving around in a clunker fitted with a government license plate.

While coasting south on Route 22, the boys made yet another poor decision that would help seal their fates. Instead of heading straight for California, dealing microdots along the way to pay for gas, Ricky and Jimmy chose to go back to Long Island and sell as much of their stash as possible in one shot. They knew they were heading back into the lion's den, but if they could make some quick cash, it would be worth the risk.

As Ricky and Jimmy inched closer and closer to Northport, investigators from the Suffolk County Police Department were carefully removing the remains of Gary Lauwers from Aztakea Woods.

The two were now on a collision course with fate.

When they pulled into town that evening, the usual festivities were already in full swing. Dozens of teenagers were crowding in and out of the New Park, smoking weed and drinking booze. Ricky and Jimmy knew most of them, and they all were prime candidates for microdot sales.

Across town, crime scene technicians from the Suffolk County Police Department were wrapping up their day of removing Gary's remains from Aztakea. Due to heavy decomposition and a quickly setting sun, the technicians were unable to remove all the bones from the shallow grave. Instead they bagged up what they could and put a tarp over the hole in the ground. To keep any would-be visitors away from the grim site, the Suffolk County Police Department found an officer brave enough to stand guard overnight in the pitch-black woods.

As the night wore on back in the New Park, Jimmy became visibly uneasy. He knew the longer he and Ricky stayed in Northport, the higher the chance there was of getting caught. He also suspected they were being watched.

He wasn't wrong.

Only a few hundred feet away, detectives from the Suffolk County Police Department were sitting in an unmarked car parked on Main Street, keeping an eye on their two suspects.

The Northport Village Police Department had already picked up Albert Quinones, and while Suffolk County hadn't yet collected a signed statement from him against Ricky and Jimmy, the detectives sat waiting for headquarters to give them the go-ahead to arrest the two.

A short while later, Ricky and Jimmy managed to slip away from the New Park without the detectives noticing. As the sun began to rise over Northport Harbor, the two fired up the Pontiac and drove over to Kings Park to sell more microdots. After spending a little over an hour there, they blew another opportunity by heading back to Northport instead of making a clean escape from the Island. While they were on their way back, the arrest warrant was finally issued at four thirty a.m. Since the detectives staking out the New Park eventually noticed the two had vanished and left to search for them elsewhere, Ricky and Jimmy were able to enter the New Park undetected.

Soon after they arrived, two friends who had followed them from Kings Park showed up ready to fight. Ironically, they were there to confront Ricky over allegedly stealing some drugs from a mutual friend. Once Jimmy saw the two pull up, he grabbed Ricky and ran to the parking lot. There, they jumped into the Pontiac and drove off as fast as they could, hoping to avoid a brawl. Ricky drove north on Bayview Avenue and made a slight left onto Bluff Point Road. Figuring they had lost the two kids from Kings Park, they pulled over in front of a house just north of the Northport Yacht Club. The club had been a crown jewel of the village for more than eighty-five years. Coincidentally, Joseph Morrell—

whose skeletal hand Ricky had gawked at while hanging out with Randy Guethler—had been one of the organization's presidents many decades before. Ricky parked the car, crawled into the back seat, and stretched out his legs, hoping to sleep off the angel dust high.

A few minutes later Sergeant Ed McMullen of the Northport Village Police Department pulled up behind the Pontiac.

Independence Day 1984 would be Ricky Kasso's final night of freedom.

Chapter 35

"YOU'VE GOT NOTHING ON US! WHAT ARE YOU hassling us for?!"

Ricky screamed and spat as he was pulled from the Pontiac by Suffolk County detectives. Surging from a sudden burst of adrenaline—not to mention the PCP he had smoked earlier—Ricky wasn't going down without a fight. He quickly reached into his pocket. Luckily, one of the dozen investigators on the scene saw this.

"Hey, he's reaching for something!" he shouted.

Ricky was subdued and placed into handcuffs before he could hurt anyone. When his pockets were searched, a switchblade was found.

In contrast to his friend, Jimmy decided to cooperate.

"I always do square business with the cops," he told Suffolk County Detective Jim McCready as he was cuffed.

Ricky was placed in the back seat of a car with Northport Police Officer Gene Roemer and Detective Lieutenant Robert Dunn, commander of the Suffolk County Homicide Squad, and was taken to the Suffolk County Police Department headquarters in Yaphank. Jimmy was driven in a separate car. The investigators didn't want to give the two a chance to collaborate on a cover story—assuming they hadn't already.

When they arrived at eight thirty a.m., Ricky was charged with the second-degree murder of Gary Lauwers. He was then brought to another room for mug shots to be taken. Ricky lowered his head and leered at the camera, and its flash threw a quick burst of light at the gaunt face draped by wavy curls of greasy brown hair. He was then fingerprinted and locked in a holding cell until McCready and Dunn were finished speaking with Jimmy.

After Jimmy made his statement, Ricky was led into the interrogation room. Although he was still high on angel dust, he had calmed down significantly and decided to confess.

"Late at night, me and Albert Quinones, Jimmy Troiano, and Gary Lauwers all walked up to the Dunkin' Donuts," he said as McCready began writing the statement on a Suffolk County Police Department notepad. "We bought some donuts and went up to Aztakea Woods. When we got up there, we decided to start a fire, and Gary donated one of his socks to start the fire. I asked him to donate his jacket, and he said he'd cut off his sleeves. We did that and got a nice little fire going. We were all talking about killing Gary."

This revelation was significant. Jimmy had already told Detective McCready that Albert had advance knowledge of Ricky's plan to kill Gary. Ricky's statement gave credence to this claim, but now also directly implicated Jimmy. McCready silently made special note of this in his head. The thirty-seven-year-old detective suspected Jimmy of participating in the murder more than he cared to admit, due to the savage nature of the attack. Earlier, word had been passed down from the Suffolk County Medical Examiner's Office that Gary Lauwers had been stabbed twenty-two times *at the very least*, based on the holes in his jacket alone.

"Gary said that he got bad vibes—that we were going to beat him up," Ricky continued. "Gary didn't hear us talking about killing him. When Gary said that he got bad vibes, I grabbed him around the neck. Gary said he'd fight me one on one as long as Jimmy and Albert didn't jump in. I said okay and then bit him on the neck. We were wrestling around on the ground, and I made Gary say, 'I love you, Satan.' I was holding him on the ground and Jimmy kicked him in the ribs. I bit him on the ear. I looked up at Jimmy and Jimmy told me to cut his throat."

McCready's eyes lit up. He now had even more information to link Jimmy to the murder.

"I then took out my knife, held it in two hands, and stabbed Gary in the right side of his back," Ricky said. "The knife went all the way in. Somehow, he got away and ran through the woods. I caught him and brought him back to where the fire was. I had dropped my knife when I chased him, and Troiano found it. Troiano gave me the knife, and I stabbed Gary in the back and front a whole bunch of times."

There was now little doubt in McCready's mind that Jimmy Troiano would soon be charged as an accessory to Gary's murder.

"Me and Troiano dragged Gary back into the woods," Ricky said. "We started to cover him up with leaves and he sat up. I bugged out and started to stab him in the face."

"How many times did you stab him?" McCready asked.

"I didn't count how many times," Ricky answered impassively. "I'm not really sure. When I finished stabbing him in the face, we both finished covering him up with the leaves. I don't know what I said, but a whole bunch of Satanic things just rolled out of my mouth."

The next words to roll out of Ricky Kasso's mouth would haunt the investigators for decades to come.

"We heard a crow caw, which is the sign of the devil," Ricky said. "I knew Gary was dead then. Me, Albert, and Troiano then went back to the area by the fire. I knew I had lost my Satanic star and we looked for it, but couldn't find it. As we looked for the star, we saw blood spots on the ground and kicked dirt over them. We all then left. We went to Albert's house, where I took a bath. I changed my clothes and took the clothes I was wearing and threw them in someone's garbage can near Albert's house. The clothes were full of blood."

"What about your shoes?" McCready asked, looking up from his notepad.

"I'm wearing the shoes I had on that night," Ricky said. "I don't think I had blood on them."

"Where's the knife, Ricky?" McCready asked. Jimmy had already told him that Ricky said he had thrown it into the water, but he wanted to see if Ricky would tell him the same story.

"I threw the knife into Northport Harbor near the New Park gazebo the next night," Ricky replied. "It's straight out from the wood forest playground. The handle is black and 'Flasher' is on the blade."

Curiously forgetting his earlier assertion, Ricky then added, "I must have stabbed Gary forty times or more. I went back to the body three times before I buried it with Jimmy. I had a shovel up there, and the fourth time I went up there, Jimmy and I buried it. We showed the body to Mark Florimonte because he didn't believe me. I also showed it to Richard Barton. Troiano told Mike Higgins about it."

"But *why* did you do it, Ricky?" McCready asked.

Ricky thought for a second.

"Gary had been ripping people off for money and drugs in town," he told McCready. "Nobody liked him, and he got what he deserved."

The investigators were shocked by the sheer callousness of Ricky's words. Sure, they had dealt with hardened criminals before—Detective Lieutenant Dunn had been one of the investigators to question Ronald DeFeo Jr. during the Amityville murder investigation nearly a decade before—but this was a scrawny seventeen-year-old. Ricky wasn't even old enough to legally drink, yet he had spent the past three years making his name as a drug dealer. Now the Acid King had upgraded to murder and seemingly couldn't care less. Ricky signed the statement McCready wrote out for him and was brought back to his cell.

McCready made sure word of Ricky's allegations about Jimmy made it back to Detective Louis Rodriguez, who was en route to Aztakea with the suspect. Rodriguez, a fifteen-year veteran of the department, had been called in early by Suffolk County Detective Sergeant Richard Jensen. Rodriguez's last shift had ended less than twelve hours earlier, but he agreed to come in and assist with the investigation. Jensen wanted Rodriguez to photograph the Aztakea Woods crime scene and told the dark-haired homicide detective to bring Troiano along while Kasso was being questioned by McCready—the logic being that by having him accompany Rodriguez, the exact location of the murder could be determined. This idea would later come back to haunt Jensen.

Rodriguez drove Jimmy to Northport while fellow detective Robert Amato followed closely behind. When they got to Aztakea, Rodriguez pressed Jimmy about what had really happened the night Gary was murdered.

Finally Jimmy sighed and said, "You might as well know I had a part in it. Ricky did all the stabbing. I held him, but Ricky did all the stabbing."

Rodriguez pulled out his notepad and began jotting down Jimmy's words. Once he was done, the detectives exited their vehicles and had Jimmy show them the clearing where Ricky built the small fire and later killed Gary. A Suffolk County Police photographer snapped photos of Jimmy pointing toward the patch of dirt where Gary was first stabbed. Suddenly Jimmy noticed something out of the corner of his eye. He walked over to a nearby sprouting of green leaves and found a tuft of Gary's hair lying on the ground. He bent down, picked up the clump of blond hair, and handed it over to Rodriguez. Stunned, the detectives immediately bagged it to be entered into evidence.

Jimmy then led the detectives over to the spot where he and Ricky hid Gary's body. Until the day before, it had been a small, remote pocket of Aztakea that was easy to miss. Now it was a wide-open area. Crime scene technicians from Suffolk County had cleared away much of the brush and poison ivy plants that had once shrouded the body, leaving behind the blue tarp that had covered the grave the night before. There, Rodriguez and Amato had Jimmy pose in front of the shallow grave, pointing at it with a stick. Directly in front of him was the black imprint left on the ground by Gary's decomposing body. The photographer took special care to ensure it was in the shot.

When they got back to police headquarters, Rodriguez took his notes and typed up a statement for Jimmy to sign. Jimmy quietly read the pages until he came to the part where he handed the knife back to Ricky during the murder. He looked up at Rodriguez and said, "I don't want to be seen holding the knife in this."

Rodriguez now had a tough call to make: stay firm and risk

Troiano ending his cooperation or let this one detail slide. In the end, Rodriguez took a risk and chose the latter. Jimmy reviewed the modified statement, which read:

> On Thursday, July 5, 1984, during the morning hours, I was taken by detectives of the Homicide Squad to Yaphank, where I was told that a guy I know as Gary Lauwers' body was found murdered in Northport. The detectives asked me a lot of questions, and I told them some answers, but not everything. Not that I wanted to lie to them, but since they hadn't asked certain questions, I didn't offer a lot of things. I made it look like I hadn't done too much during the killing of Gary; that Rick Kasso had done most of it. When I finished telling those detectives the first story, I left there with Rodriguez and Amato and headed for Northport Village. It was during this time that I realized I should tell it all, that is, how the murder of Gary Lauwers went down. I knew that if I did this, I would end up feeling better.
>
> I took Rodriguez and Amato into the woods to show them where the fight had started that night in June, the 16th, Saturday about 2:00 a.m.
>
> Before we went there, me, Rick, Albert Quinones and Gary, had been at a Dunkin' Donuts, and Albert had told me that Rick wanted to beat up Gary, who had taken some angel dust from Rick. When we arrived at the woods known as "Aztakea Woods," Albert told me Rick was going to kill Gary. I decided I didn't care because Gary should not have

taken the dust that belonged to Rick. In the woods, Rick started a fire and Gary gave him his socks and then the sleeves on Gary's jacket. I cut the sleeves off the jacket with either Rick's knife or my knife. Gary was on the ground, saying that he felt he was going to be beat up or something. I saw Gary and Rick start to fight. All of a sudden, I heard Gary say, "I love you, mom." When I looked, Gary was on his knees and Rick was stabbing him in the back. I was pretty high, but I'm sure it was around this time that I went to Gary's side, and as hard as I could, I kicked him in the rib area. I know I broke some ribs because I felt that side cave in. Gary managed to run from us, and we chased him into the woods. Rick and I dragged him back, and I believe during this time, we took turns cutting hair off Gary's head. I guess I cut about three pieces off. Rick was holding Gary as I did this, and Rick told Gary to repeat "I love you, Satan," which Gary did, even though he was really hurting. I knew that Gary had to be killed or he would rat us all out if he lived. While I held him, Rick also cut some hair off and stabbed him some more. I didn't see Albert Quinones do any of this. I guess he was just watching. I saw Ricky put Gary in a headlock, and Gary was saying something like, "Please don't kill me." Ricky stabbed him some more. Like I said, I was glad because Gary could not leave those woods alive. Ricky was saying some shit about Satan over Gary's body. He's into things about Satan and the Devil. I saw Gary lift his head slightly, and Ricky went buggy and

> started stabbing Gary in the face. I don't have any idea of how many times, but it was a lot. We—Ricky and me—dragged Gary into the woods and covered him with leaves and branches. Rick realized he had lost his Satanic star, which was on a chain. We couldn't find it in the dark. About this time, the three of us left the woods and Gary, and went to Albert's home, where I showered. I left them and went to Kings Park. That night, I saw Ricky Kasso, and he told me he threw the knife he killed Gary with into the harbor off the "New Park" dock in Northport. Today, Thursday July 5, 1984, I was photographed pointing at several spots where this killing took place. I also pointed out and had my picture taken at the spot where Rick and I buried Gary Lauwers with a shovel this past Saturday, June 30, at about 11 a.m. We found chunks of Gary's hair, and I had my picture taken pointing at them.
>
> I wish to add that I am 18 years of age with a date of birth of December 10, 1965, in Schenectady, N.Y. I now live with my adopted parents, Mary and Vincent Troiano. I am currently unemployed and gone through the ninth grade in Northport Junior High. I have read this statement of four pages and I swear it is true.

After reading it, Jimmy scribbled his name on the bottom of the last page and handed the confession back to Rodriguez, who asked, "How do you feel about this boy being killed?"

Jimmy shrugged.

"I don't care."

Despite the omission of Jimmy handing the knife back to Ricky and *again* failing to recall the actual date of the murder, the detectives now had a much more incriminating statement from him, along with a series of photos showing him pointing to the key locations of the crime. At one forty-five p.m., Jimmy Troiano was placed under arrest and formally charged with second-degree murder.

Around this same time, over on Tanager Lane, the phone inside the Hayward home rang. It was for Johnny. Dorothy had just found out about Gary's body being discovered in the woods. When she told Johnny, he exploded in a fit of rage. He knew it had to have been Ricky. Tears streamed from his eyes as he screamed, *"I'll kill Ricky!"* Johnny punched a hole in the wall and grabbed a large pocketknife. Darting out the door, he left the phone dangling from its cord. His mother ran out after him, but it was no use. Johnny was faster than her and guided by raw, primal emotion. His best friend in the whole world—the closest thing he ever had to a brother—was now gone forever, and he was sure it was Ricky who had taken him away.

Word had also gotten to the kids living at Merrie Schaller's house. Two of Gary's friends who were living there, Glen Wolf and his friend Mike McGrory, grabbed a couple baseball bats and headed downtown. Someone told the two that Jimmy Troiano had been involved, so they decided to find him and bring him in to the cops. A Northport patrol officer noticed Glen and Mike entering the New Park armed with the bats and pulled over to stop them.

"What are you guys doing?" the officer demanded.

"We're trying to find the guy who helped kill our friend," Glen replied.

"We got him already," the officer told them. "Go home."

Up the block, Johnny Hayward was frantically searching for the beat-up Pontiac. After an hour of looking, he finally ran into a friend who told him that Ricky and Jimmy had already been arrested.

"The cops got them in a car at the end of some street," the friend told him.

Johnny sighed and said, "I'm glad they got arrested before I fuckin' found them, because I would have *killed* Ricky."

Still in shock and completely defeated, Johnny decided to walk back home. The courts would have to handle Ricky and Jimmy now.

Chapter 36

BY THE NEXT MORNING, FRIDAY, JULY 6, WORD OF THE murder and subsequent arrests had reached the *Northport Observer*, *Newsday*, the *New York Post*, and the *New York Daily News*, all thanks to a press release issued by the Suffolk County Police Department. Shortly after Jimmy was booked the day before, Northport Police Chief Robert Howard told Suffolk County's Chief of Detectives, John Gallagher, that an official statement should be typed up. Gallagher invited the Northport Village Police Department to write a press release, but Howard quickly declined.

"No," he told Gallagher. "You guys do it. You have the experience."

Howard was referring to Suffolk County's own in-house professionals—people like William McKeown, the department's assistant to the commissioner for media relations—a relative luxury Northport's small office did not have, or even *need* up until this point. It wasn't as if the Truman Capotes of the world were banging down the door every time a garbage can was lit on fire or a case of beer was stolen in the village. However, McKeown, for all his talents, would not write the official press release.

For reasons unknown, Gallagher decided to bypass McKeown and write this crucial document himself. A couple hours later, around three thirty p.m., a secretary from Gallagher's office called the Northport Village Police Department with the press release he had typed up. Officer Art Molin answered the phone and recorded Gallagher's secretary as she read the statement to him. After the call was finished, Molin gave the recording to Northport Village Clerk Rita Salerno, who rewound the tape and made the following transcription:

> Today, July 5, 1984, homicide detectives arrested one Richard Kasso who has no known address and by his own admission lives in the streets, but whose parents reside at 40 Seaview Avenue, Northport, N. Y.
>
> Kasso was arrested on the charge of murder Second Degree in the stabbing death of one Garry [*sic*] Lauwers, age 17 years of 15 West Scudder Place, Northport. Lauwers, unemployed, had been missing, although not officially reported as such, since June 15, 1984.
>
> Kasso, also 17 years of age is a member of a satanical cult and worships and partakes in rituals honoring the devil.

It is believed Lauwers stole 10 bags of a narcotic commonly known as angel dust from the defendant Kasso.

Kasso learned of the theft and sought revenge against Lauwers. The revenge turned out to be the death of Lauwers.

This came to the attention of the Suffolk County Police Department as a result from a call from the Northport Village Police Department. The Northport Village Police on Sunday, July 1, 1984 had received an anonymous phone call indicating that a body was buried in a wooded area commonly known as "Aztaki [*sic*] Woods" in the Northport area. The wooded area is known to the Northport police department who conducted a preliminary search and additionally made attempts to identify the anonymous caller. The searches on Sunday and Monday were unsuccessful. However, they felt that a continuing investigation should be made and Chief Robert Howard requested aid from the Suffolk County Police Department.

On Tuesday afternoon, homicide detectives and canine units from the Suffolk County Police Department responded to the wooded area described. Because of inclement weather and heavy rains no search was made.

Again on Wednesday, July 4, 1984 at about 1:30 under the direction of Chief Howard the search was reinstituted. At about 2 p.m. a canine [K-9] dog located a skeletal remains of a human body buried in a shallow grave in this wooded area in another direction than that which was searched by the Northport Village Police.

The remains were tentatively identified as the victim, Gary Lauwers and indications revealed that he had been stabbed numerous times. The condition of the body indicated that it had been left in the woods for approximately two weeks and further, had been recently buried. The body was pronounce [*sic*] dead by the medical examiners [*sic*] office and removed to the morgue for future examination.

Homicide detectives and Northport Village police officers, under the direction of Northport Village Police Chief Robert Howard conducted and pursued an intense investigation.

Information uncovered, revealed that the defendent [*sic*] Kasso stabbed the victim numerous times and dragged his body, thinking he was dead, to the place where it was located. When Kasso began to leave the site, Lauwers sat up and according to Kasso, stated I love you mom. These are the last words uttered by the victim.

At this point, Kasso returned to the where Lauwers sat and inflicted further stab wounds into the facial area, cutting out his eyes.

Kasso further indicated that on this last stabbing of the victim he heard a crow cry out. This was an indication to him as a satin [*sic*] worshipper, that the devil had ordered him to kill Lauwers.

Investigation is continuing to determine if and how

> many accomplices were involved in this murder.
>
> Additionally, detectives of the Suffolk County Police Department are presently searching for the murder weapon believed to be in the waters off the Northport Village dock area.
>
> James Troiano, age 18, of 2 Barry Drive, East Northport, was also charged with murder Second Degree in this crime.

Aside from resembling a middle school book report more than a proper press release, the document's contents were incredibly troublesome. Gallagher had merely *assumed* Ricky was part of a "satanical cult" based on the demonic overtones contained in his confession, but he presented this hunch as fact by saying it in an official Suffolk County Police statement—despite a total lack of evidence.

Molin and Salerno, however, were unaware of this. They printed up dozens of copies of their transcript and sent them to various news outlets. Back at Suffolk County Police headquarters, William McKeown had no idea this was happening. A copy of Gallagher's release made its way to his desk shortly after it was phoned in to Northport, and he was horrified by what he read.

"My English teacher would have killed me if I wrote like that," McKeown later told an interviewer.

Unaware that Gallagher's press release had already gotten out, McKeown immediately went to work editing the document. While a number of issues in the release were cleaned up, McKeown's revision wasn't without errors. He incorrectly identified the Lauwers family as residents of East Northport, and the misspelling of Aztakea Woods remained. Most crucially, McKeown wasn't privy to Ricky's or Jimmy's confessions, and had no idea that *neither* of them had made any reference to a "cult" in their statements. As such, Gallagher's fanciful allegations made it into McKeown's version. Two hours after Gallagher's secretary called the original draft in to Northport, McKeown's updated statement was released to the press.

He had no idea how much damage had already been done.

When Chief Howard, who was currently on a monthlong vacation, stopped by headquarters to check on things the next morning, he found a copy of Gallagher's press release sitting on his desk. When Howard read the document, he immediately ordered his department to stop handing out copies.

"There is no way I would have released that," Howard later said during an interview. "Our procedure for press releases is based on that of Suffolk County's. You are *never* supposed to give out the substance of an admission, confession, or *any* statement by a defendant. Based on procedure, it was wrong."

Despite Howard's best efforts, it was now far too late. In the fifteen hours since Rita Salerno transcribed the phone call from Gallagher's secretary, the department had already handed out nearly fifty copies of the press release. To make matters even worse, McKeown's updated release never even made it to Northport. Now, nearly every major newspaper in the tristate area had a copy of the original and had already written articles based on the flawed document for their morning editions.

Mark J. McGuire, a young reporter for the *Northport Observer*, had accurate details of the case—thanks to the friendship he enjoyed with Chief Howard—but his articles on the murder wouldn't be released for another week. Being a weekly paper, the *Observer*'s next issue wouldn't hit newsstands until July 12.

Newsday, however, was already printing that day's edition, and for just thirty cents, the residents of Long Island could gawk at the front page boasting, "2 Held in Ritual Killing of Teenager in Northport." The large spread featured a photo of the New Park's wood forest playground, almost comically adorned with *SATIN* graffiti, a shot of a dazed Jimmy Troiano being led into a police car, and a curious portrait of Ricky Kasso.

No photos were taken of Ricky during his arrest, and his official mug shot hadn't been provided with either press release, so *Newsday* got creative. Someone in the newsroom remembered Rex Smith's interview with Ricky for *Inside Newsday* only three months before and grabbed a copy of the Sony U-matic videocassette containing the segment. When Ricky appeared on screen to discuss his recent grave-digging arrest, the tape was paused, and a *Newsday* photographer snapped a shot of the boy, clad in a leather jacket and a bandanna wrapped around his head, his eyes calmly turned to Smith. This would do for now. No one on staff knew it, but another shot of Ricky would come later in the day—one that would make history.

The *Newsday* article unsurprisingly contained all the sensational and inaccurate statements contained in Gallagher's bungled press release. After all, they had no reason to question its veracity. When staff writers Jim O'Neill and Dennis Hevesi called the Suffolk

County and Northport Village Police Departments for further comment, things got even worse. O'Neill and Hevesi were unable to reach Gallagher but spoke with Detective Lieutenant Dunn, who was still reeling from the shock of hearing Kasso's confession in person. While speaking with the reporters, Dunn began to dramatically exaggerate the key details of Gary Lauwers's murder.

"You've got a whole group of Satanic worshippers," Dunn boldly claimed. "This was a sacrificial killing. They built a roaring fire in a field near the woods. They cut the sleeves out of his shirt and burned them, and they took his socks off and burned them. I don't know what this is supposed to mean, but this was what they did. It's pure Satanism. They were chanting while they did this. Just before they killed him, they forced him to say, 'I love Satan.' After he did say that, they killed him. Then they dragged him into the woods. Around two weeks later, they came back and buried him."

Suffolk County District Attorney Patrick Henry joined in on the circus, telling reporters, "This act of degeneracy makes other murders look like a day at the beach."

When Jim O'Neill called Chief Howard to ask if a Satanic cult really had been operating in Northport, Howard replied that he had only heard rumors over the years. He told O'Neill that the closest incident he could recall was the burnt goat fetus found in the New Park gazebo in 1981, which had been incorrectly attributed to the Knights of the Black Circle.

"Isn't Kasso the same guy who was arrested for robbing graves?" O'Neill asked.

When Howard confirmed this, O'Neill had enough to satisfy

himself that the cult angle was rooted in truth. All this—from Dunn's melodramatic blow-by-blow of the murder, to Howard's recollections of the burnt goat—would make it into O'Neill and Hevesi's front-page article. The groundwork was now laid for a dangerous amount of misinformation to reach the public. *Newsday*'s story got picked up by the Associated Press, which made it available to larger outlets like the *New York Post* and the *New York Daily News*.

Using the *Newsday* article as their feeble foundation, the *Daily News* printed a story of their own. It was nowhere near as large as the front-page spread *Newsday* offered, but Jerry Cassidy and Stuart Marques's article, titled "Nab Devil Cult Teen in Slaying," contained enough sensational and lurid details to shock their considerable circulation base. The story featured the press release quote about Northport's "Satanic cult," attributing it directly to Gallagher, and combined elements of Ricky's grave-digging arrest with the murder. Cassidy and Marques incorrectly claimed that Ricky had been arrested the day before wearing a pentagram and carrying "a list of the hierarchy in Hell." The two topped off the story with a little bit of original research, mentioning Randy Guethler's own grave-robbing arrest in April, giving the mistaken impression that Ricky had been his accomplice.

The *Post* went even further. While quoting Chief Howard in their article "2 L.I. Teens Seized in Bizarre Devil Cult Slaying," reporters Maralyn Matlick and Joy Cook set the stage for the media's biggest screwup in the case—connecting Ricky to the Knights of the Black Circle. Howard opined to the reporters that Ricky was "the head of the group" responsible for the "ritual killing" of Gary. Somewhat naively, Howard was merely alluding to the four teenagers known to be in Aztakea that night—Ricky Kasso, Jimmy Troiano, Albert Quinones, and Gary Lauwers—and not any organized "cult." Unfortunately, Matlick and Cook rather deceptively placed Howard's mention of this nameless "group" right next to his comments about the Knights of the Black Circle.

"There was a group of high school kids back in 1981 who called themselves the 'Knights of the Black Circle,'" Howard was quoted as saying. "That group, we believe was responsible for the charred carcass of a goat we found in Cow Harbor Park."

Granted, Howard was also briefly quoted as saying he believed that the Knights had "died out," but in the very same paragraph, Matlick and Cook tacked on Howard's mention of Randy's and Ricky's graveyard activities.

"Then earlier this year," the quote read, "two cemeteries were broken into."

For hasty or less intelligent readers, this careless clump of quotes implied that Ricky was the "leader" of the Knights of the Black Circle, had a three-year history of killing and burning animals, and had robbed graves. To hammer this spectacular imagery home, Matlick and Cook peppered their article with quotes from William Keahon, chief of the Major Offense Bureau at the Suffolk County District Attorney's Office.

"He took a breathing young man," Keahon charged to Judge Gerard D'Emilio, "mutilated him, and used him as a sacrificial animal. In my eleven years as a prosecutor, I've never seen such a hideous and vicious taking of a life."

The arraignment was notable for another reason. That afternoon Tony Jerome, a thirty-two-year-old freelance photographer, grabbed his Nikon and drove down to Suffolk County's 4th District Courthouse in Hauppauge, hoping to get a shot of the accused devil worshippers that he could sell to the newspapers. Shortly after he arrived, a white police van pulled up. The back doors swung open to reveal a group of prisoners chained together by their handcuffs. Once a Suffolk County police officer began to lead the accused criminals out of the van, Jerome and several TV news reporters got their first view of Ricky and Jimmy, who were easily the youngest ones in cuffs by several years. Ricky got up from the wooden bench inside the van, hopped down to the ground, and sauntered toward the courthouse entrance.

"That walk he was doing—that sort of *lope*—was the Northport tough-guy, dirtbag walk," Brendan Brown says. "It was a sort of a march that everyone knew how to do here. It was because you were wearing Timberland-style construction boots and they were a little too heavy. The 'dirtbag uniform' was tan Timberland boots or black biker boots with corduroys or jeans, a concert T-shirt, a flannel shirt, and a denim jacket. I know what I'm describing has been rehashed and repurposed into a contemporary fashion, but *here* in 1984, not everybody wore that. That was an identifying *uniform*."

As Ricky approached the courthouse entrance, he looked to his left and saw Jerome waiting with his camera. He leered at Jerome, growled, and continued inside. Jerome captured the exact moment their eyes met in a photograph that would soon become a pop culture icon. Ricky's face, wide-eyed, mouth agape mid-growl, would confirm every paranoid suburban parent's worst fears—these so-called "Satan kids" *were* out there. Long-haired dopers on a mission for Lucifer, all thanks to that god-awful devil music. Ricky's borrowed AC/DC T-shirt all but underlined that notion. For those who hadn't seen Ricky in a while, the photo was even more shocking once it graced the front page of nearly every major newspaper in the country. The manic and greasy-haired teenager didn't even resemble the Ricky they knew. He looked so *thin* and *evil.* Given the context, most were ashamed to admit it, but there was no way around it—Ricky looked *possessed*.

By the time Ricky got into the courtroom, however, his demonic facade had faded. As Judge D'Emilio read the charges against him, Ricky scanned the room for any sign of his parents. Vincent and Mary Troiano were at the courthouse to support their son, but Dick and Lynn Kasso were nowhere to be found. Ricky's parents would later tell the newspapers that a detective told them not to bother coming to the arraignment, saying it wouldn't be worth the four-hour drive. When Ricky realized that no one was coming, he lowered his head and stood in silence for the remainder of his time in the courtroom. Judge D'Emilio ordered both Ricky and Jimmy to be held without bail pending a hearing the following week. When Robert Luckey of the *Daily News* photographed Ricky leaving his arraignment, the wild-eyed boogeyman of Northport had vanished and been replaced with the hollow shell of a teenager slowly realizing his life was effectively over.

Chapter 37

"YOU'VE HAD MURDERERS SLEEPING IN OUR HOUSE! How could you do that with your little sister here?!"

Matthew Carpenter had no idea what his mother was talking about. This changed when she threw the copy of *Newsday* down onto his bed. Ricky and Jimmy were staring back at him under the headline "2 Held in Ritual Killing of Teenager in Northport." Suddenly everything came together in his mind: Gary going missing, Ricky's Satan talk, the warning not to carry a knife, the terrible nightmares. Ricky was a killer and Jimmy had, at the very least, helped—and he had let them sleep in this very room.

"You see what your *friends* do?!" his mother cried, hammering the point home.

Matthew panicked, fled the house, and ran to the pay phone down by the roundhouse. He dropped a quarter in the slot and dialed his girlfriend, Carol, asking her to meet him downtown.

When she arrived, Matthew told her everything he knew about Ricky's arrest and suggested fleeing Northport. Carol agreed, and with what little money they had, she and Matthew hopped on a train headed toward Manhattan.

Over on Seaview Avenue, just two doors down from the Kasso home, word of Ricky's arrest reached Grant Koerner. When he saw the newspaper photos of his childhood friend wearing an AC/DC shirt, Grant's first instinct was to run upstairs and take down some of the rock posters adorning his bedroom wall. He may have only been thirteen years old, but he was smart enough to see the storm coming.

A mile away, on Cherry Street, Brendan Brown was sitting in his backyard with his friend Adam, going through his tape case filled with AC/DC bootlegs and rarities. A few moments later, Brendan's mother stormed outside in her nightgown, clutching a copy of that morning's newspaper.

"Do you know these boys?!" Mrs. Brown cried out. "Do you know anything about these boys?! You don't go in that park, right?!"

When Brendan looked at the photos on the front page, he froze. There was the "dirtbag" who had been menacing him for the past year. To make matters worse, Ricky was wearing an AC/DC shirt in the photos, and here was Brendan sitting with a whole cache of the band's albums.

"Suddenly, 'dirtbag' became a totally different thing," Brown recalls. "'Dirtbag' wasn't just a dirty-looking kid walking around in an AC/DC T-shirt anymore—'dirtbag' was now *Satanic*. 'Dirtbag' was *homicidal*. 'Dirtbag' was *drugs*. When you're ten or eleven years old and you're just starting to find your musical identity, having the *whole world* suddenly tell you it's the worst thing ever is pretty weird."

However, this was only part of it. Brendan's mother was now so fearful of the teenagers in the New Park that she arranged for Brendan to go to school in Mineola, nearly thirty miles away, effectively cutting him off from any chance of a social life at home. For her, the risk was simply too great.

"This ruined people's *lives*," Johnny Hayward says. "I had girlfriends that I saw in school one day, and the next day they were gone. After the shit that happened here, their parents packed up their families and moved. That happened with a *lot* of people."

While the scared citizens of Northport had the option of fleeing the ensuing mess, Ricky couldn't run from the reality he had created. He and Jimmy arrived at the Suffolk County Sheriff's Office Correctional Facility in Riverhead around two p.m. on Friday, July 6. The four-story hunk of concrete surrounded by barbed wire was a cold reminder of the severity of their actions. Jimmy had been here before, but a less-than-sympathetic jury might ensure that this facility was the last building he and Ricky ever inhabited.

An hour later a coworker of jail psychologist Dr. Richard Dackow handed him a copy of a newspaper detailing Gary's murder along with Ricky's and Jimmy's arrests, and noted that the young prisoners were downstairs. Normally Dackow visited new inmates the day after their arrival, but he knew Jimmy from his previous stay and wanted to check in. When he found Jimmy in the holding pen, he was surprised by his demeanor. After skimming through the alleged Satanic elements of the article, Dackow expect to find two raving lunatics. Instead he found Jimmy curled up in the fetal position on a bench inside the holding pen. Jimmy refused to move or even make eye contact while Dackow tried speaking to him through the bars. The few times he said anything were only to express his frustration and hopelessness at the situation he was in. Based on this behavior, Dackow ordered that Jimmy be brought to the jail's sick bay, where he could be kept under suicide watch.

When Dackow spoke with Ricky, he was taken aback by how calm he appeared. In a way, he was almost disappointed by Ricky's placid behavior. If he had been foaming at the mouth while speaking in tongues, it would have helped Dackow make sense of Gary's brutal murder. However, there would be no such revelations. Ricky made good eye contact, was respectful, and spoke coherently. The only noticeable change came when Dackow mentioned reading about him in the newspaper. Ricky lit up and asked for a copy. Dackow was reminded of eager children at Christmastime as Ricky excitedly pleaded to see the press he had received. He told Ricky he could probably get a copy once he was brought to his cell.

"Are you having any thoughts about hurting yourself or others?" Dackow asked, trying to bring the conversation around to more serious matters.

Ricky replied that he was not.

"Have you ever tried to hurt yourself in the past?"

"No," Ricky replied, stretching the truth. "My parents put me in South Oaks last year, but that was for drugs. Is there a drug counselor here I can talk to?"

Dackow replied that there was, but since it was Friday afternoon, he asked Ricky if he would mind waiting until Monday morning to speak with them.

"Sure," Ricky replied.

"You know," Dackow said, "the article I read was pretty negative. Some of the other inmates here might be aware of what you did. Some of them even knew Gary. Are you concerned about this?"

"Nah," Ricky replied. "I'm not even sure what really happened that night. I was high on PCP. It sounds like the newspapers are making a bigger deal out of this than it really is."

Dackow didn't find Ricky to be suicidal and declined to send him to the sick bay with Jimmy. However, as special protection for him against the other inmates, Dackow assigned Ricky to administrative segregation. While this meant he would be on the same cell block as prisoners who were accused of rape, child molestation, and murder, it also meant Ricky would be checked on every half hour by a guard—twice as often as the inmates in general population.

When Ricky was brought to his cell, his belt and shoelaces were removed as a precaution. He was offered dinner shortly after speaking with his mother via telephone, but declined. A little while later, he was permitted to leave his cell and watch television before bed. When the evening news came on, a special report about his arrest aired. The news anchor started off by incorrectly pronouncing Ricky's last name as "Kay-so." Incensed, he leaped to his feet and shouted, "Goddamnit! The bastards can't even get my name right!" before returning to his cell.

A few hours later, around twelve thirty a.m., Ricky sat in his cell, waiting for the next round of check-ins by the guards. This time they didn't show. Suddenly the entire cell block began to chant in unison.

"Hang up!"

No guards.

"HANG UP!"

Still no guards.

"HANG UP!!!"

Ricky stood up, took a sheet from his mattress, and tied it around his neck. Just as Corrections Officer Ronald Horton finally entered the cell block to belatedly begin his rounds, Ricky secured the other end of the makeshift noose to one of the uppermost bars of his cell door, climbed as high as he could, and jumped. A distinct *thud* was heard by a prisoner in the neighboring cell, and then silence. Within thirty to forty seconds, the sheet cut off the blood and oxygen flow to Ricky's brain, rendering him unconscious.

Horton found Ricky hanging from the door about five minutes later. He immediately cut the boy down and called for help. After mouth-to-mouth resuscitation failed to bring Ricky back to consciousness, he was rushed to Central Suffolk Hospital, two miles away. An IV was administered while doctors went to work with a defibrillator, administering electric shocks to Ricky's chest.

Despite exhaustive efforts made to save his life, Ricky Kasso died at 2:17 a.m., taking any chance of justice for Gary Lauwers with him.

Chapter 38

THE DETECTIVES CALLED DICK AND LYNN IN ARGYLE around four in the morning on July 7. They informed them of Ricky's suicide and told them they would have to return to Suffolk County and formally identify the body. Dick and Lynn were already planning to drive back later that morning, as they had spoken to Ricky twice over the phone since his arrest. At first Ricky had downplayed his involvement when speaking with his mother, claiming, "The detectives told me I killed him. . . ."

Lynn didn't believe him. She had witnessed Ricky's downfall firsthand over the last two years, and though she might have been ashamed to admit it, she wasn't surprised that he had killed someone. Only a few short hours before his own death did Ricky finally admit to his mother that he had killed Gary.

"Mom, I was absolutely out of my mind on mescaline," he said. "I was out of control. I didn't know what I was doing."

As the call went on, Ricky eventually showed his true colors.

"He ripped me off, Mom," he said, trying to explain away the horrible thing he had done.

Now, instead of driving back to Long Island for more answers, Dick and Lynn would be returning to claim their son's body. Once the sun rose, they got dressed and threw a few things in the car, ready to drive back. Dick's sister, Sue, who had driven up to visit a few days before, agreed to stay with Kelly, Jody, and Wendy while their parents attended to matters back home.

When Wendy woke that morning, she shuffled into the living room and switched on the television. As she sat half-awake watching a rerun of *The Muppet Show*, Lynn walked up behind Wendy and placed her arms around her youngest child.

"Your brother just killed himself," she whispered in her ear. "Your father and I have to go home and identify his body."

Before Wendy could ask any questions, Lynn got up and walked out of the house. Kelly and Jody soon followed, leaving the cabin to go play with some friends. Left alone to deal with the news, Wendy broke down and fled back to her room. There, lying on her bunk bed, she wept. At eleven years old, Wendy could barely wrap her head around what her brother had done back in Northport. Now, before she could make sense of the charges against him, Wendy's brother, who adored her more than anyone else in the world, was gone. She didn't feel like being alone with this thought. Wendy left the bedroom and sat in her aunt Sue's lap, bawling. Sue tried to console her, but it was no use. Wendy felt awkward crying in front of her aunt. She wished her mother was there to hold her and tell her everything was going to be okay—even if it was a lie. When Wendy hopped down from her aunt's lap, the realization fully hit her: Ricky was dead and was never coming back—and neither was the boy he had killed.

It was all too cruel and quick.

After a quiet drive marred by unforgiving rain, Dick and Lynn arrived at the Suffolk County Medical Examiner's Office in Hauppauge later that afternoon. Once they identified Ricky's body, Dick and Lynn had his remains transported to the Brueggemann Funeral Home in East Northport. In the past, Ricky had told his parents and several friends that he wished to be buried in his leather jacket, but Dick and Lynn opted to have their son cremated instead. Over the phone, Dick told Paul Papa, one of the funeral directors, that they did not want a funeral service for Ricky, and that he would pick up the ashes sometime in the future.

The Kassos then returned to their home on Seaview Avenue to pick up some paperwork for Ricky's cremation and check on the elderly couple renting the house for the summer. While Dick searched inside, his wife walked over to the Koerner residence. Grant's mother, Betty, maintained a close friendship with Lynn and rushed to greet her. When Betty opened the door, the two quietly embraced each other.

"I don't know why they didn't have him on a suicide watch," Lynn said softly, her voice cracking through the tears. "Don't think I'm hard or cruel, but it's over—and it's better this way. He's at peace."

Betty invited Lynn inside to sit in the living room. Normally one for spirited conversation, Betty held back, allowing her friend to speak uninterrupted. She knew nothing she could say would soften the blow of the last forty-eight hours.

"The body's going to be cremated," Lynn said. "No service. They'll save the ashes for me."

Then Lynn paused, almost completely overwhelmed by emotion.

"I just keep thinking about his hands," she told Betty. "Those were the hands that I washed when he was a baby, and he used those hands to kill someone. . . ."

After talking for a few more minutes, Lynn asked if Betty would take care of her houseplants until they returned in the fall. Betty agreed, and they walked to Lynn's house, where Dick was still rummaging through drawers, trying to find Ricky's birth certificate and other documents.

"Lynn, we have to find those papers!" Dick called out to his wife as she walked by. "We really have to settle some things!"

Betty told Lynn to go do whatever she had to and that she would take care of the plants.

As Lynn walked away, Dick turned to Betty and said, "You know, we're really worried about these plants right now. They're *very* important."

Amused by Dick's sarcasm, Betty winked at him and went about helping collect the rest of Lynn's things. As she moved about the house, she passed the bedroom that had once belonged to Ricky, long since taken over by Kelly. A sudden and unexpected sensation came over her. In that moment, the full depth of the situation finally hit Betty—the boy who had played with her own son in their sandbox for years was now dead. Dead and a *murderer*. There would be no second chances for the child who had countless sleepovers with her son, and had even helped her collect pinecones at Christmastime so they all could make wreaths together. Ricky's short life was over, and he had taken another's with him. What was once a completely normal suburban home now felt like a tomb. Betty quickly grabbed the last of Lynn's plants and raced back to her house.

After the Kassos said their good-byes to Betty, they retired for the night inside their home. Despite the growing controversy, the elderly couple renting the Kasso house decided to stay, so Dick and Lynn caught a few hours of sleep in another part of the house. Early the next morning, the two drove off as the sun rose over Northport. They couldn't have left a second sooner. The newspapers had already gone to press by the time word reached them of Ricky's suicide the day before. However, on that Sunday morning, every major newspaper in the tristate area would carry the latest terrible update in an already horrific case right on its front page.

Any hope the citizens of Northport had for this dark stain on their community to go away quickly and quietly was about to be destroyed.

Part Five

THIRTEEN WAYS OF LOOKING AT A BLACK SPOT IN THE WOODS

Truth is stranger than fiction, but it is because
Fiction is obliged to stick to possibilities; Truth isn't.
—Mark Twain,
Following the Equator

Chapter 39

SATAN TEEN KILLS HIMSELF IN JAIL . . .

CULT SLAYING FIGURE FOUND HANGED . . .

RITUAL KILLING SUSPECT HANGS HIMSELF IN JAIL CELL . . .

ARRESTED SATAN CULT LEADER KILLS HIMSELF . . .

SATANIC CULT MURDER SUSPECT FOUND HANGING IN CELL . . .

The news of Ricky's death shocked the world almost as much as the headlines about nonexistent devil cults scurrying about Long Island. For those following the developments, it felt as if the air had suddenly been sucked out of the room. What did this mean for the case? Would the truth ever be known now that Ricky was dead? Were there other "cult members" lying in wait, ready to strike now that their supposed "leader" was gone?

And what about his accomplice?

There would be no front-page pictures of Jimmy Troiano

grinning maniacally at the camera, proud as a peacock. No further tales of crow caws or Satan's demands. The world wanted to see Ricky Kasso in a courtroom, his dark deeds dissected and analyzed before his very eyes—the same eyes that pierced the soul of society. The public wanted juicy blurbs straight from the mouth of a teenage "Satan killer"—something to whisper in horror to their friends, neighbors, and coworkers, as their heads shook in disbelief. However, with one cheap prison-issued bedsheet, Ricky Kasso denied the world this grim pleasure.

One final act of defiance.

The public would now have to settle for James Vincent Troiano in the hot seat. Sure, Jimmy's hazy, drug-polluted recollections may have only amounted to dragging Gary back to the fire and kicking him while Ricky hacked away, but it would have to do.

In the end, someone needed to pay.

Someone had to be held accountable for what had happened to Gary Lauwers.

Despite the tricky position that they now found themselves in, the prosecution wasn't about to cut Jimmy loose just because Ricky was dead. Everything continued as planned, with Ricky's role in Gary's murder being treated as an afterthought. It was almost as if Ricky Kasso never even existed. He might as well not have. With his suicide, Ricky's confession would now be inadmissible in court, due to the United States Constitution's Sixth Amendment Confrontation Clause, which guaranteed Jimmy the right to face any accuser. With Ricky lying in the Suffolk County morgue, this was now impossible. It was a considerable hit to the prosecution's strategy, but they felt they still had a chance of a conviction, thanks to the combination of Jimmy's second confession and the aid of Albert Quinones, who had agreed to testify in exchange for the guarantee that he would never be charged in Gary's murder.

Hinging a high-profile criminal case on the sworn statements of two drugged-out street kids was a risky move, but it was all the prosecution had.

Life for the media, however, wasn't nearly as bleak. As the days wore on, the story grew and became more fantastic. As early as Saturday, July 7, major papers like the *Post* and the *Daily News* were no longer using Northport Police Chief Howard's recollections of the Knights of the Black Circle as a brief aside to contrast and compare the rumors of Ricky having his own small Satanic collective. Instead they somehow jumbled the two elements together and started telling the world that Ricky Kasso was the *leader* of the Knights, and that more than a dozen of its members stood before a "roaring" fire, "chanting" as Gary was sacrificed to the devil. Not having Ricky around to refute these tales only made them that much easier to print.

And print they did.

The *Daily News* devoted its front page and several accompanying articles to Ricky's suicide, declaring Northport to be a place "where evil dwells." The *Post* and *Newsday* both ran articles, as well as the *New York Times*, which offered a large spread detailing Gary's murder and Ricky's suicide. To top it off, ABC, CBS, and NBC all produced television segments on the case for their nightly news programs.

This surge of coverage was attracting significant attention—not only from the public, but from other media publications as well.

One such publication was *Rolling Stone*. The magazine's managing editor, Robert Wallace, had taken special note of the growing controversy surrounding the "Long Island Satan murder," and felt the magazine should run their own story on the case. While the newspapers were quick to blame hard rock bands for Gary's murder, coloring their articles with quotes from AC/DC's "Hells Bells" and Ozzy Osbourne's "Rock 'n' Roll Rebel," Wallace felt the magazine might have something more substantial to offer. *Rolling Stone* had always prided itself on being a champion of the counterculture, and the media's recent attack on rock groups—all thanks to Ricky's AC/DC shirt—certainly opened a figurative door for the publication to have a say in the matter.

Wallace had one person in mind for this assignment; twenty-six-year-old wunderkind David Breskin. In the past year, Breskin had made a name for himself at *Rolling Stone* as the first journalist in many years to get famous jazz musician Miles Davis to sit down for an interview. More importantly, however, Breskin had just finished a piece about the recent wave of teenage suicides sweeping America. The young writer had proven to Wallace he could handle a tough assignment, but also approach a community shaken by tragedy and make its citizens comfortable enough to talk on the record.

These were the qualities Wallace needed for the Northport story.

When Wallace telephoned Breskin, asking if he would be

interested in traveling to Long Island to cover the case for a long-form article, he certainly found the offer tempting. He too had been following the sensational newspaper coverage and smelled bullshit. At the same time, however, Breskin was worried the assignment might pigeonhole him as the "teen death guy." He had just finished his suicide article, which already had been a tough subject for him to report on, as he was still haunted by his father taking his own life a few years earlier.

In the end, the prospect of writing about such an interesting case for a much beloved publication won him over, and Breskin agreed to go to Northport. *Rolling Stone* set Breskin up with a press pass and an expense account to cover transportation, food, supplies, and lodging.

By now it was obvious the Kassos were not going to allow a public memorial service to be held for their son, so ten of Ricky's friends who weren't afraid to openly mourn the most despised teenager in the country decided to hold their own gathering. Clad in AC/DC shirts, they quietly left their Northport and Kings Park homes and walked down to the New Park. There, they clung to one another as they wept and carved remembrances into the wooden benches nearby. One girl, a fourteen-year-old friend of Ricky's named Denise, noticed the word *Satan* written on one of the benches. She tearfully grabbed a blue marker from her pocket and crossed it out, replacing it with *I love you, Ricky*.

Another friend approached and added, *Good luck, Jimmy*.

The next morning David Breskin picked up a rental car for his trip to Northport. He then drove back to his apartment on

Riverside Drive in Manhattan, packed up his Sony Pressman tape recorder, a sack of fresh Sony cassette tapes, several spiral notebooks, and a bag of clothes. Breskin was careful to select his wardrobe for this assignment. Dress shirts, jackets, and ties for interviewing police, parents, and lawyers; and ratty jeans, concert shirts, and Converse Chuck Taylor high-tops for the crucial act of talking to the teenagers who had known Ricky and Gary. With his long, curly hair and boyish looks, Breskin felt he could easily pass for "one of them," given the proper attire. He loaded up his rental car and headed east on I-495 toward Long Island.

Chapter 40

DAVID BRESKIN SAT ALONE IN HIS RENTED ROOM AT the Chalet Inn & Suites in Centerport, clutching the telephone's receiver in his hand. He stared at the open phone book in front of him, debating whether to dial that phone number again. Circled in pencil was the listing for the Lauwers family. He had already dialed the number four times but hung up before it even rang.

How do you casually speak to the parents of a boy who was so brutally murdered? he wondered. Still, this was the job he had been sent to do, so Breskin toughened up. On the fifth try, he finally called the Lauwers home. His anxiety was temporarily alleviated when Gary's brother, Michael, answered the phone instead of his parents. Michael was polite but brief, telling Breskin that his family wasn't granting any further interviews. Breskin understood and thanked Michael before hanging up.

The young writer set his notebook down and turned on the

television. As they had for the last two nights, the three major networks—ABC, CBS, and NBC—were all airing coverage of the case, along with the local New York networks. One man being interviewed caught Breskin's attention: Dennis McBee. McBee was a youth worker with the Youth Development Agency of Northport/East Northport, and Breskin was struck by his thoughtful answers in the face of a veritable media circus. He looked up the YDA's number in the white pages and decided to give McBee a call when he woke up.

The next morning, after showering and grabbing a quick breakfast, Breskin called McBee at work. McBee agreed to an interview, hoping *Rolling Stone*'s popularity with young adults would help bring the true story of what happened to a national audience. Breskin threw on his "professional outfit"—a suit jacket, slacks, dress shirt, and tie—and drove over to meet McBee at the Youth Development Agency on Diane Court in East Northport.

When Breskin parked his car, he activated his Sony Pressman recorder and spoke into the microphone, marking the first tape.

"The tenth of July, 1984. 'Knights of the Black Circle.' Long Island. Day One."

After being led upstairs, Breskin sat across from McBee and said, "So, tell me about the Knights of the Black Circle."

"Well," McBee replied, "soon after I was hired here about two and a half years ago, rumors started that this group had organized, and they were basically kids who were going through some rough times. Minor crimes; breaking and entering here and there, public drunkenness—things like that. They were high school students, many of them very heavily into *tripping*. They would get together and have a big bonfire. Out of that, apparently, a few animal sacrifice incidents occurred, with a fringe group somehow connected."

"Did the fringe group have another name?" Breskin asked.

"Not that I ever heard," McBee replied. "It was very difficult to get information on this from the kids. They talk about who was *dealing dope* a lot easier than they talk about the Knights. The Knights did their best to sort of project this badass image and they were very successful at it. This fringe group started to get a little more bizarre, and the Knights died out. Ricky Kasso was part of this fringe group. He was a very disturbed kid—using dust an *awful* lot, from what I hear. Rumor has it he was one of the bigger suppliers of drugs at the high school, and this past spring, he was arrested for attempting to dig up a grave."

Breskin pulled the previous day's issue of *Newsday* from his bag and hurriedly flipped through it until he found a tiny correction notice on page four.

"But I just read it was another guy, Randall Guethler, who apparently dug up the hand and the skull, and not Ricky," Breskin said.

"Well, *no*," McBee replied, embarrassed that Northport had seen two similar teenage grave-disturbing incidents in less than six months. "Ricky was trying to dig up a grave, but was unsuccessful. While the police were investigating *that* incident, they found that a mausoleum had been broken into a few months earlier, and a skull and a hand had been taken. That's where Randy's name came in."

"Were Kasso and Guethler friends?" Breskin asked.

"Yes," McBee said. "The story was they were using these things in various rituals. I don't see them as a *true* Satanic cult. The symbolism they used were the symbols that all of us know about Satanism. They weren't deep, dark symbols that *true* Satanists are aware of. That's kind of irrelevant, though. They *thought* they were Satanists, and I think that's enough."

Breskin agreed.

"If you believe it, it's real," he said. "It's sort of like Satanism *lite*."

"Yeah," McBee replied. "And a lot of it was rebellion in terms of them wanting to freak adults out and scare society."

"Did you know about these rituals in the park?" Breskin asked. "Had you seen anything yourself?"

"I had never seen anything myself," McBee admitted. "Going back a bit, a goat was burned in the park. Before that, various dogs or cats had been mutilated. There were a lot of people whose pet cats had disappeared."

"This happened in Indianapolis, too," Breskin said, recalling a recent news story. "In a big way. *Hundreds* of dogs and cats."

"I see animal mutilation as an early warning sign that something's *wrong*," McBee opined.

"Were Kasso or Troiano involved in animal mutilation?" Breskin asked, trying to connect the dots.

"Word has it that Kasso was *definitely* involved in it," McBee replied, "but nobody wants to talk. I made several attempts to talk to Ricky up at the high school, but all he had to hear was that I worked for a social service agency and he was *gone*. If you hang out in the smoking area at the high school, the kids think you're either a pusher or a narc. In most cases, I've been pretty successful. But the group that Ricky hung out with? There's just no breaking through *that* crowd."

"What about Kasso and Troiano living on the street or in a car?" Breskin asked.

"For a nice upper-middle-class suburban community," McBee replied, "we have quite a few kids who live out on the streets. *Throwaways*. Some as young as fourteen are on the streets, or they move in with a friend for a little while. Kids who may come from the nicest of families, but they've still been thrown away. They've been cast aside as much as the family garbage is every night. They don't fit into the pattern, and therefore no one wants them around."

"In a community of seven thousand five hundred people, how many kids, would you say?" Breskin asked. "Ten? Fifteen?"

"I know at least a dozen," McBee said.

"That's a *lot*," Breskin said. He was beginning to see a pattern of teenage nihilism, driven—at least in part—by a feeling of low self-worth emanating from their homes. Breskin suspected this was the root of Ricky's issues. He had already read a few newspaper articles hinting at the possibility.

"Did you read what the Kasso family's reaction was when the detective called?" he asked McBee. "The detective said, 'There's no need for you to come down to Long Island. I'll call you back once he's arraigned.' And they took his advice! Their son had just been accused of *murder*!"

"I can tell you that, from what I hear," McBee offered, "long before this happened, someone who is renting their house asked them about their son. They said they didn't have one. I heard this through somebody who knows someone at the real estate agency who handled it."

"Are the Kassos still upstate, or have they come back?" Breskin asked.

"Not that I know of," McBee said dryly.

Breskin couldn't believe his ears.

"They haven't come back?" he asked. "So, there's been *no* funeral for him?"

"No," McBee replied. "It says something about the family. I don't care what the kid's done—it's their son and he's *dead*."

Breskin shook his head in disbelief.

"Do you know much about what happened at this 'ceremony,' other than what's already been reported in the papers?" Breskin asked. "Were there *really* a dozen people there chanting 'I love you, Satan'?"

"That's basically what I've been hearing," McBee replied. "Word has it there were as many as twelve people there. Other kids say there were only two. I'm waiting to see what comes out of the grand jury hearing this week."

"Did Lauwers go up there willingly?" Breskin asked.

"From what I hear, he was lured into the woods," McBee replied. "Rumor has it they planned the murder that afternoon.

There have also been rumors that an older person was involved in this. Supposedly, one of Northport's older and less desirable characters, who had moved away from the area and moved back in, was in charge of the cult—but no one will give me a name. No one will give me *anything* on this. There were rumors about a guy in his thirties who wore a Satanic belt buckle and looked like a street character hanging around Northport Village, but he's nowhere to be seen recently. It's disturbing that there were people who knew somebody was brutally murdered—*tortured to death*—and nobody told anyone."

"It does make me wonder what they say about TV and how people don't know what's real and what's not," Breskin said.

"The cops tried to say this was all to blame on rock videos," McBee replied dismissively. "You can't blame rock culture as a whole. *John Lennon* is part of rock culture, and I can't imagine John Lennon encouraging these things."

"Well, 'Helter Skelter' goes back to Manson," Breskin joked.

"Christianity caused the Inquisition, so I guess you're right," McBee laughed.

"What about Ricky's suicide?" Breskin asked. "Did that shock people?"

"Quite honestly, a lot of kids were happy to hear it happened," McBee replied. "It was like, 'At least we don't have to worry about Ricky Kasso on the streets again.' On the other end, we have to deal with another element that's trying to make Gary into this sweet, innocent baby."

"'Baby'?" Breskin asked incredulously. "Who talks like that?"

"Some people who knew him," McBee replied. "They're making him out to be this sweet, innocent kid who never did anything wrong in his life and was brutally murdered for no reason."

"Was there a viewing for Lauwers?" Breskin asked.

"Today," McBee replied. "Two o'clock."

"Two o'clock?" Breskin checked his watch, wondering if he could make it in time. It was now 1:11.

"It's down at the Nolan Funeral Home on the corner of Laurel and Main," McBee offered. "I'm going to try and get out of here early so I can buzz down there just in case anything crazy happens."

"I want to talk to these kids," Breskin said hurriedly. "None of the news coverage ever comes from the kids. If I'm going to present this differently, I think there should be more kids in the story and fewer authority figures saying, 'What a great town we have!' That means I need to get in touch with people you think would be worth talking to."

After mulling it over for a moment, McBee decided to help Breskin.

"I would suggest talking to Chief Howard first," he said. "He knows the families. He knows the kids."

"What about the mayor?" Breskin asked. "Is he in the same building?"

"Well," McBee said, "he runs the funeral parlor where the wake is this afternoon."

The tone of the conversation suddenly shifted. This strange little detail added a new level of absurdity to the situation.

"The *mayor* runs the funeral parlor?"

McBee nodded.

Breskin exhaled loudly. The idea of the local undertaker being the mayor of Satantown, USA—"where evil dwells"—was like something out of a cheap paperback.

McBee chuckled.

"Small-town America at its best, right?" he said sardonically. "In terms of kids, there are two avenues. One: I would certainly welcome you to hang out downstairs at any time and feel free to talk to kids. The other place I would suggest is down at Cow Harbor Park. During the late afternoon and early evening, the gazebo down there is a gathering spot for kids."

Breskin wasn't too sure about hanging around a youth agency or a known drug-peddling spot for a scoop. It made him feel more like a predator than a journalist.

"Maybe the best thing for me to do is just hang out with you," he suggested.

"That would be fine," McBee replied. "I don't have any problems with that."

McBee shook Breskin's hand and saw him outside. He wouldn't be able to join Breskin on his trip into the village, but one of the YDA's teenage volunteers, Mercedes McGrory, offered to ride with Breskin to Northport and give him directions. Mercedes and her brother, Mike, lived at Merrie Schaller's house, and she offered to introduce him to a few people who had known Gary and Ricky.

"I think the press has just blown it up so much," Mercedes told

Breskin as she sat inside his rental car. "The Knights of the Black Circle *were* involved in Satanic rituals, but it was nothing organized, and Ricky and Jimmy had nothing to do with the Knights."

"But didn't Ricky and Jimmy use the name?" he asked.

"No," she insisted. "That's the thing; the first couple articles in the paper said it was just some kids who were involved in a Satanic cult. Then, a couple days later, the articles said, 'Kids in connection with the Knights of the Black Circle . . .' Then, the following day, they said they were *members* of the Knights of the Black Circle. That's the way things have become twisted around. It's just so frustrating that it's being blown out of proportion. . . ."

When Breskin pulled into downtown Northport, he half expected to see a hellish landscape, ripe for murderous teenagers like Ricky Kasso to sprout out of the ground, ready to attack. Instead he was greeted by your typical picturesque seaside village, complete with rows of mom-and-pop shops lining Main Street. Most of its citizens were trying to go about their day, avoiding the throngs of reporters and cameramen all racing down to the New Park. Someone had tipped off *Newsday* about a few local teenagers trying to clean up the Satanic graffiti on the wood forest playground, and word quickly got out to other agencies.

As Breskin parked his rental car, he noticed the swarm of journalists crowding around two teenage boys, Brian Higgins and Tom Sullivan. Brian and Tom, who had both known Ricky and Gary, had gone down to the New Park equipped with sandpaper and paint, determined to destroy the graffiti the Acid King had left behind. Most of their friends were happy to join in. For them, it was an easy way to show solidarity with the Lauwers family, along with the villagers whose lives were being torn apart by an invading press.

For a few select others, however, Brian and Tom were merely placing a Band-Aid over a horrible truth no one could deny.

One of Ricky's friends walked past the park and said, "They're scratching away his *life*. . . ."

Breskin decided to skip Gary's first viewing and walked up to Brian just as another reporter finished up interviewing him.

"*Satin,*" the shirtless teenager said, pointing to the spray paint he was sanding away from a wooden beam. "S-A-T-I-N. It was in a couple of other places too."

"Is that because he didn't know how to spell 'Satan'?" Breskin asked.

"Exactly," Brian replied, wiping the sweat from his brow. "He wasn't smart."

Glen Wolf, who had earlier been introduced to Breskin by Mercedes McGrory, approached the two.

"You wanna go up to the scene of the murder later?" he asked, strapping on his guitar.

"Yeah, sure," Breskin replied.

"*Don't go up there,*" Brian snapped. "There's *nothing* there. It's just the woods."

Brian was tired of all the people gleefully wandering into Aztakea to gawk at the spot where Gary was murdered, like it was some cheap sideshow attraction. Breskin quickly changed the subject to avoid confrontation.

"How did you get involved in this?" he asked.

"I just had the idea because Gary was a friend of mine," Brian replied. "I'm just sorry that it took this for us to realize that this stuff shouldn't be here. I just came across the idea, told Tom Sullivan about it, and we started organizing a committee to get rid of it all. I've been down here for almost three hours now."

Brian turned to Glen, pointing his sanding block in his friend's direction.

"This man right here is very smart," he continued. "He brought a sign to the Northport Firemen's Fair saying 'Demolish Satanism in Northport.' He stood right in front of the gate all night long. I heard a cop patted you on the back?"

"Yeah," Glen scoffed, rolling his eyes. "The same one who gave me a ticket for walking in the road instead of the sidewalk a few years ago."

"How do you feel about what happened to Gary?" Breskin asked.

"I'm sorry that it had to happen," Brian replied, "because Gary was a good friend of mine."

Suddenly Glen Wolf, his friend Karl Blessing, and a few other kids convened inside the gazebo, pulled out their guitars, and began to strum. Breskin walked over as they all started to sing Simon & Garfunkel's "He Was My Brother" for Gary. Breskin hung around a little while longer as the impromptu band started playing the Who's "Won't Get Fooled Again," followed by Led Zeppelin's "Stairway to Heaven." When the group was finished, Breskin overheard Mercedes McGrory tell a friend that she needed to get back to the YDA. He told her that he would give her a ride back, as he wanted to talk to Dennis McBee some more. As the two were leaving, Breskin told Glen he would meet him back downtown later in the afternoon.

Back at the YDA, Breskin struck up a conversation with Gary's friend Anthony Zenkus, who also volunteered for the organization as a youth worker. Anthony gave Breskin his honest appraisal of the alleged occult aspects of the murder. The writer wanted to hear more, so he invited Anthony to join him for dinner over at the pizza place next door.

After grabbing a few slices and drinks, the two sat at a table inside the tiny restaurant and resumed their conversation.

"A few people I know showed me *The Satanic Bible*," Anthony told Breskin, "and from what I read, it's basically a modernistic appraisal of man, saying man is *the* highest creature, and you have to love yourself more than anything and screw everybody else to get ahead."

"Sounds like capitalism to me," Breskin replied.

"It is," Anthony agreed. "Dennis said it's a celebration of capitalism. I was looking at it a week ago, and it denounces any kind of animal or ritual sacrifice. It says, 'That's not what we're about. We're about getting ahead in life.'"

"So, you're telling me Satanism is Horatio Alger warmed over?" Breskin asked.

"No," Anthony replied. "All *Anton LaVey* is about is making money. I'm sure there really are sick cults out there, though. Listen to Joel Martin on WBAB. He interviews Long Island necrophiliacs and Long Island vampires. I think there's a *power trip* in Satanism. It's got a set way to say, 'Hey—now you're powerful. Now you can strike back at the people who screwed you over.' There's a lot of lost people everywhere. It's something to believe in."

"You're a very sophisticated person," Breskin said, still surprised by Anthony's intelligence for his age.

"As I sit here eating pizza with my hands," Anthony laughed. "Now, I see where the media is coming from because it's not every day where someone is killed in this way, where the eyes are gouged out. They *mutilated* the body."

"You wanna know why they're hooked on the 'Satan' thing?" Breskin asked. "They need an *explanation*. Anything this bizarre, this strange, and this *crazy*, needs an explanation. Every suicide of a young person needs an explanation. Drugs, family—whatever."

"I mean, it's displacement," Anthony replied. "These kids live here, and they live on the *streets* or other people's houses. They're just pushed aside."

"Is Northport unusual in that regard?" Breskin asked. "Are there street people in, say, Scarsdale? When I was growing up in a suburb a lot like this, there were no street kids."

"I'm telling you, these people are everywhere," Anthony insisted. "These people weren't terrorists. I mean, if you walked by, they'd say hi to you. It's not like the Knights of the Black Circle are riding around on motorcycles, shooting up people's windows. Things like that just don't happen. If you read *The Satanic Bible*, it has a lot to say about power and wealth—things these people don't have. I hate to be analytical, but it seems like Satanism is a way to realize stuff they don't have. They're being just like their parents. It's so capitalistic."

"What else have you heard about Ricky?" Breskin asked.

"This is secondhand information," Anthony replied, "but someone I know said the cops supposedly told Kasso he was going to die anyway, so he might as well kill himself."

"I don't believe in capital punishment," Breskin said, "so I don't think he deserved to *die*, but you can't do something much worse than what he did. I mean, on that level, who gives a shit what drugs he took beforehand? He's still responsible for the action of *taking* those drugs."

"I agree," Zenkus said.

"All the people who have talked to me have been very open like you," Breskin said, "but no one wants to tell me who was in the Knights. People say the Knights don't even really *exist*, yet no one wants me to find them."

"The Knights of the Black Circle had nothing to do with this," Anthony insisted. "Ricky was too clicked out—even for them."

"But in an existential way," Breskin replied, "everybody is responsible. Everyone *saw* what the kid was doing."

"In a way," Anthony said. "Especially since he robbed a grave. The papers called it 'Satanism.' That's *not* Satanism. A *true* Satanist doesn't rob graves or sacrifice animals. I just thought it was some freaked-out kid and then *this* happens. He should have been checked out."

"He *was* checked out," Breskin told him. "The psychologist said he was just 'antisocial.'"

Anthony shook his head at the suggestion.

"'Antisocial' means sitting in a corner at a party," he insisted. "'Sociopathic' is robbing graves. There's a difference."

Breskin took a sip of his drink.

"Well, I want to talk to those psychiatrists," he said. "That's the tangent of the story that I'm interested in."

"It's a *good* tangent," Anthony replied. "I'm just worried that this is going to be a really negative thing for kids here. They've had enough unnecessary tragedy. Their friends have been killed in motorcycle accidents or died of cystic fibrosis. This kid Robbie Clayton got killed at a party last year, and now all *this* stuff. It's all just unnecessary. I don't know what's going to happen. I'm really scared. . . ."

After Breskin finished interviewing Zenkus, he went out and bought a copy of *The Satanic Bible*. Sitting on the bed in his rented room, Breskin flipped through the book until he came upon a chapter entitled "On the Choice of a Human Sacrifice." In this chapter, LaVey describes a "symbolic" sacrifice by writing that "the victim is destroyed through the working of a hex or curse, which in turn leads to the physical, mental or emotional destruction of the 'sacrifice' in ways and means not attributable to the magician," adding, "The only time a Satanist would perform a human sacrifice would be if it were to serve a two-fold purpose; that being to release the magician's wrath in the throwing of a curse, and more important, to dispose of a totally obnoxious and deserving individual."

Ricky made sure to end his confession by saying Gary "got what he deserved." Breskin wondered if this could have been a reference to the passage on page eighty-eight of *The Satanic Bible*. He quickly jotted down this quote in his notebook and kept reading.

On the very next page, Breskin took note of LaVey writing, "The question arises, 'Who, then, would be considered a fit and proper human sacrifice, and how is one qualified to pass judgment on such a person?' The answer is brutally simple. Anyone who has unjustly wronged you—one who has 'gone out of his way' to hurt you—to deliberately cause trouble and hardship for you or those dear to you. In short, a person asking to be cursed by their very actions."

Ricky certainly felt that Gary had wronged him. After all, he was living on the streets with very little to his name. The only money coming his way was through drug dealing, and Gary had stolen most of his stock. It wasn't just a matter of getting high at that point; it was about having the money to survive while virtually homeless. Did that excuse what Ricky had done? Of course not, but Breskin began to wonder if these writings had indeed influenced Ricky, or, at the very least, justified the murder in his own PCP-fueled mind.

Chapter 41

THE RAIN STARTED AS GARY'S SECOND VISITATION AT the Nolan & Taylor-Howe Funeral Home began. Dozens of teenagers slowly filed inside the large brick house on Laurel Avenue, tossing their cigarettes aside. Johnny Hayward was there. So was Lion, along with Dorothy, Glen Wolf, Tom Sullivan, and countless others who knew and loved Gary in life.

Another teenager who shuffled in to pay his respects was Matthew Carpenter. When he and his girlfriend Carol had returned to Northport a few days earlier, they found reporters literally sitting in trees, trying to take as many photos of the New Park as possible. Some were from London, while others had flown in from as far as Japan. He couldn't believe the attention this story was getting. When he picked up a copy of *Newsday*, he saw why. The newspapers had been labeling Ricky a Satanic cult leader for nearly a week, calling Gary's murder a "ritual sacrifice."

Before leaving for the funeral home, Matthew smoked a joint and tucked the article in his pocket.

Walking inside the funeral home, he navigated through the maze of mourners, past Gary's casket, which was adorned with a photo of the murdered boy, and walked up to Herbert and Yvonne Lauwers.

"You know this wasn't Satanism, right?" he said, pulling the article from his pocket. "This was just *drugs*."

Before Herbert or Yvonne could reply, one of Gary's friends walked up, gently placed his hands on Matthew's shoulders, and said, "You should go."

Matthew left, completely embarrassed by what he had done.

After the viewing ended, everyone walked outside for cigarettes and conversation. David Breskin was sitting there waiting. The wake was a private affair, and he didn't want to wear out his welcome on his first day by intruding inside. He quickly found Glen Wolf and they began to chat, mostly about the controversy surrounding the Knights of the Black Circle. Breskin was soon introduced to Mike Drogos, a friend of Gary's, and more importantly, a friend of the Knights. Drogos found Breskin easy to speak with, unlike the other reporters who had stormed the village.

"The papers are mostly wrong," Drogos told him. "There's only a couple people into Satanism. There's no gathering, no chanting, none of that shit."

Drogos turned to his friend Lion.

"Where's Johnny?" he asked.

"He went inside to get his jacket," Lion replied, pointing to the funeral parlor.

"I need to give this guy his number," Drogos told him. "He's where it's at. He ain't no fucking newsman. He's from the *Stone*, man."

"Rolling Stone?" Lion asked.

"Yeah," Breskin answered.

Lion walked over.

"What do you want to know, man?" he asked.

"I want to know the truth about the whole story and not just the bullshit I read in the *Post* or the *Daily News*," Breskin replied. "They'll spend a day or two on it. I'll probably spend a *month* or two on it."

As Breskin was reassuring Lion, Johnny Hayward, Dorothy, and Tom Sullivan emerged from the funeral home. Still shaken from Gary's murder, Johnny was a brooding shell of a devastated young man.

"Johnny, come here!" Lion hollered. "This guy is from *Rolling Stone*. He wants the truth, man."

The boy approached Breskin.

"What do you want?" he asked.

Breskin could see the hurt in Johnny's eyes and cut to the chase.

"I'm trying to find out the whole story," he said. "I'm trying to present it thoroughly instead of all the sensational bullshit that's in the papers."

"I used to hang out with the Knights too," Johnny replied, "but I was never a member."

"What was different about the Knights compared to anybody else?" Breskin asked.

"Nothing," Johnny insisted. "They were just a group of friends."

Lion, however, disagreed.

"You were killin' fuckin' animals," he said, staring at Drogos.

"We weren't killin' no fuckin' animals, man!" Drogos replied.

"You weren't the ones who went around killing cats and shit?" Lion asked.

"We fucked around with cats, but we never *killed* them!" Drogos maintained. "It was just a laugh! We'd fuck 'em up, throw 'em in the fire, and let them run out—shit like that."

Lion calmed down.

"I can understand," he said. "There's a lot of bullshit being said that never happened, man."

"I hate to agree with the newspapers, man, but it was the angel dust," Tom Sullivan said to Breskin. "There were never any problems like this until I saw angel dust coming into Northport."

"It's easy to blame one thing," Breskin said. "You can blame this drug, but what about all the *other* drugs he was taking?"

"It was pretty much drugs in general," Tom replied.

"Okay, but that's saying something different," Breskin said, "and that's not even getting at the *reason*, because drugs are just a *symptom*. *Why* are young people all taking drugs? *Why* do they want it? *Why* do they do it?"

"It's the culture," Glen offered.

"Okay, now you're getting to the shit that's not easy to talk about in the newspapers," Breskin said.

"He was probably trying to escape his family," Dorothy said.

Johnny agreed. "His family sucked."

"Did anyone care about Kasso?" Breskin asked. "You saw how he was getting more and more fucked up and desperate. Didn't you ever think to yourself that the peers instead of the parents or the authorities or the school principal should get him help?"

"*I* tried!" Lion insisted. "*Dave Johnson* tried!"

"We talked to him every day," Johnny said. "He just never went. Every day he'd just get up, get some drug, and be on the drug all day."

"That's not true, man," Lion countered. "He *did* make an effort to straighten his ass out. He went to take a test to enter the navy, man. He *went*, man!"

"He made an effort so he would have a place to stay!" Dorothy fired back. "He went so he could be warm and sleep and have food in his stomach! You think *Ricky Kasso* was going to take an order?!"

"How many people do you think knew about it but didn't say anything?" Breskin asked, trying to cut the tension by changing the subject.

"Too many," Dorothy replied as she broke down. "Ricky Kasso wasn't such a bad person," she said, fighting back tears, "but he did something terribly bad that no one can forgive him for, but if you really knew him . . . He had a *heart*. He was a really good person."

Suddenly a man approached the group. His outfit, notepad, and tape recorder gave his occupation away—newspaper reporter.

"What do *you* want?" Johnny seethed.

"Did you guys hang out with Gary?" the reporter asked without bothering to even introduce himself.

"Yes, we did," Lion replied, keeping his answers brief.

"*Why?*" Johnny demanded.

"I'm just asking," the reporter answered in an aloof tone.

"If you're gonna print something, get the *truth*," Johnny said. "If not, *leave*."

"Well, no one wants to talk to us!" the reporter replied.

"I don't want to talk to you," Lion replied. "There is no 'cult'!"

The reporter remained oblivious to their anger.

"What time is the service for . . . uh . . . uh . . ."

"For *Gary*!" Glen Wolf screamed. He couldn't believe the reporter had already forgotten the name of the victim—their *friend*—less than a minute after arriving.

"So, how does Gary's family feel about all of this?"

"They obviously feel awful, you *idiot*!" Lion told him.

"So, you're all Gary's friends?" the reporter asked smugly. "How many friends did Gary have?"

Breskin had enough.

"Think of how many friends *you* have and multiply that number by twenty," Breskin told him.

Lion was impressed. This was the first time in five horrible days that a journalist had stepped in to defend him and his friends.

"I'm looking forward to seeing *your* article, man," Lion told him with a smile.

The reporter adjusted his large, Coke-bottle glasses and looked Breskin up and down. "So, what paper are *you* with?" he asked.

"I'm not a reporter," Breskin replied. "I'm a writer."

"He prints the truth," Glen said, "unlike *your* shit."

The reporter saw he wasn't getting the scoop he had hoped for and walked away without uttering another word. As he made his way back to his car, Tom Sullivan shouted out, "Make the headline 'There Is No Cult in Northport!'" The reporter didn't respond. He got into his car, put the key in the ignition, and drove off wearing the same smug look on his face that he'd walked up with. Breskin saw this as a good time to duck out. These kids had dealt with enough for one day.

"All right," he said, turning toward Lion. "I'll be in touch."

Lion shook Breskin's hand.

"I'll tell you right now, man, you're welcome by us in the town," he told him. "I really like you."

"Take care," Breskin told him, and walked off.

With the wake finished and the reporters gone, Gary's friends decided to leave. Today had been a nightmare, but tomorrow—the funeral—would be worse. As his friends faded away around him, Johnny Hayward said to no one in particular, "I'm gonna go get a bottle and get my ass drunk. . . ."

Tomorrow would be good-bye.

Chapter 42

"FUCK GARY! HE DESERVED IT!"

Johnny Hayward turned to see a ten-year-old boy who lived across the street from the funeral home retreating inside his third-floor bedroom window.

"No," Johnny yelled back, "fuck *you*!"

Suddenly a reporter ran up to the teenager clad in the dark suit and shoved a camera in his face.

"Did you know Gary?!" he asked, way too excited for Johnny's taste.

Johnny just glared at him.

"What's your name?" the reporter pressed.

Johnny grabbed the reporter's camera, tearing its strap, and with all the force of a major-league pitcher, he chucked it at the pavement. The overzealous reporter gasped as the camera shattered into a dozen pieces. Before he could say anything, Johnny got in his face.

"No fuckin' pictures!" he screamed. "If I am in *one* fuckin' picture, I will sue any motherfucker who prints it!"

Another reporter standing in Johnny's path fearfully jumped backward as the boy turned around. Johnny met his friends inside and told them to come out back with him. When they got there, he pulled a joint from his pocket, lit it, and inhaled deeply. He didn't want to be sober when he said farewell to the best friend he'd ever had. Exhaling a big cloud of smoke, he passed the joint to Lion, who was standing next to him. Before the sun rose that morning, Lion had snuck into his parents' bedroom while they slept and snatched a light-colored suit from his stepfather's closet. None of the boys thought they would be burying one of their friends before graduating high school, so most of them had to borrow something decent to wear. When they were done passing the joint around, they threw the roach on the ground, stomped it out, and walked inside to begin one of the hardest days of their young lives.

Inside, Gary's casket was rolled toward the front door, to the hearse waiting outside. Johnny Hayward, Lion, Brian Higgins, Gary's neighbor Bill Kreth, and two other friends had all been asked by Herbert and Yvonne to serve as Gary's pallbearers. Floored by the terrible and important honor bestowed upon them, they all solemnly agreed. When Johnny went to lift the casket, he was shocked by how light it was. The whole experience began to feel like a charade. In that moment, everything seemed too surreal to process. He began to weep.

"Use two hands!" the other pallbearers told him. *"Use two hands!"*

"Why the fuck do I need to use two hands?!" Johnny shot back, tears streaming down his face. "He isn't in here! It's fucking *empty*!"

Suddenly Michael Lauwers walked over to Johnny, placed a hand on his shoulder, and said, "It will be okay, Johnny. Gary *is* here and he's at rest."

What Johnny didn't realize was that his best friend had been cremated and that the box of ashes had been placed inside the casket. Michael's kindness in the face of impossible grief gave Johnny the strength to carry on. He lifted with the other pallbearers and took the casket outside. Once their son's remains were loaded into the back of the hearse, Herbert and Yvonne Lauwers told the boys to meet them at their home an hour after the service ended. The funeral procession then drove to the St. Philip Neri Roman Catholic Church for Gary's final service. When they all arrived, and the casket was brought up to the altar, Father Thomas Colgan asked everyone to be seated and began reading Gary's eulogy.

"Gary was a believer," Colgan told the mourners. "Everyone eventually comes to Christ. For some, it may take ten minutes—for some, it may take ten years. Gary Lauwers was . . . *sidetracked*, perhaps, but which one of us is exempted from these pitfalls? We have the opportunity of making this right. Let us reason what has happened to ourselves. Let us understand we are not lost. Gary is not dead. He is going through a new door to a new life with Christ."

Few were moved, least of all Gary's family. A few days earlier, when Yvonne and Nicole Lauwers visited Colgan at St. Philip Neri to plan the funeral arrangements, the sixty-one-year-old priest told them, "I hope you're not having his funeral here because of the good press you'll get."

The two were stunned by Colgan's insensitivity. They vowed never again to set foot inside St. Philip Neri after Gary's funeral—and they never did.

Gary's friends saw Colgan's eulogy for what it was—a collection of empty platitudes tiptoeing around the less savory aspects of Gary's brief life, all offered up as a buffet for the quote-hungry journalists scribbling away in the rear pews. David Breskin sat among them, trying not to attract attention to himself. He remained respectful, keeping his notebook tucked away but leaving his tape recorder rolling for posterity.

Once Colgan finished, the pallbearers rose from their pews, lifted the casket, and began their final walk with Gary. The cameras clicked away as the boys emerged from the church carrying their fallen friend. With Herbert and Yvonne Lauwers following closely behind, Gary's friends placed his casket in the waiting hearse, closed the door, and watched it drive away. The crowd of reporters didn't know the limousine wouldn't be taking Gary to a cemetery. Instead Gary's ashes were driven back to the funeral home, where they were given to his family.

Outside St. Philip Neri, Gary's friends congregated on the front steps, trying to ignore the reporters and television cameramen. Glen Wolf ran up to them, pulled his sport coat over his head, and flapped his arms, telling them all to figuratively fly away before following his friends back to the funeral home. Breskin caught up with them outside.

"How was the service?" he asked.

"They didn't say enough about Gary," Lion said, criticizing Colgan's eulogy. He turned to Johnny and said, "*You* should have done it. If anyone was gonna talk about Gary, it should have been you."

"What were you thinking about during the service?" Breskin asked.

"Loving Gary and all the things he did," Johnny replied, "because you can't bring him back."

"Where do you think he is now?" Breskin asked. "Do you all believe in Heaven?"

"I don't know," Johnny replied. "If there's a Heaven, he's there. I'll put it that way."

"Yeah. I don't believe in *Satan*," Glen Wolf added.

"He and I always used to kid about it," Johnny continued. "We used to say we'd probably be dead or in jail by the time we were eighteen."

"Yeah, but he was *right*," Lion said.

"During the service," Breskin said, "the priest said, 'Now he's in a place that's beyond his wildest imagination and his best dreams.' It was almost as if he was saying Gary's death was *good* because now he's with Christ. Are you guys scared of death?"

"Everyone's gonna die, I figure," Johnny said. "If you're gonna live life like, 'Oh shit, I might die,' then you're always gonna be frightened. I say if you're gonna live, have good times all the time. Go out and have a party. Push yourself as far as you can go and have a good time. If you're worried about dying all the time, it doesn't make any sense. If I die tomorrow, I can always say I had so many good times and I lived my life to the fullest."

"What do you live for?" Breskin asked. "What do you love more than anything else?"

"My mom always says I value my friends too much," Johnny replied. "She was worried that Gary would rip off the house. I was *best friends* with Gary. I knew he'd never do anything like that."

"But he *did* . . . ," Lion reminded him.

Everyone fell quiet. The echoes of birds singing could be heard in the distance, a cruel reminder that life would go on without Gary Lauwers.

"I think we should be getting back to Gary's house," Johnny told Breskin. "I'm sorry."

"No, it's cool," he assured him.

Johnny let out a big sigh and turned to Lion.

"All right, you ready?"

Lion nodded and the group all began walking toward the Lauwers home, ready to grieve in private with his parents. As Breskin was heading back to his car, he noticed a teenager being interviewed by a reporter. When he overheard the reporter say he was from the *New York Post*, Breskin became incensed. The grieving kids he had interviewed over the last two days were having their lives ruined by newspapers like the *Post*, and he'd had enough of it. Breskin walked over as the reporter was wrapping up his interview and asked him why the paper kept pressing the idea of a Satanic cult in Northport.

"I think these were two or three whacked-out drug kids who adopted their own pseudo-Satanism ritual," the reporter replied.

"Yeah, but the *Post* was the most crucial in tying in the connection between these kids and the Knights of the Black Circle," Breskin maintained.

"I think every newspaper and every radio station I've heard made the same connection," the reporter insisted. "Probably because of all the police reports, which initially labeled this as a Satan thing."

Breskin wasn't about to let him shift the blame.

"The police reports were based on the testimony of kids who were so out of their minds on mescaline they didn't know what they were doing anyway!" he said. "The papers picked it up as *gospel* and ran with it!"

"The police station is still running with the same line too," the reporter pointed out.

"Because they're covering their asses right now!" Breskin angrily countered.

"Well, you know, personally, all I've got to say is there *is* a legitimate Satan angle," the reporter replied. "There seemed to be a little more *ceremony* attached to this than the average murder, and I think the ceremony attached to it is what makes this especially horrible. So, I think that probably answers your question."

The reporter started to walk away.

"Well, that could be," Breskin conceded. "It's a very complicated story."

"Sure is!" the reporter hollered back. "Someone's probably gonna write a book about it—maybe it'll be *you*!"

Breskin could only shake his head and laugh as he walked away. This wasn't about book deals—this was about finding the truth.

Chapter 43

"OLD ASPHALT PAVEMENT ROAD WITH LOGS PAINTED with white stripes on the sides for guardrails to kind of mark the left side of the road . . ."

Glen Wolf watched as Breskin noted the route to Aztakea into the Sony Pressman's microphone. He had finally made good on his offer to take the writer to the murder scene, and the two were now walking up the path leading into the woods. A few moments later they reached the clearing where Gary Lauwers was killed. The circular area, approximately twenty yards by thirty yards across, was mostly flat, littered with many small bushes and plants, and bordered on all sides by tall trees. Off in one corner, Breskin found the remnants of the campfire Gary helped build before his murder. Aside from a large burnt blotch on the ground, all that was left were two scorched tree branches and a portion of the wooden frame from Ricky's old couch.

"Your average fuckin' suburban wooden party spot," Glen quipped. "Senator Smith's driveway is only about a hundred yards from here."

When Breskin was done taking notes, Glen took him about fifty yards away from the murder spot to where Gary's body had been buried.

"Off the clearing where they dragged him to bury him, it's about eight feet by ten feet," Breskin told his tape recorder. "There's a little pine tree at the foot or head of the grave. There are blue tarps around here that the police left. There's a black spot which may have been caused by . . ."

"Fire?" Glen offered.

"Well," Breskin replied, "it could be *blood*."

Glen leaned over and sniffed the small tree at the head of the grave.

"Doesn't smell like it's been burned. . . ."

Breskin didn't know it yet, but his initial suspicion was correct. The black spot next to the grave was soil stained by decomposition from the two weeks Gary had lain there.

Suddenly two teenage boys walked up to the grave site.

"What's goin' on?" Glen said, greeting the visitors.

"You found it?" the older boy asked. "You found where he was?"

"Yeah, it's right over there," Glen said, pointing to the trench behind him that had since been filled in by police.

"That's what I thought," the younger boy said.

"Did you know Gary?" Breskin asked them.

"I knew him from hanging out," the younger boy said, "but I never knew his name. I knew Rick."

"Are you surprised he was capable of this?" Breskin asked.

"Nah," the younger boy replied. "Not on *angel dust*."

"How important was Satanism to him?" Breskin asked.

"Well," the younger boy said, "he *worshipped* Satan. He would read books and chant things."

"He'd sit there and chant, 'Satan, Satan, Satan,' and shit like that," Glen added.

"He was a good kid," the younger boy said, "but the drugs and Satan caught up with him."

"Tell me about your shirt," Breskin said, pointing to the older boy's Mötley Crüe tee. "People seem to be making such a big deal about these concert shirts."

"Music does have *something* to do with it," the older boy said. "Take that Sabbath song, "After Forever." Every other line is something crazy. '*Would you like to see the Pope on the end of a rope?*' Rick always used to sing that. Whenever he was in my car, he'd be like, 'Put on this song!'"

Ironically, "After Forever" was Black Sabbath bassist Geezer Butler's attempt at writing a pro-Christian song to help deflect the rumors that his band worshipped the devil.

"We used to put on any Sabbath song," the older boy continued, "like the title track, 'Black Sabbath.' That's another sick song."

"He was obsessed with their song 'Changes,'" Glen added.

"That's *old* music, man," Breskin said, surprised to hear that the so-called "devil music" Ricky had been listening to was more suited to the previous generation. "Wasn't that in the late sixties or early seventies?"

"Yeah," Glen replied. "Then Ozzy Osbourne broke out of that group and formed his own sick shit, like biting the head off a bat."

"There are some kids down in Texas who got rabies because they bit the head off a bat," Breskin said, recalling an article he had read in the paper earlier that morning.

"Serves 'em right, man!" Glen exclaimed. "I love rock 'n' roll, but I ain't gonna go bite the head off a *bat*!"

"You can take AC/DC for example too," the older boy said.

"They sing about the devil," the younger boy agreed.

"'Hells Bells,'" Glen said.

"Sing me some of 'Hells Bells,'" Breskin asked.

The three paused.

"I only know the line *'Hells bells,'*" Glen replied. "It's hard to understand what he's singing."

Breskin laughed.

"I don't like the way they're making this into a cult thing," the younger boy said, almost mournfully.

"Get ahold of today's *New York Post*," Glen told Breskin. "They put the Midway in it with a skull, handcuffs, a knife, a hatchet, rolling papers, and all that shit."

The *New York Post* had printed an article that morning by Ransdell Pierson and Paul Tharp, titled, "BARED—DEVIL DEATH CULT HQ: Post finds the head shop where Satan-worship leader did his drug deals." The huge, two-page spread featured photos taken inside the Midway of the items Glen was describing, along with the first public revelation of Ricky purchasing the murder weapon from the shop. The writers also continued to double down on their insistence that Ricky was a leader of the Knights of the Black Circle "cult," despite having failed to provide any evidence for the past six days.

"Look, I'm no fan of the *Post*," Breskin maintained, "but if the shit was there, it was *there*."

"Yeah, but it's *every-fucking-where* else, too!" Glen said.

Breskin paused. The kid had a point.

He turned back to the two boys and said, "Now, you guys have both used dust, right? I haven't, so tell me something about it. Tell me what it feels like."

"You don't *feel* anything," the older boy said. "You feel like you could rip your gut out and not even know it."

"You feel like you're floating," the younger boy offered.

"You feel like you're ten feet tall," Glen added.

"Who was the first to bring dust to this town?" Breskin asked.

"Me and him," the older boy said, surprising the journalist.

"After us, it was our friend Vinny Ivy," the younger boy said. "Then Ricky and Jimmy tried it. They liked it and they went back to the city again and again. After about two months of going back and forth, Ivy crashed his car into a wall. They were all dusted out. He lost his license and his car. Two weeks later, he got sent to Sagamore Psychiatric Center. Even though Ivy's car was wrecked, Kasso just kept going. He found other ways into the city. Once

Ivy started hanging out with Kasso, my friend of ten years suddenly starts saying, 'The devil wants me! I keep hearing voices!'"

"Ivy came over my house the night after the car accident," the older boy added. "He was screaming hysterically about seeing devils with long beards and leather jackets riding motorcycles down Main Street. He was on my floor crying hysterically."

Breskin still couldn't grasp why so many teenagers in this little village were going out of their way to experience such horrors.

"Was there something Ricky wanted that he couldn't get to with drugs?" Breskin asked.

"I think he was trying to get in touch with the devil," the younger boy said. "About three months ago, me, Ivy, and Kasso drove up to this cemetery. Kasso smoked *bag after bag after bag* of dust and started chanting, trying to get someone to talk to him. He was talking about digging up a grave. Nothing happened, so after a few hours, we just left."

"You must have liked him a lot to do that with him," Breskin said.

"He was a drug friend," the younger boy insisted. "That's all it was."

"So, you didn't have an attitude to help or save him?" Breskin asked.

"I talked to him about it," the younger boy replied, "but I couldn't stop him if that's what he wanted to do. I told him, 'Hey, if you do too many drugs you're going to be dead soon,' and he said, 'That's what I want.'"

Glen nodded.

"Gotta go sometime," he recalled Ricky saying.

"Right before all this whole cult shit started, Ricky and this other dude were in my car," the older boy added, "and they were like, 'We're trying to get this cult going. Going to the library to read up on some books. We want your mother to be the leader of it.' I'm not gonna go into this because my mother has some sort of shit you're not gonna believe even if I *try* to explain it to you."

"After the atomic bomb, I'll believe anything," Breskin reassured him.

The older boy paused.

"She has these *powers* . . . ," he told Breskin.

"She raises tables," the younger boy added. "Telekinesis."

"Yeah, he's seen it," the older boy said. "Ricky said, 'Ask her if she wants to be the head of it. I want somebody who has some kind of power to talk to people.' We've talked to dead people. We've talked to Jim Morrison through a table."

Suddenly a crow swooped down, screeching as it passed the grave. The boys shared a collective shudder, each of them simultaneously recalling Ricky's confession.

"That's a sign!" Breskin joked, trying to cut the tension.

"I think it's funny that when Ricky died, it was raining, lightning, and thundering," the younger boy said.

"All of a sudden, my door slammed open," the older boy told Breskin. "It was shut and locked tight, and it slammed open and banged against the wall. It was two a.m. 'Cause indirectly, we were the ones that got him started in this whole thing. It was just his way of coming to my house, saying, 'Hey, man, look at this shit,' you know? Also, somebody was murdered in my room many years before we moved in."

The older boy wasn't the only friend of Ricky's to experience paranormal activity in the wake of his suicide. After Ricky's friend Ronnie learned of his death, he drove out to the end of Franklin Street, shined his headlights toward Aztakea, and shouted, *"Ricky, if you're out there, give me a sign!"* Ronnie's headlights suddenly burned out—and never worked again.

"You should ask the table!" the young boy jokingly suggested.

"I don't wanna ask that shit," the older boy replied.

"What did your mother think of Ricky?" Breskin asked.

"Oh, she hated him," the older boy said. "She doesn't like any of my friends. Ricky said, 'Let's form this cult,' but I said, 'Nah, I'm not getting into this shit.'"

Before Breskin could reply, a storm cloud appeared overhead, blocking out the sun.

"We're gonna get rained on," Glen said.

"Yeah," the older boy replied. "We're gonna split."

"Well, look," Breskin said, "I know it's a corny sentiment, but take care of yourselves?"

"Yeah, we will," the younger boy chuckled.

"We'll try!" the older boy said, walking off into a sea of trees.

As Breskin walked away from the murder scene, he pulled out his notebook. Haunted by the image of the dark stain where Gary Lauwers was left to rot, he jotted down a potential title for the article: "Thirteen Ways of Looking at a Black Spot in the Woods," an homage to the Wallace Stevens poem "Thirteen Ways of Looking at a Blackbird." His article needed to be a reminder of the real-life horror surrounding the murder of Gary Lauwers—not the crap made up by the cops and the newspapers—and this reminder needed to be the very first thing readers saw.

Only then could the world truly appreciate just how tragic and unnecessary this all really was.

Chapter 44

LONG ISLAND ATTORNEY ERIC NAIBURG FIRST FOUND out about the "Northport Satan case" while flipping through the Sunday, July 8, edition of the *New York Times*. By now Ricky was dead, but Jimmy was still alive, being kept under twenty-four-hour observation in the Suffolk County jail. Naiburg saw no mention of a lawyer for the accused murderer and decided to seize this opportunity.

On Monday morning Naiburg walked into the Suffolk County Courthouse in Riverhead and asked a judge he was friendly with if Jimmy had been arraigned yet. The judge replied that he had not, so Naiburg grabbed a piece of paper and wrote, *If Troiano needs an assigned attorney, I'm here and available*, and handed it to the clerk, who agreed to give it to Judge Gerard D'Emilio, who would be presiding over the upcoming grand jury hearings.

Later that week, on July 11, the grand jury ruled that there was enough evidence to try Jimmy for the second-degree murder of Gary Lauwers. At the end of the hearing, Judge D'Emilio turned to Jimmy and said, "You need a lawyer—somebody *very* experienced. I see Mr. Naiburg is in the courtroom. Mr. Naiburg, do you accept this assignment?" Naiburg said yes. Jimmy and his family agreed to the arrangement, and with that, Naiburg secured one of the most controversial cases of his career.

Once David Breskin found out that Jimmy had finally acquired a lawyer, he called Naiburg at his Hauppauge office and asked for an interview. The forty-two-year-old attorney believed that continued national coverage of the murder through *Rolling Stone* could be advantageous to his case, and agreed.

When Breskin was shown into Naiburg's office, he found a sophisticated, intelligent lawyer, dressed to the nines in a three-piece suit, and clean-shaven, with his curly brown hair trimmed neatly around his ears. If looks were all that mattered, Jimmy's upcoming trial might have resulted in a draw. Naiburg seemed the perfect opponent to William Keahon, the impeccably dressed chief of the Major Offense Bureau inside the Suffolk County District Attorney's Office, who had recently been assigned as the case's prosecutor.

"So, other than this case being an interesting one, why take it on?" Breskin asked.

"No other reason but that," Naiburg replied honestly.

"What did Troiano say in his confession?" Breskin asked.

"I haven't seen it," Naiburg admitted. "I can't talk about the confession until I find out what the *police* wrote. Defendants don't write their own confessions; police write them for them. Defendants just sign them."

"Was it taped?" Breskin asked.

"Are you *kidding*?!" Naiburg scoffed. "It's too difficult, apparently. We're only talking about the Suffolk County Police Department, who have millions and millions of dollars at their disposal. They can't afford a Sony like *that*!"

Naiburg pointed to Breskin's tape recorder.

"No confession is ever taped. *Never*."

"Why don't they use tape?" Breskin asked.

"Ask the police officers," Naiburg said. "See what kinds of answers you're gonna get. Queens County *videotapes* their confessions. Suffolk wouldn't hear of it."

"Have you seen the medical examiner's report?" Breskin asked.

"Not yet," Naiburg replied, "but I don't know how much information they're going to get from a body *that* decomposed. From my understanding, there were no maggots left when they exhumed the body, and that's an indication they've already done their work. It takes about four generations of maggots to decompose a body, and there were none left at that point."

"Is the autopsy report available to the public?" Breskin asked, hoping to get a look at it. He had a sneaking suspicion that the police were exaggerating the aspects of Gary's murder, particularly the alleged removal of his eyes. "I imagine there would be photos."

"They always take pictures," Naiburg said, skipping the first half of Breskin's question. "They take pictures, they draw diagrams. They take the defendant down to the scene and tell him, 'Point to this, point to that,' and then they give the photos to a jury and say, 'While he was pointing, he was telling us he did it.'"

"Did they take your client and do that?" Breskin asked, unaware that Jimmy had been photographed at the scene while in custody.

"Mm-hmm," Naiburg replied, nodding intently. "When he was first arrested. The police spent twelve hours with them before they notified their parents, who would have stopped them from talking, I'm sure. An attorney would have been contacted, so why do it, right? They're homicide detectives—they have a case to build. . . ."

Chapter 45

ON SATURDAY, JULY 14, BRESKIN CAUGHT A BREAK. Thanks to half a week spent gaining trust in Northport, he finally secured an interview with one of the original cofounders and leaders of the Knights of the Black Circle: Paul McBride, aka "King." Paul asked Breskin to meet him at one of the small baseball fields on Kew Avenue in East Northport, only a block over from the YDA.

When Breskin arrived, he found Paul, a short young man with long brown hair, waiting for him under a large tree in the southwest corner of the northernmost field. Sitting next to him was Chrissy, one of Gary's ex-girlfriends. Breskin said hello and asked if she minded being interviewed for the story as well. She said she didn't, but asked to be called "Baker" in the article, which Breskin agreed to.

"So, tell me about the beginning of the Knights of the Black Circle," Breskin said as he sat down in the shade.

"There's a lot I *can't* tell you," Paul replied. "We have jackets with colors on the back, so we look like a gang, but we're not. It's a group of people who have a belief in a certain thing, but I can't tell you about it. It's a secret. I can tell you one thing, though—we did *not* do sacrifices. We never hurt nobody at all."

"What about Ricky and Jimmy?" Breskin asked.

"Troiano and Kasso were *never* in the Knights," Paul replied. "One guy in the Knights knew Kasso a long time ago when he was straight, but dropped him when he started getting fucked up. The papers are saying Kasso was the leader of the Knights. That's *bullshit*!"

"But Ricky wanted to be in the group, didn't he?" Breskin pressed. "I heard that he was sort of a fringe member, but the group didn't take him."

"He never asked," Paul insisted. "I met the guy *two times* for a total of seven minutes altogether, and he was already really fucked up."

"I knew him before he was doing dust and all that," Chrissy said. "He really wasn't that bad of a guy, you know?"

"He wasn't," Paul agreed, "but he fucked up."

"When the dust started coming into town and everybody started doing it," Chrissy continued, "he and Vinny Ivy and those guys used to go down to the graveyard and hang out. All Vinny Ivy talked about was the devil. They'd bring a tape recorder along with them and tape themselves tripping on acid and mesc. They said the devil possessed the tape and that there were all these different voices and stuff on the tape. Vinny Ivy said he went to a priest about it and the priest said everything could have been true."

"Have you ever tried dust?" Breskin asked.

"Once," Chrissy replied. "You're not the same person when you try it. You feel like somebody's standing next to you. Maybe when Ricky was on dust, the person standing next to him was the devil."

"What's the difference between what you're involved in and what *they* were involved in?" Breskin asked.

"We're not out to hurt anybody," Chrissy insisted. "We're just out to have a good time and party with our friends."

"You can hang out with friends and not call yourselves anything," Breskin said, challenging the innocence of her explanation. "Why the name?"

"It makes us more united," Paul said. "We're like a family. We don't have families, so we have to stick together."

"Do you have a mom and a dad?" Breskin asked.

"I have my mom," Paul replied.

"And you don't think of *her* as your family?" Breskin prodded.

"Well, yeah, of course," Paul said. "She's my mom, but she's always at work. I never see her no more."

"You have any brothers or sisters?" Breskin asked.

"Brothers," Paul replied curtly.

"So, you have *something* of a family," Breskin said.

"That ain't no family," Paul replied dismissively. "Nobody talks to nobody."

"Who's left in the group?" Breskin asked. "Who are the other guys?"

"They're all lords," Paul replied. "I'm the King. There's Lord Merlin. Lord Algol. If you read up, Algol is a star in the sky. It's called the 'Demon Star.' It's a big giant star with two small stars around it. When the small ones meet, the big one turns black and you can't see it, so that's why they call it the Demon Star. We got Lord Nigel and Lord Sigil. That name came out of a book."

"What sort of books did you read?" Breskin asked.

"If you want to read a good book, read *Life Forces* by Louis Stewart," Paul said. "It talks about yoga, meditation, white magic, black magic—anything you want to know. Good book."

"Would you describe what you do as 'devil worship'?" Breskin asked.

"Not what people consider," Paul replied cryptically.

"Well, why don't you tell me what it *really* is, though?" Breskin said, becoming frustrated. "You see, I keep trying to find out what it really is as opposed to all the bullshit that's in the papers, and no one wants to tell me."

"The image that's going around is that we sacrifice animals, and now *humans*," Paul replied. "That's bullshit. Like I said, we have our own beliefs. This is our religion and *nobody's* going to stop us. We don't harm nobody, so they have no right to stop us."

"Someone told me your group fucked around with cats," Breskin said.

Paul and Chrissy laughed.

"Merlin never liked cats," Chrissy replied. "He would chase 'em and stuff to scare the shit out of 'em."

"I never hurt a cat," Paul insisted. "I love cats. Not as much as dogs, though. I love dogs."

"Yeah, I'm a dog person, myself," Breskin said.

Paul suddenly lit up.

"Oh!" He said. "Do you like Labrador retrievers?"

"Yeah, I love those," Breskin replied. "My brother has one."

Paul smiled. If there was anything he truly loved in the world, it was his black Labrador retriever.

"Do you believe in an afterlife?" Breskin asked, curious to see if the Knights' leader held any belief in the supernatural.

"I think whatever you truly believe is going to happen when you die is what's going to happen to you," Paul replied.

"What do you think it's going to be for you?" Breskin asked.

"For me," Paul replied, "it's gonna be like this really classic *Playboy* cartoon from 1966 that had a group of people sitting around a pool. Girls and guys are drinking, and there's a guy sittin' there dressed up in a tuxedo—has the horns on and all, like a devil—and he's saying, 'You didn't actually think hell would be *that* bad, did ya?' Something close to that."

"So, that's what you think it's going to be when you die?" Breskin asked, surprised by the corniness of Paul's response.

"No," Paul said with a laugh. "I like that cartoon, though."

Breskin sensed he was being messed with, but forged on.

"Why was Ricky the way he was?" he asked. "What was he looking for that he didn't find? I mean, everyone's looking for *something*."

"Maybe he found it," Paul replied nonchalantly.

"What I heard is he wanted to be the devil's right-hand man," Chrissy added. "I heard he was going to chase Gary's soul. He said he would kill himself in jail. Everybody knew that. Some God-loving person probably would have killed him in jail, so he probably just figured he would kill himself so that he could go to Hell and be with the devil."

"King, what are some of the most important songs to the Knights?" Breskin asked. So much noise had been made in the press about rock music's role in Gary's murder, and Breskin wanted to know what the Knights actually listened to.

"One of my favorite songs is 'Time Has Come Today' by the Chambers Brothers," Paul replied, surprising Breskin. "I was listening to that today. Also, 'Earache My Eye' by Cheech & Chong."

Another strange surprise. Breskin was expecting heavy metal. Instead he got a psychedelic soul single from the mid-sixties and a stoner comedy record.

"We're just out to have fun, you know?" Chrissy insisted. "We're not really concerned with what people say about us, we just want to set the record straight so that nobody starts coming after us."

"Maybe one night you should come see what we do," Paul teased.

"I'd *like* to see what you do!" Breskin said, losing his cool. He was tired of games. These kids were being blamed for an incredibly gruesome murder on the front page of nearly every national newspaper, and it all seemed to be some big joke to them. "I've been asking, but you won't tell me what you do!"

"I told you," Paul said calmly. "We just mainly hang out and have a good time any way we can."

"It's really been hard to have a good time this last week or so, though," Chrissy added.

"I'm sure," Breskin said, defeated. He knew he wasn't getting the definitive answers he had hoped for. "Well, is that it?" he asked.

"I guess so," Chrissy replied.

"Is that it, *King*?" Breskin asked.

Paul nodded and walked away with Chrissy in tow.

Chapter 46

ANY FRUSTRATION DAVID BRESKIN WAS FEELING over the interview with Paul McBride evaporated when a Northport teen gave him the phone number of Rich Barton, the fourteen-year-old boy who had been taken to see Gary's remains and later sheltered Ricky before his arrest.

Breskin figured if he could get closer to Ricky's inner circle, it might lead to understanding the terrible deeds the Acid King had committed. None of the explanations offered seemed to hold much weight. The Satan angle was superficial and corny, mostly being pushed by overzealous cops and unscrupulous journalists. Blaming it on drugs alone was just as infantile. There were millions of drug addicts in America, and as far as he knew, none of them were sacrificing their friends in the woods. There had to be some ugly truth lurking below the surface of this crime, and maybe Rich Barton could reveal what it was.

Breskin called the Barton house and asked Rich if he was willing to talk, and the boy cautiously agreed—but only after receiving permission from his mother. When Breskin arrived later that day, Rich invited him into his kitchen to talk.

"The cops told me not to say anything about what happened," he said sheepishly as Breskin switched on his tape recorder.

"Don't be nervous," Breskin told him. "I'm nothing to be nervous over. There's no legal reason for you not to say anything. All the things you've told them, they went and told the press anyway. So, how long did you know Ricky?"

"About a year," Rich replied.

"I know you weren't there when Gary was killed," Breskin said, "but were you at the park?"

"I was down at the park that night," Rich replied. "I went up to Aztakea three hours earlier with Rick and Jim. We tried to make a fire, but we couldn't. It was wet. And then we tried to get out of the woods, but we couldn't 'cause we were all fucked up on mesc. They took ten hits. I only took one. I guess when you take mesc, your eyes go bad, or somethin'. We had the tunes cranking—Sabbath, Ozzy, Judas Priest. When we finally got out around nine thirty, I said, 'Fuck it, I'm going home to trip out by myself.' They went back downtown."

Suddenly the doorbell rang. Rich got up to open the door and found Lion waiting outside.

"How's it goin', Rich?" Lion asked.

Rich shrugged and led Lion into the kitchen, where Breskin was waiting.

"So, I know there was a bunch of kids down in the park," Breskin continued without missing a beat, "and a group of them went to Randy Guethler's party."

"Yeah," Lion said. "That was me, Glen Wolf, Liz Testerman, Marlene, Mike McGrory, and I don't know who else. Randy had a case of beer in there 'cause it was his birthday. We were out till, like, four or five o'clock in the morning. After the party got beat, we all left and sat down by the water."

"So, when was the first time Ricky said something to you that didn't sound kosher?" Breskin asked Rich.

The boy replied in detail about the horrific afternoon where Ricky brought him to see Gary's body rotting in the woods.

"I didn't tell anybody," he said, "but I couldn't escape it. It came up every two minutes. I wasn't gonna tell the cops. I thought Ricky was gonna kill *me*."

"You kept this all to yourself for *two weeks*?" Breskin asked. "You must have been a *wreck*! Was it hard to sleep?"

"I had bad dreams about going up there at night," Rich replied. "We were hanging out in Aztakea, getting wasted, and all of a sudden, someone pops up, grabs me, and drags me into the woods. It was Gary, and his face was all mangled and stuff. He took me into the woods, and I woke up. I had another one where I was sleeping in my room, and Gary came through my door and killed me with a knife. I was sitting there with my mouth wide open, saying, '*Holy shit!*' He just comes in and stabs me. Doesn't say nothing. I died right away."

"How did you try and escape all of this in your mind?" Breskin asked. "If you thought about it all day, you'd go crazy."

"I couldn't escape it," Rich replied. "I tried to just do something else."

"After I found out, Rich and I went to Adventureland," Lion said. "We did things to block it out."

The doorbell rang again.

This time Rich returned with Albert Quinones and Mark Florimonte.

Breskin did his best to appear calm. He had been in Northport for nearly a week trying to find out what had really happened that fateful night in Aztakea, and now the only free witness to the crime—that he knew of, at least—had just walked through the door. In an even stranger turn of events, Breskin hadn't even been aware of Albert's existence until the day before. The police had made serious efforts to prevent the press from knowing about their witness, but this was all undermined by Eric Naiburg.

Jimmy's lawyer had quickly discovered there was another person in the woods that night—and that he had been secretly offered immunity by the prosecution. A sharp litigator, Naiburg used this to his advantage by revealing Albert's name and involvement to several reporters. As far as he was concerned, if the public knew there were other people present at the murder aside from Jimmy, it might take the heat off his client.

Good news for Naiburg; horrible for Albert.

Now the world knew he had watched Ricky Kasso kill Gary Lauwers—and had done nothing to stop it. Albert knew some of Gary's friends would be out for blood. Not Breskin, though. He was looking for answers, not vengeance. With Albert Quinones now standing in front of him, Breskin hoped this would be the moment where he finally learned the truth.

"I'm not gonna harass you or anything like that," Breskin gently told Albert. "I'm just trying to put all the pieces together."

"Everyone's getting all these different rumors, man," Albert replied. "It's making me look worse."

"What did Jimmy do to make him as responsible as Ricky?" Breskin asked Albert, trying to take the focus off him.

"The cops are saying Jimmy held Gary down while Ricky stabbed him," Albert replied. "But that never happened. He kicked him. It was a *fight*, man. No one knew what was going to happen. If I knew they were gonna do it, man, I would have let Gary know and I would have talked to Ricky and Jimmy to try to avoid it, man. It bugs me out, man. Gary already paid him his money back. Everyone was his friend. I mean, Ricky and Gary were both talking a lot, shit like that. The thing that bugs me out, man, is all of them were pushing me, especially Gary and Ricky, to take a hit of mescaline. They were all tripping. I didn't want to, but finally, I just said, 'What the hell,' so I took a hit."

"Was that one of your first times using mesc?" Breskin asked.

"I've done it a couple times," Albert replied. "It's not an *every-week* thing. It was a trip, man. Ricky treated us to donuts at Dunkin' Donuts. To me, Gary was being cool and shit. And then we went up to Aztakea around midnight, because they wanted to go to a good tripping area, and they've got a little field where you can trip out. See, Ricky was getting pissed off, because he couldn't start a fire, so Gary just takes off his socks, puts them in there. After Gary made a fire with his socks, they wanted to make it bigger. And Ricky comes out with a remark, 'Why don't you just burn your whole jacket?' The guy's like, 'How 'bout I just cut the sleeves off and use my sleeves?' It was fucked, man. So he took off his jacket and just chopped off the sleeves. I guess he was going to make it into a vest."

Breskin sat silently, knowing where the story was heading next.

"All of a sudden Gary goes, 'I have funny vibes that you're going to kill me,'" Albert continued. "Ricky was saying, 'I'm not going to kill you. Are you crazy?' and shit like that. I was just tripping out, man. I was peaking. They were just fighting. Punching each other and shit, and I didn't think anything was going to happen. I mean, I could see Ricky's point too, which is that he was friends with Gary, and he just turns around and steals ten bags of dust. So, they were just rolling on the ground and shit, and Gary got up to his feet after Jimmy ran up to him and kicked him in the ribs and shit, and Gary had gotten up to his feet, and Ricky just bit him in the neck, bit him in the ear, and then he just stabbed him. It was a *trip*, man; I can tell you that. If you've ever tried mescaline, it's a trip. You hallucinate, man. You sit there and stare out, and you look at the trees, and it looks like they're bending down and shit."

"We were on the Long Island Expressway the other day," Mark added, "stuck with a flat tire for four hours, tripping on mesc. I looked out from the windshield at these clouds, white clouds, all of them in a circle, and one big one in the middle. They were like drifting and coming closer, and they were like skeleton things. They weren't like a regular skeleton—they were all distorted. But you could see the eyes, the nose, and the mouth, like a regular skeleton."

"It was like a nightmare," Albert said. "I couldn't move, man. My whole body, all of a sudden, it just wouldn't move, it wouldn't function. It was like in shock. I was going crazy, man. I just stood there in my place, like all bugged out. I didn't know what to do."

"So, how did Jimmy help out?" Breskin asked. "He said, 'Get him!' right?"

"I don't know if he said that or not," Albert replied.

"Ricky told me Jimmy said that," Mark added. "So did Jimmy."

"It all went so quick," Albert insisted. "After Ricky stabbed him, Gary took off and ran about twenty feet, and Ricky got him, just like that. Jimmy picked up the knife after Ricky had dropped it, and he gave it to Ricky. And Ricky made Gary get on his knees and say, 'I love Satan.' Then Ricky just started hacking away at him, man. He just kept stabbing him and shit, and then Gary was just screaming, *'Ahhh! I love my mother!'* It was really fucked, man. Ricky and Jimmy grabbed him by the legs and dragged him into the woods. They came running out of the woods after they just threw leaves on him and shit. They told me that Gary sat up and Ricky started stabbing Gary in the face and shit. I didn't know what to think, 'cause no one's normal enough to do that. If you do that, man, you gotta have lost it, you know? I'd think about going to the cops, but I thought they'd try to frame me, man. They'd set me up."

"Were you afraid Ricky and Jimmy were going to do something to you?" Breskin asked.

"Yeah," Albert replied. "I wasn't going to rat them out, because what's, like, another body? Man, it's no big deal. I mean, you see them kill once, you just don't think they're not going to kill you. For those three weeks when I didn't know what to do, I was going crazy. I was afraid. I tried to avoid them, and all they did was tag. They're very persistent. They would laugh about it and shit. They told so many people. They would just make jokes. 'Oh, Gary's dead, no big deal. Let's go get another one.' They'd say, 'Let's go up there and watch him rot.' It was really fucked up, man. It really bugged my head out. I wanted them to get caught and I'm glad they got caught because they told so many people. They were crazy, man."

"See, that day, July fourth, they were searching for the body," Mark added, "and they found it. So, they wanted to find out who knew about it. They knew Albert hung with Ricky and him, so they grabbed Albert first. And they tried to find out, and Albert wouldn't tell them anything, so that's why when Albert came home, his lip was all cut, he had bruised ribs and a big bump on his head. They wanted to know the truth."

"The detectives were beating the shit out of me," Albert said. "They brought me up to this room, and they started questioning me and shit, and they were beating the shit out of me. They didn't tell me they were going for Ricky and Jim. The next day they said they were gonna let me go, 'cause Jimmy was coming in. He looked like he got away with it and shit—he was playing it cool. I told them everything. Maybe Jimmy was probably thinking that I wasn't gonna rat him out. I don't know what to think. My head's screwed up ever since that night—and it's still screwed up, man."

"Do you have nightmares about it?" Breskin asked.

"Yeah," Albert replied. "I was trying to forget about it, man, and I couldn't. I couldn't sleep. I had some really wicked nightmares, man. I had nightmares that I killed *Mark*. I just started stabbing him in the back of the head. And then a cop came in and scooped him up with this little pick or something and threw him in the garbage. It was so weird, man. It scared the hell out of me."

"I went up there with Rich," Mark said. "The really gross part was smelling it like four blocks away. It smelled like a swamp after a thousand years, something just decaying for a thousand years. Really gross, like something you leave in the corner of a house and it just starts decaying, and decaying, and decaying, and there's maggots."

"Albert, have your parents been able to get you someone to talk to about all this stuff?" Breskin asked.

"My mom wants to send me somewhere," he replied. "She sent me to talk to Father Colgan. I talked to him about it. He seemed like he didn't care about me, man. He was more worried about *Rich* than me!"

"He didn't even really say anything," Rich added. "He talked about how his brothers got killed in World War II. That's *all* he talked about."

"Sometimes, I get scared to go in my room," Albert continued, "because when I was friends with him, Ricky used to stay in my room. It was like, every time it would hit after twelve, I'd start bugging out."

"It'll be nice when things get back to normal, huh?" Breskin asked, trying to remain optimistic for the boys.

"It's never turning back to normal," Mark said sadly, lowering his head.

Rich took a sip of his lemonade. "It'll take a while. . . ."

After the interview, Breskin quickly drove back to his rented room in Centerport, rewound the tape, pulled out his notebook, and began hastily transcribing the recording. By complete accident, he had gotten the scoop so many other professional reporters and journalists had tried and failed to secure, and he was not going to take any chances with the revelations he had recorded. If something happened to the tape, he had the notebook; if something happened to the notebook, he had the tape.

Nothing was going to get in the way of finishing the story.

Chapter 47

AT SEVEN P.M. ON SUNDAY, JULY 15, 1984, NEARLY 150 residents of Suffolk County crowded into the St. Paul's United Methodist Church on Main Street in Northport to discuss how to move forward from the tragedy as a community. The meeting was the result of several concerned citizens working together with the Place, the YDA, the village police department, and the local clergy to provide a safe and constructive environment for the residents of Northport to air their grievances, voice their collective support for one another, and offer solutions to the worst tragedy to which they had ever borne witness.

In addition to the shocked villagers, a fair number of reporters showed up as well. Breskin found a pew in the rear of the church, trying not to draw attention to himself. Once everyone was seated, Reverend Bob McDonald stood and addressed the crowd.

"I've asked the television cameras not to be here," McDonald said, hoping this would encourage everyone to speak honestly. "I don't see this as a time for people to be making speeches; I see this as a time for people to be listening to each other. One of the least helpful things we can do is try to place blame for what has happened."

Northport Village Police Chief Robert Howard spoke next and almost immediately went on the defense.

"We, as the police department, have to take care of the mess that society produces," he maintained. "Lots of people ask us why we don't get rid of the people in the park, but we have to abide by the law. We don't have the right to do it as a police department. We have to honor the Constitution of the United States and not violate people's rights. Parents don't want to be contacted by us. Parents don't believe us, or they sue us. I'm very leery of parents."

Sybil Nestor, a forty-five-year-old Northport resident, agreed. "There's a tremendous lack of communication between children, parents, and the police department," Nestor charged. "You all don't back the police department. They are working for us and their hands are tied. I've seen thirteen-, fourteen-, fifteen-year-olds—boys *and* girls—out there in the park at two or three in the morning. I don't know where their parents are."

Mimi Kail, president of the Northport Village Residents Association, echoed Nestor's sentiment by suggesting a curfew in the New Park and a town-wide boycott of the Midway. Chief Howard rose to remind Kail that an eleven p.m. curfew was already in place at the park, but that his department could do little to enforce it thanks to Huntington's regulations.

Anthony Zenkus spoke up against the curfew entirely.

"Controlling youth is *not* a solution," he told the gathering. "We're not going to solve problems by *hiding* them."

Dennis McBee agreed.

"This is a problem of the whole community," he said, "not a 'youth problem.'"

Glen Wolf joined his friends from the YDA in decrying the perceived discrimination against teenagers in town.

"I'm an adult who hasn't grown up yet—a *lowlife* from Northport Park," Wolf said, confidently working the crowd, who laughed at his biting honesty. "The police are downtown hasslin' people over beer while their houses are being *robbed*. If we run people out of the park, they'll go somewhere else. Clearing partiers out of the park would put them in the woods, and *who knows* what would happen there. The root of the problem is angel dust, and the people who supply it are adults who do it for money. I smoke pot, drink, and listen to heavy metal, but I'm no dusthead, Satanist, or *murderer*."

Fifteen-year-old Michelle DeVeau—one of Gary's former flames—also spoke, giving a voice to the teens in attendance who were too cautious or embarrassed to reveal their drug habits and psychological issues.

"I started using drugs when I was ten," she said. "A lot of kids can't talk to their parents. A lot of kids don't have anybody to talk to, and so they just turn to drugs."

Breskin made note of Michelle in his pad. Her honesty and bravery stood out, and he wanted to interview her for his upcoming article.

"I don't think the youth can say, 'Get the guy who sells the angel dust and I won't use it' no more than the drunk can say 'Close the bar and I won't get drunk,'" Richard Manning, a local father of nine, told the audience. "If this meeting serves any purpose for me, I think I should leave, not with a finger pointed, but with a finger *hooked*. Let's not kid ourselves: it's our fault—*all* of us. Let's see what the heck we can do. I think, by and large, the problems exist because of attitudes in the home. You can't drink a case of beer on the weekend and then break your kid's head because he had a can when he went to the beach."

Manning's indictment of hypocrisy drew a considerable amount of applause. However, one father, twenty-eight-year-old Bob Harrison, dismissed Manning's theory. A devoutly religious man, Harrison felt there were much more sinister forces at work.

"I just want to talk about some of the influences," Harrison said. "Parents really need to listen to what their children are listening to. Some of these songs use a technique called 'backmasking.' What they do is put a message backward in the song. You know that song 'Hotel California'? Look at that album. The leader of the Satanic Church is on the cover of that album. If you look at other songs, like Led Zeppelin's 'Stairway to Heaven,' they actually have a backmask technique in that song talking about the power of Satan. That's what your children have been listening to all this time, and hidden messages can translate into action.

'Another One Bites the Dust' by Queen? If you play that backward, it says, 'It's fun to smoke marijuana.' Now, I'm a born-again Christian, and I don't know where you all come from religiously, but those things really *hurt* me. These songs urge rebellion against authority. They're trying to rip our children away from us. They're attacking our nation. Just know who you're letting into your home by letting them listen to this music."

To Breskin's surprise, a large portion of the audience actually stood to applaud, despite Harrison's accusations being completely baseless. While some fringe fundamentalist Christian groups had recently accused popular rock acts of sneaking odes to the devil into their recordings, few in the secular world actually took the idea seriously. Ricky Kasso may have played a few records backward in a half-baked attempt to hear Satan's voice, but these hijinks weren't any more responsible for Gary's murder than horror movies on TV or cheesy paperbacks from the library.

Sensational allegations aside, one person sitting in a pew that night, Betty Koerner, had tired of the squabbles about drugs, Satan, and bad parenting. She knew what these vague concepts were code words for—*Ricky*. The troubled son of Koerner's friend and next-door neighbor was dead, and now her community was looking for someone to blame. When Koerner heard all these people getting up on the pulpit to denounce "bad parenting," she knew who they were really attacking—Dick and Lynn Kasso. Having remained the couple's friend for nearly two decades, Koerner decided it was high time someone stepped in to defend *them*.

"This is a family that doesn't know if they have a home to

come back to," Koerner told the crowd. "We have to make them feel they have a home."

Koerner then read from a letter Lynn Kasso had sent, thanking her for tending to her plants and making sure the lawn was mowed. Breskin could see Mrs. Koerner was largely alone in her attempt at humanizing the Kassos. He jotted down her name in his notebook, alongside Michelle DeVeau and Tony Ruggi, who also spoke that night.

The two-hour meeting may not have solved all of Northport's problems in one go, but it gave Breskin enough names to continue his research, and he was glad for it. The *Daily News* and the *Post* would eventually abandon the village in search of some other tragedy to exploit, but Breskin would remain.

Chapter 48

"SO, WHAT WAS THE PLACE FORMED IN REACTION TO?" Breskin asked as he sat down across from Tony Ruggi. He had heard the counselor speak at the Methodist Church meeting and convinced him to go on record for the story.

"About fifteen or sixteen years ago, there was a fatal car accident involving some young people," Ruggi replied. "The investigation revealed that the kids were involved with drugs. Up until that time, the community was very unaware of drug use in the area. The typical response was that drug use was something that took place in the ghettos of the city—that it was something *lower-class* people were involved in. Needless to say, the community had to react in some way, and the agency was formed. We've been here for about fifteen years."

"I'm a big believer in multicausality," Breskin said. "I don't believe in pinning this solely on devil worship, or drugs, or any one thing, but would it be fair to assume that the kids involved in this murder, along with the kids who saw the body and didn't say anything, are heavily involved in drug use?"

"That's a fair assumption to make," Ruggi admitted.

"Did you have contact with those kids?" Breskin asked. "There's that old saying; 'You can't help someone who doesn't want to help themselves.' No truer words have ever been spoken. Nonetheless, Ricky Kasso didn't really seem to want to help himself much, from what other people have told me."

Ruggi sighed. He knew this wasn't true in Ricky's case. He had spent the past two years watching Ricky walk through the front door, trying to get his life together. While he had indeed failed miserably, taking an innocent life along with his own, Ruggi didn't believe Ricky's desperate attempts to stabilize his existence should be erased from history either.

"This is a tough area," Ruggi said, feeling the burden of what he knew.

"Remember, Kasso is not on trial here," Breskin offered.

"Yeah . . . ," Ruggi replied, lost in thought.

He hadn't originally intended to reveal his association with Ricky, but he was now having second thoughts. Who else was going to stand up for the kid? Certainly not the *Daily News* or the *Post*, who had quickly turned him into the world's most famous "Satan killer" with nearly two weeks of sensational front-page coverage. What Ricky had done to Gary was inexcusable, but Ruggi also felt the public shouldn't judge him based solely on the final month of his short life. They needed to see the whole picture.

"I knew Ricky," Ruggi finally said. "I knew Ricky fairly well, in fact. I met him when he first ended up on the street. He was typical—very confused. A lot of almost *incoherent* thoughts because of the drug use. He used to come down here in the evenings for coffee and we would talk. He was interested in music. I'd work a little guitar with him and show him some chords. He always seemed to be reaching out, but he had a basic concept that he would be dead by the time he was twenty, so he just wanted to have fun."

"Where did that concept come from?" Breskin asked. "Jim Morrison?"

"It didn't even go *that* far," Ruggi replied. "All I can say is, there were things that he felt were bad and wrong in his life, whether they were real or imaginary."

Breskin sensed the "specifics" Ruggi were avoiding were related to Ricky's parents.

"The kids I've spoken to feel like Ricky was thrown away by his family," Breskin said.

"I really don't want to say anything against the family," Ruggi replied cautiously, "but all I can say is Ricky *did* feel that way. He was very confused and was medicating himself with drugs. He was hurting a lot and the drugs were making him feel *good*. He knew the dangers of drugs. He was not a *dumb* kid. He was a very bright kid. He would say, 'I know the drugs are bad for me, but they make me feel good. I'm not going to live past twenty anyway, so I'm just going to enjoy myself.'"

"Did he *want* to live past twenty?" Breskin asked.

"No," Ruggi replied flatly. "He didn't want to because he had nothing to look forward to. He had *nothing*. He had no job, no education, no family, no *anything*, so what's the use of living? The only thing he might have had was the drugs. But last winter, there was a sudden change. He stopped doing hallucinogens. He decided he wanted to make contact with his family, go to school, and get a job. It seemed to come out of almost nowhere. He went back to his family and conformed to their rules. He cut his hair. He changed the clothes he was wearing. So, for a kid on the street, that *is* making an effort. We were very hopeful. We liked this kid. Then, something went *wrong*. Something *happened*. I mean, I've heard there were problems with the family. I heard there was a big fight over something in school. The next thing I know, he's back out on the street again. From that point on, he went downhill extremely fast. The next I heard about him was when I heard on the radio that he and Randy Guethler had been picked up for grave robbing. I remember thinking, 'This kid is really losing it now.'"

"Was he committed to the idea that he was a representative of the devil?" Breskin asked, trying to gain some further insight into the occult aspects of Gary's murder.

"We talked about the devil on occasion," Ruggi replied. "Ricky got a lot of that from library books. He got his list of the dignitaries in Hell out of a library book. He went looking for things. I think what appealed to Ricky was the idea of a loser fighting back against the establishment. He would talk about it and sometimes he would laugh about it."

Breskin remained perplexed. So many, it seemed, had seen

the writing on the wall for Ricky, yet no one made any sort of real effort to help him. Sure, hindsight is always twenty-twenty, but *grave robbing*? Public displays of Satan worship? These were not your average suburban problems.

"Did anyone say to him, 'Damn, Ricky, you really had it together there for a while—what's the story?'" he asked.

Tony nodded.

"His response was, 'It's no use. I just can't win,'" Ruggi replied. "He was defeated, at that point. I think that's why he went downhill so fast. . . ."

Once Breskin was finished interviewing Tony Ruggi, he hopped back into his rental car and drove over to Seaview Avenue for his next appointment. Parking only a few doors down from the Kasso home, Breskin was there to interview Betty Koerner. He walked up the driveway and was shown inside the two-story cedar shake home by the petite housewife.

"So, why do you think the Kassos didn't come back?" Breskin asked as he sat down with Betty and her daughter, Selina, in their living room. "Their son had just been charged with *murder*. To me, it sounded like they had tried and tried and tried to help him out and then disowned him."

"I think it was the shock of the grave-digging arrest," Koerner replied. "They had three girls up there to deal with and get emotionally set. I think they had to get adjusted to it."

"Do you think there was a great deal of guilt for not coming down and then, the next thing they knew, Ricky was dead?"

"She didn't *say* that," Koerner replied, "but I think that's only natural."

"I think there was a lot of guilt," Selina offered. "The newspapers made a point of saying Troiano's parents were at the arraignment but the Kassos weren't, and I remember Lynn saying she thought that was out of line. She didn't really say why she didn't go to the arraignment, but one of the things she *did* say was, 'This was just one more thing Ricky did. This had been going on for so long that this was the final act.' He had been cutting himself off emotionally from them for years, so it wasn't as if a normal son or daughter had done this. I think they didn't go because they just didn't want to deal with him."

"I would say things like, 'Lynn, there's always hope,'" Koerner continued, "and she'd say, 'Oh, he's so far gone. His mind is gone.' I'd say, 'Well, as long as there's life, there's hope,' and she'd say, 'Maybe so.' He came home before the holidays and he was very sick with pneumonia. He was so thin. They got him help and medication, and he was fine. The same thing happened in the spring. Lynn was annoyed at him because he never came back for his prescription. I kept reminding her, 'This is not the son you raised. Don't feel responsible for this. Some evil thing has taken over his body.' He just got thinner and thinner and looked so sunken. You have to wonder if the drugs didn't get him first, would his health have?"

"Did they feel he had a chemical imbalance?" Breskin asked.

"No," Koerner replied. "She never suggested that to me. She felt his mind was gone."

"Yeah, but you know how some people think they are born alcoholics?" Selina said, trying to better explain Breskin's point.

"No, she never said anything like that," Koerner replied. "She just felt he was gone on drugs. Kelly and Jody were disgusted and ashamed. The family is *not that way*. They're not drinkers. They're good people."

"I've heard rumors that Ricky was cremated because Dick and Lynn couldn't find a funeral home that would take him," Breskin said.

The rumors were unfounded. The Brueggemann Funeral Home took care of Ricky's final arrangements with zero fuss, as they had provided their services for the Kassos in the past. However, with Dick and Lynn refusing to grant any further interviews, no one outside the family knew this.

"That is *sick*!" Koerner gasped. "She did not say that to me, but if it's true, that's sickening! If there was going to be a service, I wanted to go in support because I felt there probably wouldn't be flowers because of the way the media played up all this cult nonsense about this *terrible murderer* who had killed this *Ivy League kid*! The newspapers used Gary's eighth grade picture where he looked like a Harvard graduate. The media played it up like Ricky was some wicked, vicious *animal* and that's why these terrible threats have come upon the family! Gary was a bad kid too, no better than Ricky! They were all into *bad* stuff!"

"What kinds of threats?" Breskin asked.

"For the past three summers," Koerner replied, "Dick and Lynn have rented out their home to a nice elderly couple with no children. The threats they got were just horrifying. People called up in the middle of the night and said, *'Murderer! Killer! We're gonna cut your balls off! We're gonna kill your wife, cut out the eyes out of all of your daughters, and burn your house down!'* They finally decided to move out a few days ago."

"I was told Mr. Kasso told the renters that he didn't have a son when they asked about his family," Breskin replied.

Koerner understood the origin of that rumor.

"When I spoke to that man," she replied, "he said he had seen a picture of Ricky in the house but didn't ask any questions because he didn't know if he was dead or not. He said this was the first he had heard of their son."

"Some people think the Kassos are a good and decent family," Breskin said, "but I've also heard from a *lot* of kids that Mr. and Mrs. Kasso didn't give a damn for Ricky and had disposed of him. They had tried and tried, and then they gave up."

Breskin understood that Lynn and Mrs. Koerner were good friends, but at some point, she had to at least acknowledge some sort of truth lying at the root of these rumors. Koerner, however, didn't waver in her loyalty to Dick and Lynn.

"No, they did *not* give up," she firmly insisted.

"I'm just saying what I've heard," Breskin countered. "I'm putting as many pieces together as I can. . . ."

Chapter 49

CHIEF ROBERT HOWARD REACHED INTO THE PLASTIC cooler sitting outside in his backyard and pulled out a can of soda, turning his eye toward David Breskin.

"You want a drink?" he asked.

"No, I'm fine," Breskin replied as he parked himself in one of Howard's folding lawn chairs.

Howard, still on vacation, looked more like someone's laid-back uncle than a seasoned police chief.

"What's your experience been with drugs in this town?" Breskin asked.

"We average about two hundred and fifty to three hundred arrests a year in this department," Howard replied, setting his drink down beside him. "One year in the late sixties, we had seventy arrests for marijuana possession. Last year, we had *one*."

"The kids tell me if a cop sees them in the park smoking a

joint," Breskin said, "they look the other way and the kids look the other way. It's just understood."

"They're not *supposed* to look the other way," Howard replied with dismay. "But if we bring someone in on a simple marijuana possession charge, the courts automatically dismiss it. Even if you make an arrest, you have to release without bail. You could compare it to a traffic ticket. It's sort of a waste of time and paperwork. The police enforce what society wants us to enforce. We get the message. This isn't unique to Northport Village. The press has been pushing that we have Satanic worshippers, drug use in the park, and that the police do nothing about it."

"Yeah, well, the 'Satanic worshippers' quotes come straight from the Four Musketeers—Dunn, Henry, Keahon, and Gallagher," Breskin countered. "I've not only seen the quotes in the *Post* and the *Daily News* but also in the *New York Times*."

"Dear *God*, I hope they've been misquoted," Howard sighed.

Breskin reached into his bag and grabbed a newspaper.

"Here," Breskin said, opening the paper to read aloud. "It says, 'The cult, according to Assistant DA Bill Keahon of Suffolk County, is known as the Knights of the Black Circle. It has about twenty teenage members and held gatherings for several years in the Northport area involving the sacrifice of animals.'"

"If Keahon said that, he is *certainly* misinformed," Howard scoffed. "I think I know Northport Village and what goes on here a little better than *he* does. I'm sure he probably might not have even known where Northport was prior to this case."

"He does now," Breskin laughed.

"Yeah," Howard chuckled. "I don't know where he's getting his information from. It isn't from us. Even if there *were* devil worshippers, as long as they're not violating any criminal statutes, there's nothing wrong with what they're doing from a police perspective. It's freedom of religion."

"Do the Suffolk County people shoot their mouths off on an average murder case as much as they did with this one?" Breskin asked.

"I can't answer that," Howard replied, nervously laughing. "What you gotta understand here is we work with the county very closely. After you leave, we'll still have to work with them. However, if I had known it would get this out of hand, I would have answered 'no comment' to every question from the start. It just got too carried away. As a small-town police department, we're not used to walking into the office and seeing fifteen TV crews in there. Usually, we have our coffee and say, 'Oh, what happened last night?' and go through the reports."

"'So-and-so's garbage can got run over . . . ,'" Breskin offered.

"Right!" Howard said. "The normal things on the blotter. Maybe a stolen car here or a burglary there."

"So, take me back to the beginning," Breskin said. "How did you first hear about this murder?"

"I got the call on Monday morning, July 2, from my lieutenant," Howard replied. "There was a report from a girl that someone had been killed and their body was dumped in the woods."

"A girl?" Breskin asked. "So, it would have been a *peer* of these kids and not a parent? The press reported two different stories about how the police were notified, and I haven't been able to nail down which one is correct."

Howard froze, realizing he had just screwed up. The identity of Jean Wells was supposed to remain secret—and he had just inadvertently given Breskin a big clue.

"I guess one could make that assumption," he replied coyly, trying to cover his tracks. He took a quick sip of his drink and lit a cigarette.

Breskin took the hint.

"We found the grave site on Wednesday," Howard continued. "He was *surprisingly* decomposed. More than we would think for that length of time."

"From what I understand, there really was not much left of Gary," Breskin said.

"No," Howard replied quietly. "Mostly skeletal. It was one of those things where you go, *'Blech!'*"

"I would imagine it was one of the most difficult things to deal with," Breskin said, "even for the hard-core professionals."

"Probably not," Howard replied frankly. "You know what the worst one was? We had a woman dead in her eighty-degree house for two weeks. *That* was the worst one. You take Vaseline, put it up your nose, and try to pretend it's something else. I honestly thought this would only make page five in *Newsday*. When they came and talked to me, they were the ones who put forth the idea of a Satanic cult. Jim O'Neill said to me, 'Isn't this the same guy who was arrested for robbing graves?' They tied it together and

BOOM! That set off all the other papers and TV, and they jumped on it."

"How did you react to Kasso's suicide?" Breskin asked.

"I actually felt sorry for the mother because I know her," Howard replied. "I don't think it was done out of depression. I think it was Richard's final blow to his parents."

"Suicide is the ultimate 'fuck you,'" Breskin concurred. "It's always directed at someone. It's an act of communication."

"And he *did* it," Howard said. "Boy, he really gave it to them. I don't feel sorry for Kasso. I figure he was a waste of life anyway. Somebody said to me, 'This is worse than the Amityville Horror,' and I said, 'Crap!' I hear Jimmy Breslin wants to do a book on this! If it's anything, it's a couple of druggie kids. I also don't think there's any cause and effect with the music. You ever watch those old newsreels when rock 'n' roll came out in the fifties?"

"Yeah, Jerry Lee Lewis was gonna make people kill each other too," Breskin replied sarcastically. "Now, there was a circle of kids who were at least *told* about the murder. How many do you believe knew about it?"

"I'd say a dozen kids had *some* knowledge of it," Howard replied. "I know who you've talked to already."

Breskin was taken aback by this sudden and unexpected revelation.

"How do you know who I've talked to?" he asked, trying to keep his cool.

Howard lit another cigarette and inhaled deeply.

"I know who you've talked to," he repeated.

"Because you've been notified that I've talked to them?" Breskin asked.

Howard remained silent.

"Look, nothing's a secret in this town," Breskin said, visibly frustrated. "I've been here long enough to know *that*."

Howard paused for another moment.

"I'm on vacation, but I check in every day," he finally replied. "I was in yesterday for a couple hours and asked what was going on, and your name was brought up along with who you were speaking with."

"You know, Officer Iannone stopped me on the street the other night," Breskin said. "I was carrying my notebook in my hand. He said, 'Hey you! You with the notebook! I know what you're doing. I'd like your name.' So, I gave him my name."

"You didn't have to," Howard admitted.

"I know I didn't have to," Breskin replied, "but at that point, I figured it was much more important to let the cops know I'm on the level than to get all constitutional about it. He said the reason he took my name was that he wanted to protect me if other people complained—that way, he could say, 'No, we know him. It's okay. Don't worry about it.' What he's *really* gonna do is run a check on my name to make sure that I'm not selling drugs and that I don't have a record. It's funny, though. Believe me, I have long scheduled a haircut, but because of this story, I can't get rid of this mop of hair."

Howard laughed and thought of his wife, Maureen, a professional hairdresser.

"We should get my wife to have you sit in a chair for her!"

"Yeah, I should," Breskin replied, "but I have to keep it long so the kids will trust me."

"Well, the assumption in the department is that you're working for the defense," Howard finally admitted.

"That I'm working for *Naiburg*?"

Breskin was stunned by the absurdity of this idea.

"Could be," Howard laughed. "You just don't know. Cops are paranoid."

"You know," Breskin replied, "one thing I am concerned with is how these kids have been ostracized by their community. There has been no outreach to these kids."

"This was *disastrous*," Howard said. "I wouldn't doubt the Lauwers family is going to move. When I talked to the parents, they had absolutely no idea their kid was involved with this group at all. We went into that house and probably shattered their image of their kid."

"Well, Gary's parents told the papers he didn't ever do drugs," Breskin replied. "Parents disbelieve *too*."

Howard agreed.

"They're the worst ones to get to believe anything!" he said. "It's always, 'Not my son! Not my daughter!' It's always somebody else's kid. 'Go get them out of the park, but leave my kid alone!' The problem is, it's their kids and they don't acknowledge it."

Howard lit yet another cigarette.

"I really feel sorry for my kids because I don't believe 'em," he laughed. "Everything they say is a lie, and that's from dealing with kids for years. It's hard not to think everybody in the world is a scumbag. You can get that way from the constant lawsuits and being dragged into federal court on *crap*. The last time we went to federal court was because we caught a kid in the park with a beer. We got sued for eleven million dollars. Any cop faced with this is going to say, 'Screw that!' If the police don't have to deal with kids in the park, they're not going to."

Chapter 50

"YOU LIKE TO DISCOVER PEOPLE. THAT'S WHAT A Gemini does."

David Breskin sat on the grass inside Northport Village Park, having tarot cards read for him by a teenage girl. Nearby, a local cover band was playing the Temptations' "Just My Imagination" as balloons were inflated, faces were painted, and refreshments were served. It was July 22, 1984, and the third annual YDA Summer Festival, sponsored by the Youth Development Agency of Northport/East Northport, was underway.

"You usually meet people who want to get close to you," the girl continued, as her friend Michelle DeVeau sat down beside her. "But you don't like people getting close to you because as soon as they start knowing everything about you, it frightens you. You don't like people reading through you and that bothers you. That's probably why you wear sunglasses—you don't like people to see your eyes."

"No, it's just very bright," Breskin quipped. "I squint a lot. What about my love life?"

"You and your girlfriend are going to break up," she told Breskin. "This card means the end of a love affair."

"I'm gonna have to tell her that," he chuckled. "She's in Paris right now."

Once the tarot reading ended, Breskin focused on Michelle. He had been hoping to interview her since she'd spoken at St. Paul's a few nights before, and now, sitting in the Old Park as the band began to play Pure Prairie League's "Amie," he would finally have his chance.

"I hear you knew Gary pretty well," Breskin said, turning on his tape recorder.

"Gary and I were really close," Michelle replied. "I knew him for about four or five years. He was a sweet guy. I'd always come down here looking for him because he was fun to be with. I used to call him 'Billy Idol.' I was in love with the guy, you know? I still got one of his hickeys. It won't go away."

Michelle pushed her long brunette hair out of the way to reveal the mark on her neck. Breskin smiled.

"Yeah, I see it," he replied.

"If it ever goes away, I'm going to kill myself," she joked.

Suddenly Michelle remembered Ricky's suicide and thought better of the quip.

"I'm only kidding about that," she assured Breskin.

"Gary got beat up a lot, right?" he asked.

"Yeah," Michelle replied. "He was a skinny little guy—an easy target. Gary was a wimp. He was more into peace than fighting. He fought to get people to like him. Why does anybody fight? He'd bought a knife for protection, but I don't think he carried it around. Gary told me Ricky told him he was gonna kill him, supposedly."

"If Gary thought Ricky was really going to kill him," Breskin said, "why did he go up into the woods with him that night?"

"Gary was gullible," Michelle replied. "He was the kind of guy who would believe anything anybody ever said to him. He was very insecure."

"Did Gary get on okay with his folks?"

"All I know is his mom and dad are really nice people," Michelle replied. "I'd talk to his mom on the phone every once in a while. 'Hello, Mrs. Lauwers. Is Gary there?' And she would say in her accent, 'Oh no, Gary's not here. You know boys, Michelle; they're never home.'"

"They don't think he was involved with drugs, according to the papers," Breskin said.

"Gary's parents were blind to the drugs," Michelle replied. "Like most parents. He did them to be accepted—like most kids. He liked getting stoned, but he didn't like all the other stuff."

"But he *did* steal ten bags of angel dust," Breskin countered.

"That was for money," Michelle insisted. "He told me he smoked some of it, didn't like it that much, and gave it to other people. He'd get stuff and share it with everybody because he wanted to be liked."

"What about Ricky?"

"I couldn't deal with that asshole," Michelle replied, disgusted. "He was a prick. People worship him, which is really sick. I've seen thirteen-year-old girls running around with *Ricky Lives* on their T-shirts."

"What, in Magic Marker or something like that?" Breskin asked.

"No," Michelle replied. "They went to places and got them made. I was gonna kill them. They put around graffiti: *Ricky Lives, Dead or Alive*. I'm putting around *Gary Lives in Our Hearts*. I also put the chorus from 'Fire and Rain' by James Taylor. I heard it on the radio the other day and someone dedicated it to Gary. I sat there and just started crying."

"How did you find out about him dying?"

"I was over my grandmother's house and my mom and dad both came in," Michelle replied. "I knew something was going on. They said, 'We have something to tell you.' First thing I thought was 'Somebody's dead.' They said, 'Gary died.' I ran into my grandmother's kitchen, grabbed the biggest knife I could find, and booked out into the backyard. I just started hacking away at a tree, started freaking on a tree. I was like, *Why him?*"

"You know, it was healthy for you to do that to the tree instead of yourself," Breskin offered.

"That poor tree . . ." Michelle chuckled. "When I found out Gary died, I imagined him the last time I saw him: in his denim jacket, a Billy Idol T-shirt, his jeans, his Led Zeppelin pin, and his Beatles pin. My parents have been watching me with a fine-toothed comb—looking at my wrists, making sure I don't come in stoned."

"What do you think happens when you die?" Breskin asked, still trying to figure out the obsession with death among Northport's teens.

"I know Gary went to Heaven and Kasso went to Hell," Michelle answered confidently.

"What about Troiano?" Breskin asked. "He's still around."

"I hope he *dies*," Michelle fired back. "I really do. There's not many people I wish death on, but *him*? I wish death on him, okay? My dream is to get the hell out of here. I want to go somewhere there are no sickos and you don't get hurt by people. I think my generation is a bunch of lowlifes. No ideals. I'm more like a hippie than anything else. I'd like to be in Woodstock."

When the band was finished playing, Michelle led Breskin over to the bandstand to show him all the new graffiti that had appeared since Gary's murder.

Breskin noticed one inscription that said, *There is no Satan crowd downtown. Kasso was a waste.*

"Who wrote that one?" he asked.

"Randy Guethler," Michelle replied.

Breskin eyed another—*To Gary: I love you and I will never forget the fun we had and the time I spent with you. Gary Lauwers will live in my heart forever!—Squishy*. Next to the inscription was a drawing of a tearful eye, a heart, and a cross.

"Who's 'Squishy'?" Breskin asked.

Michelle blushed.

"Me." She smiled. "He used to call me Squishy."

"Why 'Squishy'?"

"Long story," Michelle said cryptically as she led Breskin back out onto the lawn. "Don't worry about it."

As the two walked out of the bandstand, they passed one more piece of hand-carved graffiti, long since painted over by the village. It read:

Oh, I wish I was a little bar of soap, bar of soap
I'd go slidey, slidey, slidey over everybody's hidey
Oh, I wish I was a little bar of soap, bar of soap.

The lyrics to this old campfire song had been left there many years before by a young Ricky Kasso.

Before drugs.

Before Satan.

Before murder.

Chapter 51

COLM CLARK SAT RUMMAGING AROUND IN THE darkness of David Breskin's rental car, looking for the brown paper sack of beer in the back seat. He and another friend of Gary's, Dan Petty, had agreed to give Breskin an interview in private, and sat with him in his rental car in the Foodtown parking lot.

"They should be back there somewhere," Dan said.

Colm eventually found the bag and pulled out two bottles, handing one to Dan.

"You want one?" Colm asked Breskin.

"No, I've got one, thanks," Breskin replied before taking a sip from his bottle of St. Pauli Girl. "Was Gary ever into the Satan thing like Ricky was?"

"He was," Colm replied, "but it was just the *appeal* of it, not the actual thought of Satan, and all that. He'd write stuff like '666.'"

Suddenly a black cat jumped out of the window of a car parked nearby.

Dan jumped up in his seat.

"*Holy shit!*" he exclaimed. "That cat just climbed out of the window."

"That's all we need tonight: a black cat. *Right?*" Between screeching crows and black cats, David Breskin was fed up with ominous animals echoing Gary's murder. "So, when Gary wrote '666,' did he know what it meant?"

"He had this upside-down cross and this little brown book about Satan," Dan replied, "and he was just saying all these stupid things, but he never really knew what it meant. He'd read it, but he didn't really understand it. He really *was* starting to turn his life around, though. He started playing basketball and was thinking of going into the army or the marines."

"What happened that made Gary start getting his act back together?" Breskin asked.

"It was slow," Dan replied, "but you noticed him getting more and more friends. He started gaining relationships up at Merrie's, but he sorta fucked that up when he stole pills from Liz Testerman. She was taking Librium for her back or something. He said, 'I don't want you taking these anymore,' and took a handful of them. I think, after that, he realized he had to face some consequences. Everything was piling up—the things with Ricky and Liz—and I think he realized he shouldn't have done that."

"Did Gary hang out with people like Kasso because he wanted to be accepted?" Breskin asked.

"He hung with Kasso *sometimes*," Dan replied, "but it wasn't like they were really good friends or nothin'. I don't know how *anyone* could be friends with Kasso. He seemed like the type of person who would turn his back on you for drugs or money."

"He was hanging out with Kasso the night he stole the angel dust," Colm added. "Kasso beat him up and gave him, like, two weeks to pay."

"It wasn't that bad," Dan insisted. "It wasn't as bad as the time Gary beat up *Muxie*."

"Yeah," Colm agreed. "Truthfully, by that time, I didn't even want to hang out with him. It was a stupid thing that he did. So many people were looking for him. He owed other people money too. Gary would tell you just about anything just to get what he wanted, sometimes."

Dan nodded and took another sip of his beer.

"Gary would do things for the moment," he said. "He wouldn't think about what was gonna happen to him the next day. He'd totally fuck somebody over and not think about the consequences of it. Sometimes he stole money from his parents. He'd get eighty dollars and go out and buy a twenty-five-dollar bong and spend the rest on weed and smoke it all that night."

"Didn't Gary pull a BB gun on someone?" Breskin asked.

"Yeah," Colm replied. "I was there when that happened."

Dan shook his head in frustration.

"Those were the kinds of *stupid* things Gary did that made you not want to him hang out with him!" he exclaimed.

"Didn't he take a butane torch and burn the kid who reported him for doing that?" Breskin asked.

"No," Colm replied. "I was there when that happened. That was this kid, Mike Muxie. It was his BB pistol. Gary and this other kid, Steve, in just a total spur-of-the-moment thing, decided to gang up on him."

"We all hung out with Muxie and we were just starting to get sick of him," Dan added.

Breskin's eyes darted to his rearview mirror as he heard a car pull up behind him. He watched the blue-and-white Ford LTD roll to a stop and its driver's-side door open. A uniformed Suffolk County Police officer exited.

"Here's a cop," Breskin said.

"Oh, great . . . ," Dan said, setting his bottle down between his feet.

"We're not doing anything wrong, are we?" Breskin asked, trying to remain calm. "We're not driving anywhere."

Breskin shut off his tape recorder as the officer approached the driver's-side window. Breskin rolled it down, handing the officer his license and registration. The officer didn't mince words. He had been patrolling the area and saw the three of them sipping from bottles while sitting in Breskin's rental car. He shined his flashlight into the back seat and found the beer. After Breskin thoroughly explained himself, the officer declined to arrest him, instead issuing a ticket for "contributing to the delinquency of a minor" before returning to his vehicle.

"So, why did Gary start with the drugs?" Breskin asked as he switched his tape recorder back on. "What sort of need did that fulfill in him?"

"To feel accepted?" Dan guessed.

"It wasn't striking out against his parents," Colm insisted, "because the only time his parents started getting pissed at him was when he started doing drugs and dropped out of school and stuff. I *think*. I'm not really totally sure what his parents thought of him."

"He was just always like that," Dan said. "Since he was a little kid. He was always the kid that started the little forest fires. Stuff like that. He's the kid that climbed up the tree very high."

"Knock over garbage cans," Colm added. "Something like that."

"Drugs just seemed to be the natural course for him to take," Dan admitted.

"Was Gary different stoned than when he was straight?" Breskin asked.

"Sometimes," Dan replied. "He would get stoned and get really into it. He'd start doing funny things."

"Gary was just kind of like a *personality*, you know?" Colm recalled. "Like an entertainer. The things he'd do, like making up rap songs."

"If you want to hear the way Gary was," Dan said, "you should hear this tape we made down at the Path. On the tape is pretty much the way he was."

"I'd love to hear that," Breskin said. He looked at the dashboard clock. It was midnight. He looked at his interviewees, already stressed from their brush with the law, and said, "Why don't we just end there. . . ."

When Breskin later returned to the *Rolling Stone* offices in Manhattan to update his editors on the progress of the story, he showed the ticket he'd received in the Foodtown parking lot to Jann Wenner, the magazine's cofounder and publisher.

"'Contributing to the delinquency of a minor'?" Wenner read with a smirk. "Man, we've been doing that since we started publishing!"

In the end, Wenner agreed to pay the young reporter's ticket.

After all, Hunter S. Thompson's business expenses were far more unusual.

Chapter 52

ON MONDAY, JULY 23, DAVID BRESKIN LEFT HIS HOTEL room and drove over to the Suffolk County Police headquarters, thirty miles away in Yaphank. He had an afternoon appointment with Detective Lieutenant Robert Dunn of the homicide division and was eager to take him to task for the wild claims he'd made to a rabid press. Once he arrived, Breskin was shown into Dunn's small office. Outside the door, a small plaque reading THOU SHALT NOT KILL hung from the wall. Inside the office, however, Breskin noticed a second plaque bearing a quote from Shakespeare's *Henry VI*: THE FIRST THING WE DO, LET'S KILL ALL THE LAWYERS. Breskin chuckled as he took a seat across from Dunn's desk and switched on his Sony Pressman.

"So, what about you telling the papers about 'a whole group of Satanic worshippers,' and all that?" Breskin asked, cutting to the question he most wanted answers to.

"I think 'group' is a proper word," Dunn replied, calmly trying to defend his sensational remarks. "After listening to these boys talk, there certainly were strong ritualistic overtones. There's no question about that, in my mind. It came right from their very mouths. The methodology involved, the taking of parts of clothing, the locks of hair, making him say he loved Satan, the utterings of incantations of some sort."

"But this is coming from Kasso and Troiano," Breskin countered, "both of whom were taking hallucinogens *daily*. Couldn't they have just been giving you a load of crap?"

"Well, how can I comment about that?" Dunn asked, becoming visibly frustrated. "In my opinion, as a reasonably experienced investigator, they were telling the truth."

"What about the connection you made between this and rock videos?" Breskin asked, adding, "Off the record, I can't stand heavy metal music."

"Some of it I find good, really," Dunn told a surprised Breskin. "I think Rush is *excellent*. I think their early records are quite good."

Breskin couldn't help but laugh at the absurdity of the situation. Sitting before him was the detective lieutenant who had, just days before, told the *New York Post* that rock music videos were partly to blame for the murder of Gary Lauwers—and now here he was, professing his love for Canadian rock gods Rush.

"I don't want to limit it to rock videos, though," Dunn continued. "That statement was made as the result of the community saying, 'How could this happen in Northport?' Not 'How could this happen?' I don't have MTV, but from time to time, I've had to turn away from some of the films on NBC or ABC that we allow to come into our homes. I mean, people see *violent* death and they have no sense of pain, anguish, or motive. Somebody just opens a shower curtain, and some guy comes out and chops them to pieces with a hatchet. 'How can this happen?' Well, what did you watch on television last night? You have to wonder about their naïveté."

"What about the prison psychiatrist not putting Kasso on a suicide watch?" Breskin asked. "Don't you think a kid who had committed the sort of murder he had, and went on with life for two weeks—and *bragged* about it—seems like a suicide risk?"

"No, not necessarily," Dunn said. "Do you feel that harkens a suicidal tendency?"

"Definitely," a stone-faced Breskin replied.

Dunn paused, sensing a challenge from the young journalist.

"Based on *what*?" he asked incredulously.

"Based on three months of studying teen suicide," Breskin replied without missing a beat.

Dunn backed down and sighed.

"I wish I was aware of the same body of knowledge," he said. "I've had inmates who have killed six people, and you might say the state of their depression would be *awesome*, but they were not suicidal."

"Well, the interesting thing is suicide doesn't always come out of intense depression," Breskin clarified. "Often before the suicide, a suicidal person seems very calm, very cool, very in charge—because they've already decided. A lot of people commit suicide on the way *up*."

"I truly wish we were able to see that," Dunn said. "It was an accidental human error. It was a matter of the psychiatrist's evaluation of Kasso. There was some discussion in the newspapers having to do with Kasso's potential suicidal tendencies. We were *not* made aware of them. I understand Mrs. Kasso agrees that she did not make us aware of that, despite what the papers say. Had she done so, we would have made a sincere effort to notify those who were responsible for his care."

Notification or not, there was still a significant issue with the Suffolk County Correctional Facility's monitoring of Ricky. While he was not on an around-the-clock suicide watch, he was still supposed to be checked in on every thirty minutes. What the press and the public did not know was that the jail had failed to do even that. Several national publications quoted Sergeant Ronald Brooks, a Suffolk County sheriff's spokesman, as saying Corrections Officer Ronald Horton had checked in on Ricky at twelve thirty a.m.—thirty minutes before the suicide—and that he "appeared to be sleeping normally."

None of this was true.

The inmate check logs for the night of Ricky's suicide clearly showed no one had checked on him for quite a while before he was found hanging in his cell. Even though this fact was easily traceable, the powers that be decided to cover it up and hope for the best.

"What was his demeanor like when you questioned him?" Breskin continued.

"I'd say calm to a *shocking* degree," Dunn replied. "It was like when I dealt with DeFeo in the Amityville case. I found Kasso's behavior somewhat odd—rationalizing what he did. I think the four or five of us were all looking at one another, saying, 'How can kids—human beings—be that cruel to a person they did grass with, or whatever else?' I mean, a kid they dealt with, talked about their girlfriends with, and about what kind of a car they'd like to have, and how come they never went to college, and why their mothers didn't understand them. I think we were in a state of shock, just as the public was. We're hardened to looking at and smelling these things, but there does come a point where we're just as shocked as anybody else, and maybe a little bit more shocked. I had veteran detectives tell me that was the cruelest death they had seen. The boy died a *cruel* death."

As Breskin finished jotting down his notes, his mind turned to rumors that some of the street kids had told him. The idea of more people than the established four being in Aztakea that night was beginning to bother him. What if the daily papers *were* right about ten to fourteen teenagers watching Gary's murder? Not a Satanic cult, *of course*, but the usual gang of suburban kids who all showed up for what was advertised as your typical Northport beatdown, but instead were subjected to a brutal killing. After all, these kids had already proven they could keep their mouths shut if they needed to. Not a single person who had been brought to Aztakea by Ricky and Jimmy to view Gary's remains had the courage to call the police or tell a parent. It took the bravery of one girl with secondhand knowledge to bring the whole house of cards tumbling down.

"Are you *damn* sure there were only four people up there?" Breskin finally asked.

"No, I'm not," Dunn replied to Breskin's surprise. "I'm definitely not sure."

Chapter 53

"CAN YOU TELL ME, IN WHATEVER LENGTH OR BREVITY you wish, where your involvement in these events began?" Breskin asked, holding the phone to his ear.

On the other end was Dr. Richard Dackow, the thirty-eight-year-old prison psychiatrist who had evaluated Ricky and Jimmy once they got to Riverhead.

"When Kasso came in around two o'clock," Dackow replied, "he was interviewed by two different officers who described him as calm, relaxed, and well-oriented. Someone told me about the article in the newspaper around three o'clock and I quickly scanned it. I thought they might have some problems. I saw them both in the holding pen area. I spoke to them for about five minutes each. I was very much concerned about Troiano. I could see there was a significant deterioration in him from the last time I saw him. He was angry about being in this situation and was feeling very hopeless about it. I ordered that he be put in sick bay. Now, we get around ten thousand admissions a year and maybe we'll place a hundred of those in sick bay, because that's only a four-cell area. That's the only place where we have constant observation in the facility."

"I understand the jail has an outstanding reputation for suicide prevention," Breskin said.

"In my eleven years of working at this facility," Dackow replied, "this was the first time I've ever had a client commit suicide. After I spoke with him, Kasso was assigned to administrative segregation. That has double the coverage of a normal housing area and the checks are twice as frequent. He was assigned there because my impression of him was that he was very calm and very cool. He wasn't frightened. He expressed no remorse over the killing."

"I would assume that, in the jail, 'good riddance' was the sentiment largely felt," Breskin said.

"Actually, a lot of the people I know down there were really upset about it," Dackow countered. "One fellow asked to be moved to a different cell. He wanted to be away from it."

"Was Troiano kept in that sick bay cell?" Breskin asked.

"He's still there," Dackow replied. "I don't foresee him ever moving out of that area."

"Have you had the opportunity to talk with him since Kasso's death?" Breskin asked.

"I've briefly spoken with him once since then," Dackow replied, "only because I was down in the area to talk to someone else the day after. His only concern was how it would affect his case. There was no expression of remorse or anything like that. I asked him if Ricky told him he had planned to commit suicide, and he said Ricky told him that if it looked like he was going to do a lot of time, he might do it. However, one hypothesis is that he killed himself by mistake."

"How would *that* have happened?" Breskin asked, setting his pen down to pay very close attention.

"He had a rather *negative* type of charge," Dackow replied.

"That's the understatement of the year," Breskin chuckled.

"He was probably a rather unsympathetic character in the eyes of his fellow inmates," Dackow continued. "All of the prisoners in administrative segregation are accused of crimes that if they wore them around their neck, they would be in real jeopardy—not just in jail, but if they went to a PTA meeting and told you what they had done. Primarily child molesters, sexual abusers, murderers. Not a group that should be too eligible for casting stones. One way you can gain sympathy is to make a suicide gesture. There are some things that tend to corroborate that. I understand the suicide gesture he had made at South Oaks was pretty much like that. He had also used suicide gestures to manipulate his parents with the ketchup on his wrists. I understand from one of the other inmates that he had heard a thump just as the officer was making the rounds. Four or five minutes after he heard the thump that he assumed was Kasso, the officers had him down and were applying CPR. Because of the locking devices, that's about how long it takes. He may have, in fact, been trying a suicide gesture anticipating that he'd be rescued and didn't plan it particularly well."

This revelation stunned Breskin. What if Dackow was *right*? What if, despite all his tough-guy talk over the past few years about killing himself if he was ever arrested, Ricky actually had no intention of dying? This added a whole new layer of tragedy to an already horrific story. He thanked Dackow for his time, turned off his tape recorder, and began packing his bags for home. There, he would begin the long and arduous process of transcribing the thirty-seven hours of interview tapes he had spent the last three weeks recording. With those transcripts in hand, Breskin would have the foundation for the most dramatic and controversial story he would write as a journalist.

Chapter 54

BY THE END OF JULY 1984, MOST OF THE DAILY newspapers had abandoned the Ricky Kasso case. Within a week of discovering Gary's remains, the Northport Village Police Department had issued a gag order, forbidding its officers from giving any further comments to the press, with the Suffolk County Police Department soon following suit. This sudden lack of new information, coupled with the heinous massacre of twenty-one people inside a San Ysidro, California, McDonald's on July 18, caused most news outlets to move on.

A few publications, however, refused to let go of the story.

On July 31 the *National Enquirer* ran their "investigation" of the killing. Surprisingly, Ricky did not make the front cover, losing out to Elizabeth Taylor, Peter Lawford, and a tease for the *Enquirer*'s thrilling exposé about people who had fallen in love with their telephones. Somewhat less shockingly, the tabloid milked the Satanic element of Gary's murder for everything it had and made up even more lurid claims to pad out its pages. The article reported local children supposedly being doused with gasoline by Satanists who threatened to burn them alive, along with choice quotes from Chief Howard, Detective Lieutenant Dunn, and Dick Kasso—all pilfered from the pages of *Newsday*, the *Daily News*, and the *Post*. In an even stranger turn, the *Enquirer*'s spread featured a heroic tale in which Northport's mayor, Peter Nolan, was quoted as rescuing a puppy who had been buried in the sand by cult members.

The story was a complete fabrication. In reality, the dog—a German shepherd belonging to local resident Peter Pavarini—had fallen between some large rocks near the water after wandering away from home the previous April, and Nolan never spoke with the tabloid, as he was away in Oregon while its reporters were snooping around town.

With David Breskin still at work on his own article, the only reprieve from media sensationalism came two weeks later when *Newsday* released their own long-form study of the tragic lives of Ricky Kasso and Gary Lauwers. Titled "A Shared Secret: Murder in Northport," the article hit stands on the morning of August 12, 1984, and was the result of a month's research conducted by Rex Smith, Thomas Maier, Michael Naidus, and others, with Smith helming the writing duties. While the article showcased some of the most factual reporting on the case since the *Northport Observer*'s initial coverage, it still contained some mythmaking.

This time, however, the lies and exagg
Kassos, not the reporters. Determined to s
minimized his own role in Ricky's downfall by
he had been violent toward him for years. Lynn
the many times she and her husband kicked their
own home, claiming to have always told the local p
took Ricky in that "he had a very good home and we wa
to come home."

Dick Kasso went a step further by coldly disparaging
very people who fed and clothed Ricky by saying, "Parents
it because they are having communication problems with their
own kids. It earns them points in their kid's [*sic*] eyes by showing that they care about their kid's [*sic*] friends."

He even lied to the reporters about the incident in front of the Midway the day before the murder, claiming he had offered Ricky the chance to come home and eat when he asked for a quarter to buy breakfast. The half dozen or so people who had actually witnessed this interaction knew Dick was full of crap, especially when they read the part where Dick said he drove back to give Ricky two dollars because he "felt guilty." He conveniently left out telling Ricky to never contact his mother or sisters ever again.

When David Breskin picked up a copy of the paper, he wasn't shocked by what the Kassos had told *Newsday*. He was, however, surprised to see Rich Barton quoted in the article. Barton had been notoriously wary of the press—even Breskin, initially. When he saw that Rich had finally agreed to sit down with the paper, Breskin picked up the phone and dialed the Barton house.

sked Rich if he would be willing to talk again and the boy
ed, telling the journalist to meet him in the Crabmeadow
rying Ground. Breskin grabbed his tape recorder, hurried over
a rental car agency, and drove back to Northport.

"This used to be our hangout," Rich said, pointing to the broken headstones surrounding him and Breskin. "We used to have séances here. We'd get wasted and trip out. Ricky came here every day."

"Who else was here when Ricky tried to dig up the grave?" Breskin asked.

"I was," Rich replied. "So was Albert, J. P., and Gary. Ricky dug seven feet down. Everyone was into it. It was pretty scary. Ricky eventually got tired and stopped."

"Are you glad you talked to *Newsday*?" Breskin asked. "Do you think it was worth doing?"

"Yeah," Rich replied. "I just wish they didn't call me 'Richie' in it."

Breskin nodded, his mind beginning to wander elsewhere. He was still haunted by the idea of Gary Lauwers being murdered in front of a crowd of cheering kids, as a few Northport and Kings Park teenagers had suggested to him.

"I know everyone says there were only four people up there," Breskin said, "and I am *begging* you to be as honest with me as you can—is there anything you know that would suggest there were more than four people up there that night?"

"No," Rich replied. "There were four people up there."

Breskin thought for a moment.

"If you knew that there were more people up there, would you tell me?" he asked.

"Yeah," Rich replied.

"Can you find out for me *for sure* that there was nobody else up there?" Breskin asked.

"I tried to find out if there were any other people up there," Rich said. "There's this one kid who thinks he's a detective. He's funny. He's like, 'Well, I went up there and I looked at all the different footprints, and I saw five different sets of footprints. They were all fresh and there were three different kinds of beer there.'"

"But it was two weeks after the murder," Breskin replied. "How could he have known?"

"Yeah," Rich agreed. "I told him he didn't know what he was talking about, and he was like, 'Yes, I do!'"

"You've known Jimmy longer than Ricky," Breskin said. "Did you say anything about Jimmy during the grand jury hearing?"

"No, McCready was telling *me* stuff to say about Jimmy," Rich replied. "He was telling me to say stuff about him cutting locks of Gary's hair and kicking him. I never knew any of that."

"That's important stuff," Breskin said. "Mark Florimonte told me the same thing: that McCready told him to say Ricky and Jimmy cut the locks of hair from Gary. Did he ask you to say anything else?"

"Nah," Rich replied. "He just asked me to tell that story."

"Are you sad that Ricky's dead?" Breskin asked, watching the sun slowly set behind the tall trees bordering the graveyard.

"Yeah," Rich replied.

"Can you picture Ricky at age forty-seven after thirty years in jail?" Breskin asked.

Rich laughed. "He'd be calling me like, *'Hey! What's up, man?! I just got out!'*"

"What about you?" Breskin asked. "What do you want to be when you grow up?"

"A cop," Rich deadpanned before chuckling. "Nah, I'm just kidding. I'm thinking about going into the army, or something."

"Then you *really* get to kill people, right?" Breskin joked, making light of the daily newspapers accusing the boy and his friends of being part of a murderous Satan cult.

"Yep!" Rich laughed as the two walked away from the graveyard before going their separate ways.

Later that evening Breskin caught up with Dan Petty, who had finally found the tape he and Gary had recorded during the summer of 1983. Dan invited Breskin back to his house to listen and make a copy. Standing in Dan's bedroom, Breskin set his Sony Pressman down next to the teenager's boom box, anxiously waiting for him to press play.

The tape began with the jumbled sounds of kids talking over each other, laughing, demanding a lighter to spark up a joint. Then, suddenly, a voice rose over the cacophony.

"And now, an interview with Van Halen!"

The voice started humming the guitar riff from the band's 1978 song "Ain't Talkin' 'Bout Love."

"Hi, I'm Sid Vicious," the voice continued, now in a faux British accent. "I'm here to interview Van Halen—a so-called teenage pop group. Actually, I think they *suck*. Let's hear what the band says."

The voice now switched to a high, squeaky inflection.

"Hi! I'm David Lee Roth!"

The boys on the tape all laughed.

"The reason I talk like this is . . . *I have no nuts!*"

In the background, Dan yelled out, "No, that's Geddy Lee!"

The voice then returned, this time lively and animated.

"Hi. Eddie Van Halen here. I don't know how to fuckin' play these guitars. Our music sucks! We don't even play it, man! We've got the band from *The Little Rascals* playing in the background! That's right! The same guy who did the Buckwheat theme did our fuckin' songs, so thank *them*, man!"

The boys all howled with laughter.

"My name is Gary Lauwers," the boy said, resuming his natural voice. "I'm here at the Path in Northport, Long Island. I'd like to introduce the people here. I, myself, am Gary Lauwers. You've got Bill Kreth. He's tokin' on the doob. Colm Clark. Dan Petty. We're all sitting here. I bought a twenty count and I'm really fuckin' high."

"I'm gonna interview everybody," Bill Kreth said, chiming in. "Gary, what are your hobbies and activities?"

"Let's see," Gary replied. "My profession is . . . I'm a *robber*. But part-time, I'm just a druggie. I like tripping on 'cid. I like to smoke pot, get laid, and have a good time, you know? We contribute this tape to the society of the man who invented acid and fuckin' drugs. Man, I dedicate this fucking tape to the man who invented 'cid and mesc. This fucking dude, man! I fuckin' took five hits once, man, and I fuckin' flipped out! Thanks a lot, man! That was fuckin' cool! That was a pisser! Man, wherever you are, fuckin' trip! Fuck the world, listen to punk!"

"Thank you, Gary," Dan laughed. "That's a very good philosophy on life."

The rest of the tape featured the boys arguing over their favorite drummers—Carl Palmer versus Ginger Baker—and finished with a group sing-along of Black Sabbath's "Iron Man," led by Gary.

When the tape ended, Breskin was left stunned. Every element involved in the murder of Gary Lauwers could be found on a recording made when he was still very much alive—the drugs, the stealing, his desperate desire to fit in. There was even an appearance by Black Sabbath, one of the many supposedly "Satanic" rock groups who were being blamed by the media for this tragedy. For Breskin, listening to the dead boy was eerie, touching, pathetic, and sad, all mashed up into one clean package of teenage angst.

Simply put, it was all there on this little time machine of a cassette tape.

Breskin turned off his Sony Pressman, thanked Dan, and headed back to Manhattan. Now that he had heard Gary's voice, Breskin was determined to give one to his peers. By the time he got back to his apartment, Breskin had decided to ditch all the interviews he conducted with adults and focus solely on the kids who had been doomed by them. As far as he was concerned, there were already enough articles like "A Shared Secret," allowing people like Dick Kasso and Chief Howard to save face.

It was time for the kids of Northport—kids like Gary Lauwers himself—to tell their own story.

Part Six

JIMMY

We are each our own devil,
and we make this world our hell.
—Oscar Wilde,
The Duchess of Padua

Chapter 55

ON FRIDAY, SEPTEMBER 7, 1984, JIMMY TROIANO visited Aztakea for the last time. His lawyer, Eric Naiburg, had successfully petitioned Judge John Copertino to allow him to take the prisoner back to the murder site so he could better understand his client's actions during the night in question. The prosecution objected, arguing there was "no legal basis" for the request.

Copertino, however, felt otherwise.

While Naiburg had presented his request as little more than routine, telling the press the trip would provide "a mind's eye view of what they're alleging occurred and where," the real reason was much more complicated. In the nine weeks since he had become Jimmy's lawyer, his client had provided him with no less than three separate accounts of the murder, each one differing from the last. Naiburg hoped a visit to Aztakea would help refresh his client's memory.

Instead Naiburg got a *fourth* version of the story.

"Jimmy," Naiburg said, "I asked you four times about what happened, and you gave me four different stories that you seem to believe, but *none of them* are like each other."

"Mr. Naiburg," Jimmy replied, "when the trees are melting, and the stars are racing across the sky, it's very hard to remember what happened."

A lightbulb suddenly went off in Naiburg's mind. "You know what, Jimmy?" he said. "That's going to be our defense—*LSD*."

Naiburg needed to convince a jury that *no one* could ever know what had truly happened in Aztakea Woods that night, let alone the prosecution. Jimmy's memory was so unreliable that Naiburg had already decided not to let his client testify on the witness stand. That left Albert Quinones. Naiburg would have to show twelve men and women that Albert's testimony was just as questionable. It was a long shot, but it was also their *best* shot. After joining the sheriff's deputies in returning Jimmy to jail, Naiburg drove back to his office and began crafting his defense strategy.

Two months later, on November 22, 1984, David Breskin's article was finally released. His editor at *Rolling Stone*, Carolyn White, felt the original title of "Thirteen Ways of Looking at a Black Spot in the Woods" was a bit too dramatic and changed it to "Kids in the Dark." With the cover touting the story as a "suburban death trip," the article made immediate waves for its unvarnished look at teenage life in Northport.

One person who took special note of the story was Eric Naiburg. "Kids in the Dark" was the only piece of published media featuring an interview with Albert—and what he had to say was damning toward the Suffolk County Police.

> ALBERT QUINONES: The detectives were beating the shit out of me. See, I don't trust them, man, I don't trust no one anymore. They picked me up at two, and they were beating the shit out of me for like two and a half hours, in Yaphank. They brought me up to this room, and they started questioning me and shit, and they were beating the shit out of me. They didn't tell me they were going for Ricky and Jim. . . .

Naiburg couldn't believe his eyes. If the cops *had* beaten a confession out of Albert, it would be inadmissible in court under the Fifth Amendment to the United States Constitution, which states that no person "shall be compelled in any criminal case to be a witness against himself."

"Compelled" was the key word here. If Albert's statement had been illegally obtained, either through violence or coercion, he would be useless to the prosecution. Without their star witness at their disposal, they would have a hell of a time trying to convict Jimmy. Ricky's confession, which laid near equal blame for the murder on Jimmy, was also inadmissible under the Confrontation Clause of the Sixth Amendment to the United States Constitution, which guarantees an accused criminal the right "to be confronted with the witnesses against him." Now that Ricky was dead, that was impossible.

With this in mind, Naiburg began drafting the necessary paperwork to subpoena *Rolling Stone* for copies of Breskin's tapes.

Chapter 56

A LITTLE MORE THAN A WEEK AFTER "KIDS IN THE DARK" was released, "Pagan Pat" Toussaint woke up, showered, and threw on a jacket before leaving his mother's house on Rutledge Avenue without saying good-bye. He walked downtown, bought a pint of gin, and headed over to the East Northport train station, where he often enjoyed drinking.

By ten thirty that morning, Toussaint had finished most of his gin and was visibly intoxicated. A concerned passerby called the Suffolk County Police Department, who dispatched Officer Joseph Jackson to report to the scene. There, he found Toussaint still sipping from the bottle of gin and issued him a summons for having an open container of alcohol in public.

Two hours later, railroad engineer Patrick Quinn pulled his train out of Greenlawn Station and headed east. As he turned a corner about half a mile from the East Northport train station, he noticed a man lying on the tracks. Quinn blared the train's horn, but the figure didn't move a muscle. Thinking quickly, Quinn threw the emergency brakes, trying desperately not to hit him. Despite Quinn's best efforts to stop in time, his train plowed over the man. When police arrived to identify and collect the mangled remains, Officer Jackson recognized them as what was left of Pat Toussaint.

The man who some recall as Ricky Kasso's occult mentor was dead.

A coroner's report declared that he had taken his own life.

A month after Toussaint's suicide, Eric Naiburg finally filed his motions to subpoena David Breskin's notes and interview tapes. Breskin's first instinct was to panic. He knew enough about the law to see the dangers in this order if it were granted. Under the First Amendment to the United States Constitution, Breskin's notes, tapes, and anonymous sources were all protected, as they had been collected during the process of news gathering. Still, if this fact was disputed—or worse, ignored—it could set a dangerous legal precedent that any lawyer could use in the future as justification to hunt down information provided in confidence to a journalist.

It was just too risky.

Breskin decided to split up his tapes and notes, handing a few each to various friends around Manhattan. For one last backup, Breskin copied his interviews with Paul McBride and Albert Quinones onto two fresh tapes, labeled them "Black Sabbath 1" and "Black Sabbath 2," and locked them away in a safe-deposit box.

If Naiburg wanted to get his hands on those tapes, Breskin wasn't going to make it easy.

Rolling Stone also cried foul and enlisted the services of their own attorney, Harriette K. Dorsen. Dorsen moved to quash the subpoena, pointing out that Breskin's work was not only covered by the United States Constitution, but also by New York's shield law. Luckily for Breskin, Judge Copertino agreed, and on March 13, 1985, Naiburg's motion to subpoena was formally denied.

The trial would go on without the tapes.

Chapter 57

ON THURSDAY, APRIL 4, 1985, JIMMY TROIANO'S TRIAL for the second-degree murder of Gary Lauwers finally began. Pacing around the small Riverhead courtroom, prosecutor William Keahon gave a thirty-five-minute opening statement, damning Jimmy as "that young man who held Gary Lauwers while Kasso stabbed him." The jury of eight men and four women listened intently to Keahon's impassioned description of the murder. His account was rife with Satanic overtones, despite Keahon admitting to the *New York Times* during the previous December that "it was not a cult murder. They did some bizarre things and the killing involved some ritualistic acts, but unlike Manson, it was not part of a cult. . . ."

When the forty-year-old lawyer sat back down in his chair, Eric Naiburg rose from his seat next to Jimmy and made a brief, eight-minute response. He had no intention of spooking the jury with fanciful tales of demonic boogeymen.

"This was a drug-induced revenge killing for the theft of drugs from Ricky Kasso," he told them. "There is no doubt that Jimmy Troiano was present when the killing took place, but there is great doubt that he was involved. I take issue that James Troiano is in *any way* a participant in the murder of Gary Lauwers. Being there is not the same thing as being guilty. Please keep that in mind. Your job, ladies and gentlemen, is not easy. Only you, as the supreme arbiters of the facts, will determine what is real and what is not—what should be believed and what should not. And, most important of all, only you will determine whether the guilt of that young man has been proven beyond a reasonable doubt. Your task is not going to be an easy one. No one is going to leap to his feet from the last row of the courtroom, admit his guilt, and relieve you of your struggle of mind and conscience. Whatever decision you finally make, you will have to live with for the rest of your lives."

Once both men finished their opening statements, the first witness for the prosecution, Jean Wells, was brought into the wood-paneled room. Clad in a lacy white dress with her long, blond hair done up nicely, Jean sat in the witness box, ready to field questions from Keahon. The usual introductory matters were gone over: Jean's name, age, and relationship to the accused. When the topic inevitably turned to Jean's drug use, the sixteen-year-old said she had first used them about two years before, starting with marijuana before moving up to purple microdots and acid.

"You feel like you're in another world," Jean told the prosecutor. "I saw trees change colors, making them look purplish. Clouds would be in the shape of dragons and you could form them the way you'd like to see them."

"How many times do you think you have taken LSD?" Keahon asked.

"Probably about seventy-five times," Jean replied. "That's why I had to go to reform school at Madonna Heights. It gave me mood swings."

"And where did you get it?" Keahon pressed.

"Sometimes from Jimmy," Jean replied.

"From the *defendant*?!" Keahon cried, hamming it up for the jury. "Mr. Troiano sold hard drugs to you when you were a *junior high student*?!"

Jean replied in the affirmative and described two incidents where she had dropped acid with Jimmy, once at the beach and another time in the woods. Jimmy sat silently as he watched his friend testify. Keahon then asked Jean to describe the day when Jimmy told her about the murder, which she did in detail before the prosecutor told Judge Copertino that he had no further questions. It was now Naiburg's turn to cross-examine the witness—and he was mighty happy that Keahon had brought up Jean's significant drug use. After all, he wasn't there to make friends, and any hint of flawed credibility was worth pouncing on to save his client's neck.

"Say you were high on drugs, Miss Wells," Naiburg proposed. "If you saw a car, how would you know it really was a car?"

"Because I *saw* it," Jean answered bluntly.

"Yes, but didn't you *also* see a tree that was purple?" Naiburg replied. "Reality, for most of us, is constant, yet when you are on drugs, your reality changes. Is that correct, Miss Wells?"

Jean was becoming frustrated. Unfamiliar with courtroom tactics, she wondered why these two lawyers were so obsessed with the drugs *she* took. After all, *Jimmy* was the one on trial here—not her.

"Yeah, but you don't see anything that isn't *there*," she insisted.

"No further questions, Your Honor," Naiburg said confidently as he turned to Judge Copertino.

After Jean exited the witness box, Suffolk County Homicide Detective Kevin James McCready was brought into the courtroom to testify about the investigation that led to Jimmy's and Ricky's arrests. He described to Keahon the discovery of Gary's remains inside Aztakea Woods along with responding to Bluff Point Road to arrest the two suspects. When it came time for Naiburg to cross-examine the detective regarding the two conflicting statements taken from Jimmy, he quickly became annoyed with McCready's answers. Every time Naiburg asked a question, the sharply dressed detective would swivel in his seat to face the jury as he answered, obviously feigning sincerity. To Naiburg, McCready wasn't taking this trial seriously.

"Mr. McCready, have you been *trained* to testify?" Naiburg asked, his voice seething with resentment. "Were you told to look at the jury to *impress* them?"

"Yes," McCready replied arrogantly.

"Well, maybe you should pay attention to the questions and forget about looking at the jury!" Naiburg replied.

Keahon jumped from his seat. He knew a threat to his case when he saw it.

"Your Honor, I request a recess," he said, straightening his tie.

Judge Copertino agreed, and the jury, along with all the spectators and journalists, were escorted out of the courtroom.

When he was confident the jury and visitors had all left, Keahon pointed toward the detective, who still was sitting in the witness box, and yelled, "McCready, you're a fucking *asshole*!"

Chapter 58

WHEN THE TRIAL RESUMED ON MONDAY, APRIL 8, Dr. Stuart Dawson, Suffolk County's deputy medical examiner, was called to the witness stand. Dawson had performed the autopsy on Gary's remains after they were removed from the shallow grave in Aztakea. Reading from the report he wrote after the examination, Dawson described the body to the jurors as "markedly decomposed," with nearly everything above Gary's waist fully skeletonized. He then noted the numerous indentations left by Ricky's knife in Gary's fourth, sixth, and eleventh thoracic vertebrae, along with eight "stabbing or cutting" injuries to the left cheek area of Gary's skull. The facial injuries were contained to a small area measuring only an inch and a half in diameter, and the wounds to Gary's back were mostly in a row, as displayed by the twenty-two cuts in his jacket.

These details, according to Dawson, strongly suggested that

Gary had been held down or paralyzed as he was murdered, and that it may have taken him "quite a few minutes to die" under these conditions—especially if he had merely bled to death.

As far as Keahon was concerned, this left more than enough time for Jimmy Troiano to assist Ricky.

Still, Naiburg wasn't about to give Keahon an easy win thanks to this testimony.

"Dr. Dawson," he said as he approached the witness box, "is it possible the knife could have penetrated the victim's heart early on during the attack?"

"Yes," Dawson replied. "That is possible."

"And how long would the victim have had before dying if this had occurred?" Naiburg asked.

"He would have collapsed within approximately fifteen seconds," Dawson said.

"So, which is it, *Doctor*?" Naiburg demanded. "If these stab wounds punctured his heart and—what is more probable—his lungs, would he have been able to jump up and run into the woods?"

"I don't know," Dawson replied frankly.

"What do you mean you 'don't know'?!" Naiburg prodded. "You said there were *eight* verifiable wounds in and around the spinal column. You said that any one of them—any *one*—could have severed the nerves, causing *immediate* lower-body paralysis. How could the poor kid have gotten up and run away with those wounds, as well as the knife holes in his heart and lungs? *How?*"

"I can't answer that," Dr. Dawson replied meekly.

"You 'can't answer that'?!" Naiburg exclaimed. "You are an expert! An *expert*, Doctor! If any of those wounds pierced the heart, Gary would have been *dead*! Not just *immobilized*, but *dead* within fifteen seconds!"

"Mr. Naiburg," Judge Copertino interjected, "might I please ask that you tone it down and allow the witness to answer."

"Yes, Your Honor," Naiburg replied, relinquishing the floor to Dr. Dawson.

"I don't know the answer to that question," Dawson calmly repeated. "I don't know how deeply the knife penetrated the body."

"No further questions, Your Honor."

The next morning, the prosecution's ace-in-the-sleeve, Albert Quinones, arrived in the courtroom, escorted by his attorney, Richard Librett. Jimmy had been dreading this moment, but both Keahon and Naiburg were equally pleased that this day had finally come. Keahon was convinced that Albert's testimony would win over the jury.

Naiburg, however, had other plans. He may not have had the Breskin tapes, but the lawyer knew enough about the boy and his drug habits to prove him an unreliable witness.

After reminding Albert of his rights under the immunity deal, along with going over his background and connection to the crime, Keahon went straight to the elephant in the room—Albert's drug use.

"Have you used drugs in the past, Mr. Quinones?" he asked.

"Yeah," Albert replied.

"And what drugs have you used before?"

"LSD, coke, mescaline, and embalming fluid," Albert said.

"Embalming fluid?" Keahon asked, perplexed by this notion.

"Yeah," Albert replied. "You put it on wood chips and roll it up like a cigarette and smoke it."

"And how did you afford these drugs?"

"I sold mescaline," Albert replied.

"Were you high on the night of the murder, Mr. Quinones?" he asked.

"I was drunk," Albert answered. "I had a few beers. Gary and Ricky made me take a hit of mescaline. They all took a bunch. Gary took three downtown and another three at Dunkin' Donuts. They all were smoking dust and tripping on acid."

"Do you think your memory is influenced by these drugs?" Keahon asked.

"No," Albert replied. "I got a good memory."

"When did you first have an idea that Kasso was going to kill Gary?" Keahon asked.

"I *didn't* have an idea," Albert insisted. "*Gary* did."

This statement directly contradicted Jimmy's first confession, which read, "We got donuts and cigarettes, and then walked up to Aztakea Woods. On the way, Albert said that Ricky was going to beat up Gary. After we got up there, Albert told me Ricky was going to kill Gary. I decided I didn't care because Gary should not have taken the dust that belonged to Rick."

"Gary told me when we were around the fire," Albert continued. "He said, 'Al, I think Jimmy's gonna kill me.'"

"Jimmy?" Keahon asked, visibly confused. "Don't you mean *Ricky*?"

"No," Albert replied. "Gary thought *Jimmy* was after him, but Jimmy heard him say that and said, 'Gary, why should I kill you? I don't have any reason to kill you.' Gary was still worried, though."

"Was that before or after the sleeves were cut from Gary's jacket?" Keahon asked.

"Before," Albert replied.

"And who cut them?"

"I think Gary cut them off himself," Albert said. "Either that or he cut one and Jimmy cut the other. Gary had taken off one of his socks and thrown it on the fire, but it didn't help much to make it burn. They cut off some of Gary's hair. It didn't make much of a fire either."

"Who cut off the hair?"

"I think Jimmy cut some off," Albert replied, "and so did Ricky."

"And then what?" Keahon asked.

"Gary got real nervous," Albert said. "He kept looking at me as if I should do something. I was sitting away from the fire. I didn't know what to do. Then Gary got up and tried to run into the woods. Jimmy tackled him, and Ricky ran over and grabbed him."

"Then what?" Keahon pressed, sounding almost as eager to hear the lurid tale as the spectators and reporters in the rows behind him.

"Then, Gary got off the ground," Albert continued, "and Ricky jumped on his back and bit him on his neck and his ear. Then, Ricky stabbed Gary in his side and Gary ran into the woods. Ricky ran after him and grabbed him by his jacket and brought him back to the campfire."

Many wondered how Ricky, who was high on marijuana, purple microdots, PCP, and LSD, could have chased Gary down in the pitch-black woods and brought him back to the illumination of the small fire.

One person with an answer to offer is Grant Koerner, Ricky's childhood friend and neighbor.

"The only way I can describe it is years of training," Koerner says today. "This is going to seem odd, but we played tag in those woods *our whole lives*. I remember playing 'Ghost in the Graveyard' in those woods until I don't even know what time—well past midnight. We had *always* been running around in those woods. Even if you ran off the path, you'd still have an idea of where things were. I hate to say it was training, but those woods were only blocks from the Kasso house. . . ."

"Did Gary say anything at that time?" Keahon asked.

"He said, 'I love you, Mom,'" Albert replied. "Then Jimmy came over and kicked Gary after Ricky threw him on the ground. Then Jimmy picked up the knife and gave it to Ricky and told him to slice Gary's throat."

"Jimmy told Ricky to kill Gary?" Keahon asked, making sure to highlight this point to the jury.

"Yeah," Albert replied. "He kept making signs to Ricky like this—"

Albert dragged his index finger across his throat.

"Then Ricky made Gary get on his knees and say, 'I love Satan,'" he continued. "Gary said he loved Satan, and Ricky started stabbing him."

Several spectators sitting in the rows behind Jimmy winced. Jimmy just sat in his chair, silently leering at Albert, who suddenly began to weep.

"Ricky started stabbing him some more," Albert continued as tears streamed down his face. "He started stabbing him in the back, started stabbing him in the chest. Then, I guess he was dead. Ricky and Jimmy went over to the body and they started looking down on it, saying, 'There is smoke coming out of his back,' and they just started *laughing*. Then Ricky picked up Gary's hands and Jimmy picked up a leg. I walked over there, and I picked up a leg, and we started dragging him into the woods."

Albert then recounted how the three walked back to his house, where Ricky washed up and borrowed a shirt before leaving with Jimmy. After this, Judge Copertino dismissed everyone for a lunch recess—not that anyone had much of an appetite after hearing the boy's tale.

When everyone returned from the lunch recess, Naiburg rose for his chance to grill Albert on the witness stand.

"Do you think your head has been messed up by drugs, Mr. Quinones?" he asked.

"No," Albert replied.

Naiburg then asked Albert to describe the strange dreams he had been experiencing since the murder. He was particularly disturbed by what Albert had been quoted as saying in "Kids in the Dark":

> I had some really wicked nightmares, man. I had nightmares that I killed him. It was weird. And I had a dream that I killed another guy. [*Author's Note: Breskin's editors at* Rolling Stone *had inexplicably removed Mark Florimonte's name in the published version.*] I just started stabbing him in the back of the head. And then a cop came in and scooped him up with this little pick or something and threw him in the garbage. It scared the hell out of me. . . .

Albert agreed to discuss the nightmares, telling Naiburg, "I was lying in my bed one night with the windows open and I heard Gary screaming outside. I got scared and went downstairs and turned on the TV. I stayed up all night. Another time I was just about to go to sleep when I looked and there was a skeleton floating over my dresser. I was sure it was Gary. It really freaked me out."

"And what about the dreams you told Mr. Breskin about?" Naiburg pressed. "Did you also dream about having killed Gary yourself?"

"Yeah," Albert replied.

Naiburg then had Albert again go over the sequence of events leading to Gary's murder.

"A while later," he said, "after we got to the place where they set the fire, Gary said that he had a funny feeling that Ricky was going to kill him. Jimmy started saying, 'Ricky, I'm not going to kill you. I have no reason to kill you.'"

"Ricky?" Naiburg asked. Only a couple hours earlier, Albert had told Keahon that Gary thought *Jimmy* was going to kill him. Now, it was back to Ricky.

"I meant Gary," Albert replied, correcting only half of the perceived error. "'Gary, I'm not going to kill you. I have no reason to kill you.' Then both me and Jimmy said, 'Don't worry, Gary; he's not going to kill you.' Then, like a half hour or forty-five minutes later, Ricky started jumping on Gary and punching him in the face. They just started rolling around on the ground. I walked up to Gary and I kicked him in the face."

The spectators gasped when they heard this revelation. Naiburg was also shocked, but no one was more disturbed than Keahon. Quinones had never once mentioned assaulting Gary that night, and neither had Ricky or Jimmy in any of their statements.

"Wait a minute," Naiburg interrupted. "Will you repeat what you just said?"

"What did I say?" Albert asked, completely oblivious to the gravity of what he'd just casually admitted.

"The part about you kicking the victim in the face, Mr. Quinones," Naiburg replied, astonished.

"Yeah," Albert replied, still unaffected by what he had said. "While Ricky had Gary down on the ground, I went over and kicked Gary in the face."

"Why?" Naiburg asked.

"I don't know," Albert replied. "I just did it."

"But that's not what you told the police in your statement," Naiburg reminded him. "You told the police you had *no part* in this murder. You said all you did was *watch*."

"I lied," Albert said, shrugging as if this were no big deal.

"So, you *did* do something, then?" Naiburg asked.

"Yeah," Albert replied. "What I told the police wasn't the truth. They beat me up. They punched me in the ribs, they punched me in the mouth, and they kicked me in my private spot and told me Jimmy had said I kicked Gary. I told them I didn't do anything like that. I wasn't going to get involved in *this*. Anyway, it was Jimmy the cops wanted to nail—not *me*. So anyway, after I kicked Gary in the face, I walked back to where I was sitting, and Jimmy ran up to Gary and kicked him in the ribs. Gary started screaming, '*You broke my ribs! You broke my ribs!*' He was screaming real loud. Gary then got up to his feet and Ricky grabbed his legs. Gary fell on the ground on his hands and knees and then Ricky held Gary down. Jimmy walked over and held Gary down, and Ricky started cutting his hair off with the knife. Then Jimmy started cutting his hair off and Gary started saying, 'Al, stop them! Don't let them kill me!' He started saying that he had five hundred dollars at home and that he would give it to him—give it to Ricky and us. They kept cutting his hair off and then Gary got scared and ran into the woods. Then Ricky ran after him with the knife in his hand. Then I ran after Ricky, trying to stop him.

I tried tripping him so he would fall, but Gary got tangled up in the vines. Ricky grabbed him by his jacket and brought him back to the campfire. That's when Ricky started stabbing Gary."

Here, Albert again contradicted himself. Earlier in the day, he had told Keahon that Gary didn't run off until *after* he was first stabbed by Ricky, whose confession also reflected these events in that order.

"And where was Jimmy all this time?" Naiburg asked.

"By the fire," Albert replied.

"So, you didn't see Jimmy holding Gary down while Ricky killed him?"

"No."

"In Jimmy's statement to the police," Naiburg continued, "he said he held Gary in a headlock while Ricky stabbed him."

"It never happened like that," Albert said dismissively.

"Then *why* did he tell the police that it did?" Naiburg pressed.

"I don't know—ask *him*."

Judge Copertino brought the day to a halt. Albert had testified for nearly five hours by this point, and Copertino felt everyone could use a break. As Keahon was gathering his papers from the table, a young woman with long blond hair approached him.

"You know, Mr. Keahon," she said, "I really don't like how you are handling this. If things keep going this way, he's going to get away with it."

Keahon was well aware of this. He had just watched Albert's contradictory testimony deal his case a major blow, and he certainly didn't need to be reminded of this—especially by some stranger.

"And who are *you*?" Keahon snapped as he turned to face the woman.

She wiped a tear from her eye and said, "I'm Gary's sister."

Chapter 59

ALBERT QUINONES RETURNED TO THE COURTHOUSE early the next morning to conclude his testimony. This second day of questioning quickly proved to be just as disastrous as the first. Back on the witness stand, Albert further confused everyone by suddenly claiming Ricky had never made Gary say he loved Satan, despite him—along with both Ricky's and Jimmy's confessions—initially stating otherwise. In light of these new contradictions, Naiburg asked Albert if any of his recollections from that night were real or simply a drug-fueled hallucination.

"It's real," Albert replied.

"But how can you be sure, Mr. Quinones?" Naiburg pressed. "Weren't you on mescaline that night?"

"Yeah," Albert replied, "but you don't see that kind of stuff on mescaline."

"And what did you see that night?"

"Lots of things," Albert replied. "I saw the trees bending down, trying to grab me. There was a swarm of bees chasing me. I even saw a lion."

"And how do you know the bees weren't real?"

"I had no sting marks on me."

"And what about this lion?" Naiburg asked. "Was the lion really there?"

"No," Albert laughed. "There are no lions in the woods of *Northport*."

Naiburg decided to jump on this and test Albert's connection to reality.

"Oh?" he exclaimed. "*Huh*. Didn't you hear? There was a circus in town—a lion escaped."

Albert fell right into Naiburg's trap.

"You mean the lion was *real*?!" he exclaimed, wide-eyed.

Naiburg smiled.

"No further questions, Your Honor."

Later, outside the courthouse, a very embarrassed Keahon was left to defend his decision to offer someone as unreliable as Albert Quinones immunity in exchange for such flawed testimony.

"I had to call him before the jury because he was the only eyewitness," he told the crowd of reporters. "We have a sufficient case without this witness. . . ."

Keahon's return of confidence, sincere or feigned, hinged on the upcoming appearance of Suffolk County Police Detective Louis

Rodriguez. Rodriguez had taken the second, more incriminating statement from Jimmy on the day of his arrest, and Keahon hoped some no-nonsense testimony from a law enforcement professional would help tip the jury's opinion in his favor.

When Rodriguez entered the witness box on Friday, April 12, Keahon asked the detective to recount his introduction to the case. Rodriguez discussed how he was asked by Detective Sergeant Richard Jensen to come in to work early on July 5, 1984. When he arrived at the Suffolk County Police headquarters in Yaphank, Jensen asked Rodriguez to take Jimmy back to Aztakea Woods and have him photographed at the crime scene. As Rodriguez testified, large prints of these photos were brought into the courtroom and displayed for the jury to see. When the topic turned to the confession Rodriguez took from Jimmy, Keahon asked the detective to read the full statement aloud, which he did while Jimmy repeatedly shook his head in denial. After Rodriguez finished reading all four pages, Keahon asked the detective how he had convinced Jimmy to make this second statement.

"It just came to pass," Rodriguez replied. "We were about to get out of the car when he told me, 'Ricky did all the stabbing. I held him, but Ricky did all the stabbing.'"

"Thank you, Detective Rodriguez," Keahon said. "I have no further questions." He returned to his seat, beyond pleased with how effortlessly this round of questioning had transpired.

Again, Keahon had underestimated Naiburg's resilience.

"Your Honor, could we have those enlarged photographs of the defendant brought back in, please?" Naiburg asked.

Judge Copertino agreed, and the full-color blowups of Jimmy at Aztakea were returned to the courtroom.

Naiburg drew Rodriguez's attention to the shot of Jimmy pointing to where the campfire had been lit.

"Why was this photo taken, Detective Rodriguez?" he asked.

"To have a record of the site," Rodriguez replied.

"And what about this one?" Naiburg asked, motioning toward the photograph of Jimmy pointing a stick at the shallow grave.

"To have a record," Rodriguez repeated.

"But, Detective Rodriguez," Naiburg replied, "hadn't your department already taken nearly one hundred photographs of this very crime scene?"

"Yes," Rodriguez said.

"Then what was the point in having more photographs taken with the defendant at the scene?" Naiburg asked.

"We needed them," Rodriguez replied cryptically.

"*Who* needed them?"

"Detective Sergeant Jensen."

"Did Detective Sergeant Jensen *tell* you to put the defendant in those photographs?

Rodriguez took his time answering.

"No," he eventually replied.

"So, you just took it upon yourself to have Jimmy Troiano in these crime scene photographs?" he asked. "Is that correct, Detective Rodriguez?"

Rodriguez again hesitated.

"Yes," he finally said.

"So," Naiburg said, "you took the defendant, when he was not even a suspect yet, and put him in these photos for the sole purpose of eventually showing them to this jury, palming them off as evidence—*didn't you*?"

Rodriguez didn't answer.

"These photos are not evidence of any wrongdoing on the part of the defendant," Naiburg continued. "They merely show that Jimmy knows how to stand still in front of a camera. They prove absolutely *nothing* else. These photos are totally unnecessary for the investigation of the case."

Rodriguez remained silent.

"Do you admit that the only reason they were taken was so you could come in here and show the jury this 'evidence,' Detective Rodriguez?"

Rodriguez finally broke.

"Yes," he admitted.

Keahon couldn't believe his ears. Pointing out small inconsistencies was one thing, but highlighting a law enforcement officer's questionable conduct to this degree bordered on the total annihilation of his credibility—and Naiburg wasn't even finished with his cross-examination.

"Now, regarding this alleged 'confession,'" Naiburg continued, "when did Jimmy supposedly admit to holding Lauwers down so that Kasso could stab him?"

"In the car," Rodriguez replied. "Just before we got out to go into the woods."

"And yet, instead of immediately going back to the precinct

and writing this new statement," Naiburg said, "you continued into the woods so that you could take those worthless photographs."

He walked back to his table and picked up a printout of Jimmy's second confession.

"'I knew that Gary had to be killed or he would rat us all out if he lived,'" Naiburg said, reading the statement aloud. "'I was glad because Gary could not leave those woods alive. I decided I didn't care because Gary should not have taken the dust that belonged to Rick.' Did my client tell you *exactly* when he had those thoughts, Detective Rodriguez?"

"No, he didn't," Rodriguez replied. "It could have been a day after the murder or two weeks later."

"But you inserted them into his statement where you thought they should go," Naiburg charged, slamming the paper back down on the table. "Isn't *that* what happened?"

"As I recall," Rodriguez said, "those recollections came toward the end of his statement. He just happened to think about them at that time."

"Detective Rodriguez," Naiburg asked, "if the defendant told you that he had seen trees melting during any of these events, would you have included that in his statement?"

"No," Rodriguez laughed. "That just doesn't make any sense."

"Did the defendant display any confusion regarding the sequence of those events as he related them to you?" Naiburg asked.

"He was confused about when the cutting of the hair took

place," Rodriguez replied. "He could not remember if it was before or after Lauwers was first stabbed. He was also confused about when the kicking of the victim took place."

"Detective Rodriguez, my client was also confused about when he picked up the knife and handed it to Kasso," Naiburg said. "There's absolutely no indication in *either* of Jimmy's statements that he ever picked up the knife."

"We talked about that," Rodriguez admitted, "but I was afraid he would stop cooperating with us if we put it in the statement. He said he didn't want to be seen holding the knife, so I left it out."

"You left it out?!" Naiburg exclaimed. "Did you hear *that*?" he asked the jury. "He just *left it out*."

Naiburg threw his hands up in exasperation and said, "No further questions, Your Honor."

Keahon sat in his chair, completely beaten down by what had just happened. Naiburg had managed to make his two most important witnesses look like total fools on the witness stand. There was no one left for him to call. No additional piece of damning evidence against Jimmy Troiano. *Nothing*.

All Keahon could do now was hope that Naiburg's upcoming defense witnesses were just as easy to discredit.

Chapter 60

ON WEDNESDAY, APRIL 17, NAIBURG CALLED HIS THREE defense witnesses for a lightning round of questioning. The first was a Northport letter carrier named John Thomas who claimed to have seen Jimmy trying to use the bathroom at the Trinity Episcopal Church as late as 11:20 p.m. on the night of the murder. Thomas insisted it was the defendant he had seen, claiming to have recognized him by his "slightly bowlegged" walk.

This recollection, for what it was worth, contradicted the prosecution's insistence that Jimmy had entered Aztakea to help kill Gary Lauwers at ten p.m. Keahon was quick to point out that Thomas's testimony did not change the fact that Jimmy was in the woods at two a.m. when Gary was killed, but in the end, both lawyers were chasing themselves down a blind alley. Thomas was talking about the night of June 16. Since the Suffolk County police hadn't made any official correction once they realized they initially had the wrong date for the crime, both Naiburg and Keahon were unaware that Gary's murder had actually taken place three nights later.

The second witness called to the stand was Dr. Jesse Bidanset, a professor of pharmaceutical sciences at St. John's University. While Dr. Bidanset admitted during questioning that he had never authored any medical papers on the effects of LSD, he did testify that his studies suggested to him that LSD users often experienced deficiencies in memory and could also be easily influenced by the power of suggestion.

When Dr. Bidanset was finished, Naiburg's final witness, Philip Quinn, was led into the courtroom. Quinn was the director of Topic House, a Long Island substance abuse treatment facility, and like Dr. Bidanset before him, was there to testify regarding the effects of LSD. Quinn, however, possessed one advantage that Dr. Bidanset did not—prior LSD use. Once on the stand, Quinn would be able to base his assertions not only on his professional work but also his former personal drug habits.

Quinn started off by telling the court that he had carefully studied Jimmy's two conflicting confessions, along with Albert Quinones's statement, and determined that "none of these boys' recollections are reliable. What they have sworn is true could only be illusion. Facts and incidents become muddled because the mind of the chronic abuser is already confused. LSD jumbles the mind, changes patterns in the sensory process, and events get reshuffled in the telling. The sequence of events is quite unreliable when you're on LSD, which creates psychotic-like episodes. Now, that doesn't mean the users are *insane*; just that the user senses that his mind functions are not normal, so he tries extra hard to *appear* normal."

"So, what you are saying is that even while they are high," Naiburg said, "they are attempting to cover it up so others won't know?"

Quinn nodded.

"Exactly," he said. "I have known abusers who have appeared normal, yet they were so high they were hallucinating out of control."

Jimmy smiled and nodded along with Quinn. Fun times.

"What they do is attempt to put things in order—to make things seem *logical*," Quinn continued. "They try to fill in the blanks, as it were, in their own mental gaps. They supply answers when, in reality, there are *no* answers."

"Then how open is the drug user's mind?" Naiburg asked. "How *susceptible* are they?"

"You can plant something in somebody's mind very quickly and very easily," Quinn replied. "Their mind is wide open to a *lot* of suggestion."

"So, if the police told Jimmy that he had helped kill Gary Lauwers, and told him that while he was still under the influence of these drugs," Naiburg said, "he would believe it to be fact?"

"Yes," Quinn replied. "I suppose so."

"I have no further questions, Your Honor," Naiburg told Judge Copertino. "The defense rests."

Despite calling only three witnesses and never allowing Jimmy himself to take the stand, Naiburg was confident in his strategy.

When the trial reconvened three days later, on Monday, April 22, the two lawyers gave their final summations. Naiburg was the first to present his closing argument, giving an impassioned speech that lasted nearly two hours.

"There *is*, ladies and gentlemen, a devil in this case," he told the jury, "and its name is LSD. It's not that LSD caused the death of Gary Lauwers—although it might have—but rather it has taken the minds of the young men who worshipped it. The devil has taken from them, and therefore from us, the ability to determine what is real and what is fantasy; what can be believed and what cannot, and what is truth and what is not. Ladies and gentlemen, I don't claim to have the answer to this mystery, but the only thing I can fathom is that someone is lying. The times or the sequence has been *organized* by somebody. It all leads me to one logical conclusion—McCready *blew* it. What to do now? Call in the best they've got—call in the guy who can get a statement from a stone wall. Call in the guy who has fifteen years on the job and has taken hundreds of confessions. Send him out with Jimmy Troiano for the *sole and exclusive purpose* of getting a statement from that young boy. I submit that there was absolutely nothing Jimmy Troiano was sure about or could relate with any certainty to the detective. Unfortunately for us, there is no tape recording or videotape of the interview which resulted in this statement. I humbly and respectfully submit that only God Almighty knows or will ever know what happened that night, and I humbly and respectfully submit that if Jimmy Troiano or Albert Quinones deserve to be punished, it is the *Almighty* who must make that decision. In this case—like no other case I have *ever* seen—man alone will never do. We cannot—no matter our frustration, no matter what churns in our gut—do anything other than, by man's law, acquit Jimmy Troiano. That is *all* we are capable of doing. I can say and do no more. I can only pray that you have the strength to do what is just. You can't convict a man because of a gut feeling. To convict him would be no less heinous than the death of Gary Lauwers. May God guide your deliberations."

After a brief lunch recess, the jury reentered the courtroom to hear Keahon's final plea for a conviction.

"Ladies and gentlemen," Keahon said, "please remember this—before the police ever talked to James Troiano, he was able to tell all of this to Jean Wells. Where's the loss of memory? Where's the confusion? There was nothing mysterious or surreptitious about the methods used by the police to obtain the defendant's statements. They did an expert job. Troiano was merely trying to con his way out of this. He lied in his first statement, hoping to hoodwink the police into letting him go free. Why else would he have been planning to flee with Kasso to California? Of course, Kasso was guilty, but Jimmy knew he was just as guilty. That was a pretty *sick* night. That was a bizarre night. That was a brutal night—a *sadistic* night. But details show it was *real*—not a fantasy. The inconsistencies are the things that make it real. When you think of the outrageousness of this night, think of Gary Lauwers screaming for his life. The defendant didn't care. He said if you take Ricky's drugs, then it's okay if you kill him. Can you imagine what that boy was *feeling*? The defendant over there showed absolutely no remorse. I ask that you return a verdict of guilty for the second-degree murder of Gary Lauwers. Thank you."

The jury deliberated for the next three days while Keahon, Naiburg, and Jimmy waited anxiously. On Thursday, April 25, Naiburg was spending his afternoon pacing around outside the courthouse, hoping for word on his client's fate. Finally a security guard named Phil stepped outside, told Naiburg that the jury had reached a verdict, and winked. A calm came over Naiburg, who was friendly with Phil. He knew guards sometimes hung out near the deliberation room, and maybe he had heard a sneak peek of how this was all going to end. Naiburg raced up the steps and back inside the courtroom.

"Ladies and gentlemen of the jury," Judge Copertino said, "have you reached a verdict?"

"We have, Your Honor," Claire Maturo, the jury foreman, replied.

"Will the defendant please rise?" Copertino asked.

Jimmy stood and stared blankly at the eight men and four women who held the remainder of his life in their very hands.

"We find the defendant . . . *not guilty*."

Jimmy's mother, Mary Troiano, fell into her husband's arms and began to weep.

"Oh my God!" she cried. "Thank God!"

Vincent Troiano held his wife close and clenched his eyes shut, holding back a river of tears. Finally, when he was ready, he lifted his head to the ceiling and quietly uttered some thanks of his own.

A few rows back, Nicole Lauwers sat stunned. She turned to her boyfriend, John, and scoffed, "Well, I guess if I ever do anything bad, I'd better call Eric Naiburg."

At the prosecution's table, William Keahon grabbed his papers, shoved them into his briefcase, and stormed out of the courtroom, quickly brushing past the wave of reporters. There was no hiding his frustration.

Jimmy, on the other hand, had shown no visible reaction since the verdict had been handed down. Suddenly Phil the security guard approached the table and said, "Hey, don't you think you should thank your lawyer?"

The dazed young man turned to face Naiburg and mumbled a soft "Thank you . . ."

After nearly a year, the "Long Island Satan Case" was finally over.

Epilogue

> When the legend becomes fact, print the legend.
> —Maxwell Scott (as portrayed by Carleton Young),
> *The Man Who Shot Liberty Valance*

IN THE AUGUST 22, 1993, ISSUE OF THE *NEW YORK TIMES Magazine*, journalist Ron Rosenbaum opened his article, "The Devil in Long Island," by recounting an anecdote related to him by former *Newsday* editor Gary Hoenig:

> Some years ago in Northport—not far from the birthplace of Pynchon, who is, far more than the frequently invoked F. Scott Fitzgerald, the true literary avatar of the Long Island soul—two allegedly angel-dusting, devil-worshiping teen-agers [*sic*] were branded as "ritual cult murderers" of another teen-ager [*sic*] in the Aztakea woods.
>
> It was one of the first such episodes in what would become an overhyped national trendlet, and perhaps the first signal that something sinister was stirring out there behind the split-level shutters of Long Island's suburbs.

> But this particular story about the unprintable photo, one I heard from a former *Newsday* editor who swears it's true, isn't about the killing itself; rather about something that happened the night after the death became public.
>
> It seems the paper had dispatched a photographer to get a nighttime shot of the supposedly spooky, satanist ritual killing ground out there in the woods, something that would capture the diabolical horror of it all. But when certain pictures came out of the darkroom, they just weren't . . . suitable. Unusable. Not because they were too terrifying (at least not terrifying in a Luciferian way). But because many photographs of the alleged cult coven's killing circle prominently featured a large boulder, across the face of which was scrawled the following somewhat-less-than-terrifying cult slogan:
>
> SATIN LIVES!
>
> A check with the *Newsday* photo library disclosed that contact sheets of all unpublished photos had been discarded. Nonetheless, 10 years later, it can be said with confidence: Satin still lives on Long Island.

Rosenbaum's article was not without errors. By this point, the Ricky Kasso story had taken on almost mythic proportions, and nine years without the benefit of instantaneous Internet fact-checking had passed. The "boulder" had actually been a wooden block inside Cow Harbor Park's wood forest playground, and the photograph *was* used, appearing on the front page of the July 6, 1984, edition. Rosenbaum later dismissed the confusion by explaining that Hoenig had "conceived a dramatic spread of murder scene photos, only to abandon the project when he discovered that the self-proclaimed Satanists couldn't even spell their dread Lord's name."

Despite the inherent flaws in Rosenbaum's apocryphal story, the piece does call attention to a key issue in the media's initial coverage of the Lauwers murder: Why were the local Long Island papers willing to print the "Satin" photos, but not the larger news outlets? The answer is, most likely, a simple one—a story about half-baked Satanists who can't spell "Satan" doesn't sell newspapers. However, the Suffolk County Police, along with the district attorney's office, telling the world that a group of cult members stood around a bonfire chanting while Ricky sacrificed Gary to the devil definitely *would*. So, the larger paper ditched the "Satin" photos in favor of Ricky's wide-eyed glare or a shot of the gazebo "where cultists hung out."

Cold hard facts rarely stand a chance in the face of confusion and a well-crafted legend.

What far too many of these news outlets fail to remember are the numerous people left behind to pick up the pieces long after the scribblers have all left town.

A true testament to their bravery and dignity in the face of unspeakable tragedy, the Lauwers family never left Northport, fully aware that one cannot outrun a devastating memory. Herbert Lauwers died from a cerebral hemorrhage in 1989. Those close to the family say he never got over how brutally his youngest child had been taken from him. After her husband's death, Yvonne remained in the little house on West Scudder Avenue, occasionally receiving visits from those who knew and loved Gary.

One of those visitors was Johnny Hayward. While Johnny had left Northport a few years after graduating high school, he still made a point to travel home to check in on his best friend's mother, doing so every year for nearly a decade and a half. One day in the late 1990s, Yvonne Lauwers turned to Johnny and asked him not to return. While she had always loved Johnny like a son of her own, the pain of seeing him—a walking relic of her son's short life—had become too much. Johnny understood, hugged her good-bye for one last time, and left. Still looking to confront the past, he walked a few blocks away to visit Aztakea Woods. As Gary had no grave to visit, he decided to pay his respects where his best friend had died. Instead he found a new neighborhood of homes built over the infamous patch of woods. Walking away, Johnny wondered if these homeowners knew what they were living on top of.

"The original development built over those woods was called 'Overlook,'" Grant Koerner recalls. "I will never forget seeing the signs and saying, 'Isn't that ironic? Yes, you are overlooking something. . . .'"

Unlike others who were once close to Ricky, Grant made it through the horrors of 1984 relatively unscathed. He grew up, became an architect, but never forgot his neighbor from Seaview Avenue.

"When I hear the name Ricky Kasso," he says, "my thoughts

immediately jump to playing together in the sandbox in the backyard; I don't jump to the murder or drugs. Some people can handle certain layers of stress, and others can't. You ever see that old black-and-white film of that bridge twisting like a rubber band? What happened with that bridge is they tested it for everything except for one frequency of wind. And, on that day, that frequency of wind hit that bridge and turned that thing into *liquid*, because it wasn't designed for that one perfect day. And I sort of think that's what happened with Ricky. You add all those combinations up, plus the inability to cope with them, or society not being up to dealing with that at the moment, and *boom*. I think it was just a bad storm of all those layers."

In 2017 the author of this book discovered through the Freedom of Information Act that the New York State Commission of Correction Medical Review Board had conducted an internal investigation into Ricky Kasso's suicide in the Suffolk County jail. It found that, despite what had been told to the media, "supervisory logs of the unit in which Mr. Kasso was housed reveal that less than minimum required thirty-minute checks were made by officers during the period immediately preceding discovery of the subject hanging in cell."

The review board ended its report by recommending that "Suffolk County Correctional Facility administration take appropriate steps to ensure that impulsive adolescent detainees committed to the facility for bizarre crimes who are known to have histories of physichaitric [*sic*] treatment and drug intoxication and/or abuse, be managed under constant supervision until extensive mental health evaluations reveal that they may be cleared for less restrictive supervision," and that the supervision of detainees be "consistent with Minimum Standards for Management of County Jails."

The four-page report, which wasn't completed until nearly two years after Ricky's death, was addressed to Suffolk County Sheriff Eugene T. Dooley, and shows copies to Louis Howard, the presiding officer of the Suffolk County Legislature; Martin B. Ashare, the Suffolk County Attorney; and Suffolk County District Attorney Patrick Henry. There is no indication that Ricky's parents or the press were notified of the report's existence or its findings. Instead there is every indication that for thirty-three years, the file sat collecting dust inside an Albany office building, almost two hundred miles from Northport.

The Kassos eventually decided to stay in the village, determined not to let Ricky's legacy affect their lives. When Dick and Lynn finally retrieved their son's ashes from the Brueggemann Funeral Home several months after his death, they placed the plastic box containing his cremains on a basement shelf next to some old Christmas decorations. He would remain there for several years, never to be placed in an urn or spread in a meaningful location. For Dick and Lynn, it was simply easier trying to forget Ricky had ever existed. Kelly and Jody seemed happy to go along with this, but consequently, Wendy was denied any closure or understanding. While her older sisters were already well-known and well-liked enough not to face any kind of harassment, Wendy was left to deal with bullies shouting, "Say you love Satan, Wendy!" every day on her school bus. Not one for confrontation, she sat in her seat, staring out the window, remembering all the times her big brother would smile and wave to her from the sidewalk as the bus drove by.

As the years went on, Dick Kasso began to behave strangely. He started having trouble completing simple tasks around the house and soon forgot who his family was. Friends recall him later breaking into the basement of a neighbor's home, thinking it was the New York Giants locker room. He was eventually diagnosed with Lyme disease, which had gone undetected for many years, and was confined to an assisted living facility. He died in May 1991. A few years after her husband's death, Lynn Kasso took Ricky's ashes from the basement shelf and privately disposed of them in an undisclosed location.

No one was told until after the ashes were long gone.

Sometime later Lynn packed up, left the house on Seaview Avenue to her daughters, and bid Northport farewell for good.

In August 2007 Yvonne Lauwers passed away at the age of seventy-nine. Four months later, Gary's older brother, Michael, died of cancer that had been initially misdiagnosed. He was only forty-seven years old and left behind a loving wife, Heather.

"I'm the only one left," Nicole Lauwers-Law says with a somber laugh.

Today, like many others, Nicole chooses to remember Gary as he was in life and not for the way he died. Her memories are filled with the images of the little blond boy whom she would take along on dates, bring home to play Legos with her own children, and drive to work as he grew into adolescence.

Albert Quinones left Northport not long after the murder, shunning all requests for interviews, including one with the author of this book. He now lives in Manhattan, where he works in construction.

Jimmy Troiano's elation stemming from his not-guilty verdict was short-lived. Immediately after the ruling, Judge Copertino ordered Jimmy back to jail without bail, pending trial for his June 1984 burglary arrest. He was later sentenced to several years in prison, and he publicly accused Copertino of throwing the book at him as revenge for being acquitted of Gary's murder.

"They're biased against me because they think I slipped through a loophole in the system," Troiano told *Newsday*. "They forget the twelve people who found me not guilty."

Unsurprisingly, Copertino denied this.

After he was eventually released from jail, Jimmy moved upstate to Albany, telling the few friends and family he had left that prison had helped him stay sober and find God. He quickly grew bored of clean living, however, and on December 12, 1991, Jimmy walked into the Albany Savings Bank on Wolf Road and robbed a teller of nine hundred and seventy dollars in cash. He initially got away with the crime, but over the next year, Jimmy racked up a variety of arrests and charges, including petit larceny, possession of crack cocaine, and third-degree burglary. He was eventually arrested for the bank robbery in January 1993, bragging to officers that he had "beaten a murder charge on Long Island and would beat this one too."

He was convicted and sentenced to further jail time.

However, Jimmy was released just in time to appear in a Discovery Channel documentary that aired in 2000. With cameras in tow, he returned to Northport for the first time in nearly two decades, walked around Cow Harbor Park, and pinned the blame for Gary's murder on Ricky alone. With a big smile on his face, Jimmy also showed off his newborn son, again claiming to be drug-free.

Less than four years later, now living in Maine, Jimmy wrapped his hands and face in bandages, covered them in ketchup, and rode his stepson's bicycle to his local CVS Pharmacy in Bath. There, he produced a firearm, which was later determined to have been a pellet gun, and handed a note to pharmacists Shannon Grady and Eric Morse that read:

GIVE ME ALL OXYCOTIN
80'S 40'S 20'S AND FETNAL PATCHS NOW!
I HAVE A GUN!
I WILL USE IT!

Morse, who usually worked at a different CVS location, had trouble opening the store's safe. Impatient, Jimmy hopped over the counter and rushed toward Morse, who was eventually able to unlock the safe. When the door was opened, Jimmy grabbed three bottles of Ritalin and ran outside. There, he was greeted by members of the Bath Police Department, who arrested him on the spot.

When he was brought to trial for this latest bout of criminal activity, the judge took one look at Jimmy's record and sentenced him to 151 months in jail, declaring him "every bank teller and pharmacist's nightmare."

As of this writing, Jimmy Troiano is serving out his sentence at the McKean Federal Correctional Institution in Lewis Run, Pennsylvania. He is scheduled to be released in October 2018.

Shortly after Rich Barton's interviews with *Newsday* and *Rolling Stone* were published, a group of Jimmy Troiano's friends broke into the Barton home, doused the basement bedroom where Ricky and Jimmy had once slept with gasoline, and lit the house on fire. Rich and his family were unharmed, but their home on Maple Avenue was completely gutted. He eventually left Northport and joined the marines, serving two tours of duty.

The international media furor over the Knights of the Black Circle gradually fizzled out, but the legend remains. Today, hundreds of websites, YouTube videos, and blog articles still incorrectly refer to Ricky Kasso as the "leader" of the "Satanic cult" Knights of the Black Circle, completely unaware of John Gallagher's press release blunder.

Paul McBride died in February 2000. Friends recall the founder of the Knights freezing to death in his mobile home after a night of drinking. He was laid to rest in Northport Rural Cemetery, where his loved ones left two small statues of the Labrador retrievers he had so loved in life.

Jonathan McCuller, the Knights' cofounder, eventually wrote and published a memoir called *The Hard Way: Book One*. Today he remains disturbed by how he and his friends were villainized by the press, and finds the ordeal hard to talk about.

Brendan Brown never forgot his encounters with Ricky Kasso. In 1995 he formed the rock group Wheatus, and five years later, their song about adolescent life in suburban Northport, "Teenage Dirtbag," hit the top ten on the rock charts in America, the UK, and Germany, while simultaneously going straight to number one in Australia, Belgium, and Austria. Brown would revisit his memories of Ricky on the 2009 record *The Lightning EP*. He still writes, records, and tours with Wheatus today.

At only twenty-six years old, David Breskin left his mark on the world of investigative journalism, with *Rolling Stone* eventually selecting "Kids in the Dark" as one of the magazine's landmark articles for their twenty-fifth anniversary collection, "The Great Stories." Not long after the article's initial release, Breskin was contacted by Chicago-based writer Rick Cleveland, who asked to adapt the story into a stage play. Breskin asked if he could cowrite, and Cleveland agreed. The theater adaptation of *Kids in the Dark* opened to rave reviews on April 2, 1987, at the Victory Gardens Theater in Chicago.

Six months later, on October 1, 1987, Dell Books published *Say You Love Satan*, a paperback retelling of the Kasso story by author and self-professed "occult expert" David St. Clair. St. Clair, the author behind titles such as *How Your Psychic Powers Can Make You Rich*, *Child Possessed*, and *David St. Clair's Lessons in Instant ESP*, traveled to Northport, hoping to interview those who had known Ricky and Gary. When his attempts were largely rebuffed, St. Clair returned home, plagiarized several sections of "Kids in the Dark" word for word—along with countless articles from *Newsday* and the *New York Times*—and filled in many of the blanks with imaginary scenes, dialogue, and characters. St. Clair nevertheless declared his book a work of nonfiction, featuring the "chilling truth behind the shocking headlines."

Most readers outside of Northport naively assumed St. Clair's book to be factual, but David Breskin knew otherwise. He initially considered suing St. Clair for using his material without permission, but Breskin's literary agent advised him to seek a compensatory settlement from the Bantam Doubleday Dell Publishing Group instead. Breskin agreed, but in a strange twist of fate, he was met at the publishing house by Harriette Dorsen—the lawyer who had successfully helped quash Eric Naiburg's subpoena for his interview tapes and notes two years earlier. Dorsen, who was now vice president and general counsel for the Bantam Doubleday Dell Publishing Group, declined Breskin's request for compensation, insisting St. Clair's actions "might not have been *nice*, but it was legal." When Breskin challenged Dorsen's assertion, the forty-five-year-old lawyer told him to sue her if he didn't like what she had to say. Fed up with the experience, Breskin stormed out of the room, exclaiming, "Long live the First Amendment!"

Breskin quit journalism shortly afterward but continues writing to this day, enjoying a second creative life as a critically acclaimed poet and record producer.

The Northport Public Library, once a refuge for Ricky Kasso's macabre interests, carries a copy of *Say You Love Satan*—albeit under lock and key. The book is kept in a fireproof safe behind the reference desk, where readers must leave their driver's license if they wish to read it within the confines of the library.

No one is permitted to leave the building with the book.

Robert Howard remained Northport Village's chief of police for another sixteen years after the case that defined his career. After retiring, he went to work part-time as a limousine driver in East Northport. On December 27, 2011, Howard suffered an aortic aneurysm while loading a customer's bags into the trunk. He was rushed into surgery but died hours later at the age of seventy, surrounded by his wife, Maureen, and his sons, Peter, Michael, and Robert. He left a lasting legacy as one of the village's most beloved residents.

Kevin James McCready died of lung cancer December 28, 2015, at the age of sixty-eight. His reputation as a Suffolk County detective was left tarnished when it was revealed that he had tricked a teenager, Martin Tankleff, into falsely confessing to the murder of his parents in 1988. After McCready's death, the Suffolk County Police Department refused to comment on his legacy as a law enforcement officer.

William Keahon and Eric Naiburg, now both in their seventies, continue to practice law on Long Island.

Michelle DeVeau eventually left East Northport and finally made it to Woodstock—just as she said she would.

In the wake of the Northport incident, the Youth Development Agency of Northport/East Northport coordinated with the Huntington Youth Bureau, the Northport–East Northport Union Free School District, and various religious organizations to provide a constructive response to the problems that had largely contributed to the tragedy. Eventually, the Youth Bureau and the Northport–East Northport Union Free School District hired a group of youth street workers to reach out to disaffected children and teenagers in the community, agreeing to split the costs of doing so.

One of these youth street workers was Anthony Zenkus.

"The response from the community was amazing," says Zenkus, now a licensed social worker and adjunct professor at Adelphi University. "You saw people come together and say, 'We can't just allow these kids to be throwaways.' Our job was to go out and connect with these disaffected kids and try to draw the message to the community that 'you matter; we're here for you; we want to help you—but we also think you have something to contribute.' I did that for two and a half years. I would walk around behind 7-Eleven and places like that. These kids would hang out late at night at the gazebo, or behind it; smoking weed and doing their thing. I would go up and talk to them. I would say, 'Look, I know you think school is bullshit, and all that kind of stuff, but what do you like to do?' There was one kid who was sitting there playing guitar, so I said, 'I sing and play keyboards. Why don't you come down to the center, and let's work on songwriting and stuff?' I put together a songwriter's workshop for these kids and we recorded a song. Those were the kinds of things that the street workers would try to do. I don't think it solved all the problems, but I think the response was a very mature response for a community, instead of saying, 'Oh, we have a drug problem,' or 'Oh, it's just a bad home,' or whatever. They said, 'Look, the community has a responsibility.' And that's what happened. I thought that was one of the unsung positives of this horrendous thing."

Despite Northport eventually moving on from the tragedy, the Kasso case went on to significantly influence pop culture, inspiring six feature films, three documentaries, the name of a stoner metal band, and nearly two dozen popular songs.

The well-crafted legend simply refused to die.

Today the only echoes of Ricky Kasso's and Gary Lauwers's short lives found inside Cow Harbor Park are a few small examples of crude graffiti scrawled on the rafters of the refurbished gazebo—*OZZY*, *Grateful Dead*, *LSD*—almost certainly left by kids far too young to have known the doomed teenagers in life.

The graffiti-covered wood forest playground was eventually torn down and replaced, and Cow Harbor Park is now safe again for children of all ages. The dealers have left, and the handful of

Ricky's and Gary's friends who stayed can now let their own kids play in the park that was once deemed a "monster" without any fear of harm coming their way.

And while most have moved on with their lives—more than happy to forget the summer of 1984—some still find themselves roaming their old haunts, looking back on the days of adolescent dreams and the Acid King.

ACKNOWLEDGMENTS

The author wishes to sincerely thank the following:

Mike Acosta, David Ambro, Mara Anastas, Ronni Arden, Dr. Jonathan Arden, Joanne M. Austin, Eric Baird, Russell Barton, Elaine Bennett, David Breskin, Brendan B. Brown, Doug Brueggemann, the staff of the Central Records Section of the Suffolk County Police Department, Dave Cullen, Jonathan de la Rosa, Larry Decker, Sue Decota, Tim Dennis, Michelle DeVeau, Bob Draffin, Nic Edwards, Patrick Edwards, Jamie E. Farrell, Susan Fensten, Rob Figueroa, Peter Filardi, Aurelia Frau, Leo Freire, Jonathan Grioli, Jim Harold, Leslie Hatton, Jeff Heimbuch, Maddy Hilker, Dally Hoover, the Huntington Historical Society, the staff of the John Hay Library of Brown University, Dave Johnson, Daniel Oxford Jones, Brian Kaufman, Janine Keleghan, Grant Koerner, Betty Koerner, Robert Kolker, William Kreth, Billy Leason, Jean Leclerc, the librarians of Northport–East Northport Public Library, Valerie MacKenna, Joe Maddrey, Thomas Maier, Dan Mallory, Tony Mallory, Nick Mamatas, Mary Marshall, Demetri Matas, Jonathan McCuller, Cecily Rappaport McGuckin, Dan McGuigan, Mark J. McGuire, Meghan McKee, Matthew Milligan, Mark Moran, Chelsea

Morgan, Amanda Myers, Eric Myers, Eric Naiburg, Robin Wheelwright Ness, Scott Neumeyer, the Northport Historical Society, Ed Opperman, David Oster, Paul Papa, Eve Porinchak, Carol Prevost, Tom Rætz, Elisa M. Rivlin, Eugene S. Robinson, Gene Roemer, Rob Romaniello, Ron Rosenbaum, Tony Ruggi, Dylan Grey Rupp, Mark Sceurman, Grace Schinmann, Richard Schock, David Schrader, Heather Shade, Jacob Shelton, everyone at the Shipwreck, Fiona Simpson, Joanne Slater-Milligan, Rex Smith, Gabrielle Sterbenz, the Suffolk County Police Department, Brian Tane, Mercedes McGrory Tidemann, Tommy Turner, Doug Varley, Alison Velea, Jeff Villasenor, Rue Volley, Glen Wolf, Kyle J. Zalinsky, Anthony Zenkus, and everyone else who helped along the way.

Very special thanks to Wendy Kasso and Nicole Lauwers-Law for their bravery and strength.

Also, my most heartfelt thanks to Mom, Dad, and the village it took—I love you.

SOURCES

Newspaper Articles

Oneonta Star Staff. "Colgate Students Freed of Charges." *The Oneonta Star*, May 23, 1960.

Kasso, Richard A., Sr. "Defends CSH Board." *The Long-Islander*, November 28, 1974.

Long-Islander Staff. "New Cow Harbor Park." *The Long-Islander*, October 7, 1976.

Ambro, David. "Grave Robber Nabbed After Long Investigation." *The Northport Observer*, April 23, 1984.

Newsday Staff. "Police/Court Digest: Grave Robbing." *Newsday*, April 25, 1984.

Green, Lynn. "Town Created a Monster." *The Long-Islander*, May 24, 1984.

Cassidy, Jerry, and Stuart Marques. "Nab Devil Cult Teen in Slaying." *Daily News* (New York), July 6, 1984.

Matlick, Maralyn, and Joy Cook. "2 L.I. Teens Seized in Bizarre Devil Cult Slaying." *New York Post*, July 6, 1984.

O'Neill, Jim, and Dennis Hevesi. "2 Held in Ritual Killing of Teenager in Northport." *Newsday*, July 6, 1984.

Kirkman, Edward, and Stuart Marques. "L.I. 'Satan Cult.'" *Daily News* (New York), July 7, 1984.

Maher, Thomas J., and Rex Smith. "2 Teens Arraigned in Murder." *Newsday*, July 7, 1984.

Matlick, Maralyn. "L.I. Cops Hunt Teenage Devil Worshippers." *New York Post*, July 7, 1984.

Kirkman, Edward, and Stuart Marques. "Cult Suspect Hangs Himself in L.I. Jail Cell." *Daily News* (New York), July 8, 1984.

Kirkman, Edward, and Stuart Marques. "Where Evil Dwells." *Daily News* (New York), July 8, 1984.

Maier, Thomas J. "Odyssey of Drugs, Desperation." *Newsday*, July 8, 1984.

McFadden, Robert D. "Youth Found Hanged in L.I. Cell After His Arrest in Ritual Killing." *The New York Times*, July 8, 1984.

O'Neill, Jim, and Rex Smith. "Suspect in 'Cult' Murder Found Hanged." *Newsday*, July 8, 1984.

Dicker, Fredric. "Satan Killer's Parents Bare Son's Private Hell." *New York Post*, July 9, 1984.

Hanrahan, Michael, and Paul Meskil. "DA Wants Cultists to Describe Killing." *Daily News* (New York), July 9, 1984.

Hinckley, David. "No Rock Exorcist Needed." *Daily News* (New York), July 9, 1984.

Hornblower, Margot. "Youths' Deaths Tied to Satanic Rite." *The Washington Post*, July 9, 1984.

Naidus, Michael, and Thomas J. Maier. "Parents Tell of Son's Descent into Own Hell." *Newsday*, July 9, 1984.

Pierson, Ransdell. "Stunned Villagers Mourn Victim." *New York Post*, July 9, 1984.

Tharp, Paul, and Charles Lachman. "4 Teens Who Saw Ritual Killing Will Face Charges." *New York Post*, July 9, 1984.

Washington Post Staff. "Town Shocked by Satanic Slaying." *The Washington Post*, July 9, 1984.

Colen, B. D. "The Drug that Triggers Rage." *Newsday*, July 10, 1984.

Hanrahan, Michael, Alton Slagle, and Stewart Ain. "Cult-Slay Witness to Talk." *Daily News* (New York), July 10, 1984.

Hanrahan, Michael, and Alton Slagle. "Son Spurned Loving Family: Dad." *Daily News* (New York), July 10, 1984.

Matlick, Maralyn, and Paul Tharp. "Satan Case Goes to Grand Jury." *New York Post*, July 10, 1984.

O'Neill, Jim, and Amy Wilentz. "1 Indictment Seen in Slaying." *Newsday*, July 10, 1984.

Pierson, Ransdell. "The Devil Didn't Make Them Turn to Drugs." *New York Post*, July 10, 1984.

Edelson, Edward. "Chemical Theory Lost in the 'Dust.'" *Daily News* (New York), July 11, 1984.

Kirkman, Edward, Don Flynn, Jerry Cassidy, and Michael Hanrahan. "Says Kasso Boasted of Cult Killing." *Daily News* (New York), July 11, 1984.

Matlick, Maralyn, and Joy Cook. "Teenager Indicted in L.I. Satan Cult Murder." *New York Post*, July 11, 1984.

Pierson, Ransdell, and Paul Tharp. "Bared—Devil Death Cult HQ." *New York Post*, July 11, 1984.

New York Post Staff. "Buddies of Slain Teen Rid Town of Sect Symbols." *New York Post*, July 11, 1984.

Naidus, Michael, and Rex Smith. "Northport Still Trying to Pick Up the Pieces." *Newsday*, July 11, 1984.

Reinecke, Bill. "Satanic Slaying Rocks a Village." *Philadelphia Daily News*, July 11, 1984.

Cassidy, Jerry, Mary Ann Giordano, and Michael Hanrahan. "Cultivating Drugs, Rock." *Daily News* (New York), July 12, 1984.

Editorial. "Our Town, Our Tragedy." *The Long-Islander*, July 12, 1984.

Green, Lynn. "Brutal Slaying Stuns N'port Village." *The Long-Islander*, July 12, 1984.

Kirkman, Edward, Marcia Kramer, and Jerry Cassidy. "Indicted in 'Bizarre' Killing." *Daily News* (New York), July 12, 1984.

McGuire, Mark, and David Ambro. "Local Police Chief Blasts Cult Claims." *The Northport Observer*, July 12, 1984.

McGuire, Mark, and David Ambro. "Northport Youth Found Mutilated in Woods." *The Northport Observer*, July 12, 1984.

Smith, Rex, and Thomas J. Maier. "Indictment in Ritual Slaying." *Newsday*, July 12, 1984.

Starita, Joe. "Ritual Slaying by Teen-agers Stuns Long Island Community." *The Reading Eagle*, July 12, 1984.

Matlick, Maralyn, and Joy Cook. "Lawyer: Accused Cult Killer Is a Sacrificial Lamb." *New York Post*, July 13, 1984.

Pierson, Ransdell. "Accused Satan Killer Pins Rap on 'Third Man.'" *New York Post*, July 14, 1984.

Gruson, Lindsey. "In Northport, A Meeting on Murder." *The New York Times*, July 15, 1984.

Smith, Rex. "Northport Searches Itself for an Answer." *Newsday*, July 16, 1984.

Ambro, David. "Residents Respond in Aftermath of Murder." *The Northport Observer*, July 19, 1984.

Lanctot, Roger C. "Shock, Dismay in Northport." *The Long-Islander*, July 19, 1984.

Blackburn, John, Charles Montgomery, and David Wright. "Teenage Devil Cult's Bloody Rampage—The Untold Story." *The National Enquirer*, July 31, 1984, pages 48–49.

Smith, Rex, Thomas J. Maier, and Michael Naidus. "A Shared Secret: Murder in Northport." *Newsday*, August 12, 1984.

Smith, Don, and Jim Scovel. "4-Hour Release Asked in Slay Case." *Newsday*, August 14, 1984.

Smith, Rex. "Suspect's Visit to Crime Site OKd." *Newsday*, September 5, 1984.

Ambro, David. "Murder Suspect and Attorney Tour Village." *The Northport Observer*, September 13, 1984.

Gruson, Lindsey. "'Satanic Slaying' Is Now Ruled Out in June Slaying of Youth in L.I Woods." *The New York Times*, December 27, 1984.

Maier, Thomas J. "Reporter's Notes Sought in Slay Case." *Newsday*, January 4, 1985.

Wacker, Bob. "Demand for Reporter's Notes Delays Troiano Case." *Newsday*, January 8, 1985.

Newsday Staff. "Youth's Statement on Northport Murder." *Newsday*, January 11, 1985.

Maier, Thomas J. "Cop Testifies on Teen's Tip in Slaying." *Newsday*, January 15, 1985.

Newsday Staff. "Magazine Snubs Plea for Slay Story Notes." *Newsday*, January 17, 1985.

Gruson, Lindsey. "L.I. Murder Trial Opens: Confession Is Described." *The New York Times*, April 5, 1985.

Maier, Thomas J. "Witness: Troiano Told Her of Killing." *Newsday*, April 5, 1985.

Gruson, Lindsey. "Jury in L.I. Case Is Given Details of Ritual Death." *The New York Times*, April 9, 1985.

Maier, Thomas J. "Slaying Witness Says He Lied." *Newsday*, April 10, 1985.

Maier, Thomas J. "Troiano Witness Again Contradicts the Prosecution." *Newsday*, April 11, 1985.

Maier, Thomas J. "Troiano's Initial Denial Was Doubted, Cop Says." *Newsday*, April 12, 1985.

Gruson, Lindsey. "Court Hears Confession of L.I. Youth." *The New York Times*, April 13, 1985.

Maier, Thomas J. "Tour of Slay Site Detailed." *Newsday*, April 13, 1985.

Maier, Thomas J. "Detective: Troiano Had No Remorse." *Newsday*, April 17, 1985.

Gruson, Lindsey. "Defense Lawyer in L.I. Murder Trial Loves a Good Murder Case." *The New York Times*, April 18, 1985.

Maier, Thomas J. "Witness Says He Saw Troiano in Church." *Newsday*, April 18, 1985.

Maier, Thomas J. "Troiano Defense Calls Last Witness." *Newsday*, April 19, 1985.

Gruson, Lindsey. "Closing Arguments Made in Trial of Youth Accused in Drug-Induced Slaying on L.I." *The New York Times*, April 23, 1985.

Maier, Thomas J. "Role of Drugs Key at Slay Trial." *Newsday*, April 23, 1985.

Gruson, Lindsey. "L.I. Jury Acquits Defendant in Killing of Youth in Woods." *The New York Times*, April 26, 1985.

Maier, Thomas J., Bob Wacker, and Martin Weston. "Teen Acquitted in Northport Murder." *Newsday*, April 26, 1985.

Maier, Thomas J. "Troiano Tells of His Role in Teen's Slaying." *Newsday*, August 21, 1985.

Young, Monte R. "Upstate Suspect Has L.I. Past." *Newsday*, January 16, 1993.

Ambro, David. "'84 Northport Murder Suspect Charged with Upstate Robbery." *The Northport Observer*, January 21, 1993.

Haberman, Michael. "Anniversary of Northport Teen Murder." *The Northport Observer*, July 7, 1994.

Magazine Articles

Breskin, David. "Kids in the Dark." *Rolling Stone*, November 22, 1984, pages 30–35 and 82–86.

Breskin, David. "Kids in the Dark." *Rolling Stone: The Great Stories*, June 11, 1992, pages 129–133.

Rosenbaum, Ron. "The Devil in Long Island." *The New York Times Magazine*, August 22, 1993, page 21.

Hanc, John. "Before Salem, There Was the Not-So-Wicked Witch of the Hamptons." *Smithsonian Magazine*, October 25, 2012.

Court Documents/Police Files

Christopher Barber's statement to the Suffolk County Police Department, taken by Officer William R. Petersen, September 10, 1983. Complaint No. 83-308168.

William E. Barber's statement to the Suffolk County Police Department, taken by Officer William R. Petersen, September 10, 1983. Complaint No. 83-308168.

Suffolk County Police Department arrest report for Gary Lauwers, September 15, 1983. Complaint No. 83-308168. Arrest No. 29233-83.

Suffolk County Police Department offense report for Randy Guethler, April 8, 1984. Complaint No. 84-123488. Arrest No. 11624-84.

Randy Guethler's statement to the Suffolk County Police Department, taken by Det. Douglas J. Varley, April 8, 1984. Complaint No. 84-123488.

Ricky Kasso's statement to the Suffolk County Police Department, taken by Det. Douglas J. Varley, April 24, 1984. Complaint No. 84-123488.

Suffolk County Medical Examiner's report for Gary Lauwers by Stuart L. Dawson, MD, July 4, 1984. Case No. 84-2370.

Ricky Kasso's statement to the Suffolk County Police Department, taken by Det. K. James McCready, July 5, 1984. Complaint No. 84-256461.

Jimmy Troiano's first statement to the Suffolk County Police Department, taken by Det. K. James McCready, July 5, 1984. Complaint No. 84-256461.

Jimmy Troiano's second statement to the Suffolk County Police Department, taken by Det. Louis Rodriguez, July 5, 1984. Complaint No. 84-256461.

Suffolk County Police Department arrest report for Ricky Kasso, July 6, 1984. Complaint No. 84-256461. Arrest No. 21450-84. Filed by Det. K. James McCready.

Suffolk County Medical Examiner's report for Ricky Kasso by Jonathan L. Arden, MD, July 7, 1984. Case No. 84-2390.

Suffolk County Police Department death report for Gary Lauwers, July 11, 1984. Complaint No. 84-256461. Filed by Det. K. James McCready and Det. Sgt. Richard A. Jensen.

Suffolk County Police Department offense report regarding the homicide of Gary Lauwers, July 11, 1984. Complaint No. 84-256461. Filed by Det. K. James McCready and Det. Sgt. Richard A. Jensen.

Suffolk County Police Department vehicle impound report for Complaint No. 84-256461, July 12, 1984. Impound No. 84-1073. Filed by Det. K. James McCready.

Toxicological Report for Ricky Kasso by Dennis J. Crouch, B.S. of the University of Utah's Center for Human Toxicology, August 17, 1984. Consultant Case No. CC-926-84.

Suffolk County Police Department supplementary report for the death investigation of Patrick A. Toussaint, December 1, 1984. Complaint No. 84-489124. Filed by Det. William J. Rudock and Det. Sgt. Thomas McLaughlin.

Suffolk County Police Department death report for Patrick A. Toussaint, December 9, 1984. Complaint No. 84-489124. Filed by Det. Michael Ryan and Det. Sgt. Richard A. Jensen.

People v. Troiano. County Court, Suffolk County, New York. March 13, 1985. Print.

Suffolk County Medical Examiner's report for Patrick A. Toussaint by Charles S. Hirsch, MD, July 31, 1985. Case No. 84-4238.

New York State Commission of Correction Medical Review Board's Final Report in the Matter of the Death of Richard Kasso at Suffolk County Correctional Facility, March 17, 1986.

James Troiano v. United States of America. United States District Court, District of Maine. September 5, 2008. Print.

Author's Note: The Northport Village Police Department refused to provide any documents under the Freedom of Information Act or assist the author in any capacity during the research for this book. Access to the trial transcripts was also denied under New York state law. The dialogue included in this section of the book was re-created using the media coverage of the proceedings, and through interviews with Eric Naiburg and Nicole Lauwers-Law.

Documentary Films

Satan in the Suburbs. Directed by Scott Hillier. Image Group Entertainment, 2000.

Books

Anson, Jay. *The Amityville Horror.* Prentice Hall, 1978.

Gethard, Chris. *Weird New York: Your Travel Guide to New York's Local Legends and Best Kept Secrets.* Sterling, 2005.

Jarnow, Jesse. *Heads: A Biography of Psychedelic America.* Da Capo Press, 2016.

LaVey, Anton. *The Satanic Bible.* Avon, 1969.

St. Clair, David. *Say You Love Satan.* Dell, 1987.

Television

Killer Kids. "Occult Killers." Season one, episode one. Produced by Jean Leclerc. The Biography Channel, May 16, 2011.

20/20. "The Devil Worshippers." Tom Jarriel. ABC, May 16, 1985.

Miscellaneous

The extensive collection of interview tapes and handwritten notes made by David Breskin during his time in Northport were graciously lent by him to the author of this book during its creation.

The staff of the John Hay Library at Brown University in Providence, Rhode Island, also dutifully provided research materials that David Breskin had previously donated to their collection. The author wishes to thank them for their diligent work.

McGuire, Mark J. "Murder in Northport: The Media Coverage of the 'Satanic Cult Killing' in July 1984" (Undergraduate Thesis for Mass Communication/Journalism at St. Bonaventure University). November 1984. The author wishes to thank Mr. McGuire for kindly locating and sending him a copy of this work.

Interviews Conducted by the Author

David Ambro

Dr. Jonathan Arden

Russell Barton

David Breskin

Brendan B. Brown

Doug Brueggemann

Larry Decker

Sue Decota

Michelle DeVeau

Peter Filardi

Wendy Kasso

Brian Kaufman

Betty Koerner

Grant Koerner

William Kreth

Nicole Lauwers-Law

Billy Leason

Dot Lennon Cutting

Valerie MacKenna

Thomas Maier

Tony Mallory

Demetri Matas

Jonathan McCuller

Mercedes McGrory

Dan McGuigan

Mark J. McGuire

Philip Morell

Eric Naiburg

Paul Papa

Tom Rætz

Gene Roemer

Ron Rosenbaum

Tony Ruggi

Grace Schinmann

Richard Schock

Rex Smith

Doug Varley

Glen Wolf

Anthony Zenkus

. . . along with several friends of Ricky Kasso and Gary Lauwers who requested and were granted anonymity. The author of this book thanks them all for their courage.

ABOUT THE AUTHOR

Jesse P. Pollack was born and raised in New Jersey and has served as a contributing writer for *Weird NJ* magazine since 2001. His first book, *Death on the Devil's Teeth: The Strange Murder That Shocked Suburban New Jersey*, coauthored with Mark Moran, was published in 2015 to critical acclaim and was nominated for a New Jersey Studies Academic Alliance Author Award. Pollack is also an accomplished musician, and his soundtrack work has been heard on *Driving Jersey*, an Emmy-nominated PBS documentary series. He is married with two children, three dogs, three fish, and a couple cats.